U0139431

From the People Who Make the Test!

The **Official Guide**
to the *TOEFL Junior* ® Standard Test
TOEFL Junior ® 标准考试
官方指南

ETS 中国 编著

北京语言大学出版社
BEIJING LANGUAGE AND CULTURE
UNIVERSITY PRESS

© 2022 北京语言大学出版社，社图号 22080

图书在版编目（CIP）数据

TOEFL Junior® 标准考试官方指南 = The Official Guide to the TOEFL Junior® Standard Test／ETS 中国编著. -- 北京 ：北京语言大学出版社，2022.10
　ISBN 978-7-5619-6138-4

　I.①T⋯　Ⅱ.①E⋯　Ⅲ.①TOEFL－自学参考资料
Ⅳ.①H310.41

　中国版本图书馆 CIP 数据核字（2022）第 160461 号

TOEFL Junior® 标准考试官方指南
TOEFL JUNIOR® BIAOZHUN KAOSHI GUANFANG ZHINAN

| 责任编辑：孙冠群 | 装帧设计：张　娜 |
| 责任印制：周　燚 | 排版制作：北京创艺涵文化发展有限公司 |

出版发行：北京语言大学出版社

社　　址：北京市海淀区学院路 15 号，100083
网　　址：www.blcup.com
电子信箱：service@blcup.com
电　　话：编 辑 部　8610-82301019
　　　　　　发 行 部　8610-82303650/3591/3648
　　　　　　北语书店　8610-82303653
　　　　　　网购咨询　8610-82303908
印　　刷：天津嘉恒印务有限公司

版　　次：2022 年 10 月第 1 版　　印　　次：2022 年 10 月第 1 次印刷
开　　本：889 毫米 × 1194 毫米　1/16　　印　　张：17.5
字　　数：298 千字
定　　价：88.00 元

PRINTED IN CHINA
凡有印装质量问题，本社负责调换。售后QQ：1367565611，电话：010–82303590

图书策划委员会

主　任：王梦妍

委　员：Emelie Cambeiro　　Jean Alderman

　　　　Yu Miao　　　　　　Eric Revesz

　　　　贾云龙　　　　　　傲日格乐

　　　　李坤宁　　　　　　陈冰洁

序 言

随着时代的发展，我们对英语学习的要求也在变化，开始更专注于培养学习者在现实世界中使用语言的能力，而不仅仅将语言作为静态知识体系来考查。特别是针对青少年这个教育体系中最庞大的群体，关注其全球视野的拓展、自我综合能力的提升，无疑是培养下一代国际化复合型人才的必要条件。而在此过程中，英语测评起到了重要的作用。它不仅能够帮助学生巩固所学知识、提高学习技能，同时还可以辅助教师完成教学反馈、发现存在的问题，从而改进教学。

托福青少测试由美国教育考试服务中心（Educational Testing Service，简称 ETS）研发，并在全球范围内推广和运用。其内容由 ETS 的英语专家和试题专家编写，重点衡量学生在以英语为媒介的教学环境下的英语沟通能力，并将分数与国际通用的语言能力等级及其描述相匹配，从而提供更加全面、科学的测评标准。这样的一个过程能够更加直接地反映考生的综合英语能力，比如知识掌握情况和语言运用能力。因此，托福青少测试作为一种测评工具，能够多维度地切实帮助广大青少年快速了解、检测和鉴定自身实际英语水平。同时，ETS 中国也致力于推动中国国际教育的发展，为教育行业相关的组织和从业者提供进一步发展所需要的材料和工具。

本系列出版物包含 *TOEFL Junior*® 考试和 *TOEFL Primary*® 考试的官方指南——全球首套由 ETS 研发的针对中国考生的青少测试官方备考教材，以及针

对 *TOEFL Junior*® 考试和 *TOEFL Primary*® 考试的官方词汇手册。编者"因地制宜",结合中国特定教育和社会背景下的教学需求以及中国青少年的发展特性,除了提供大量的实用信息、学习建议与指导之外,还首次公布了全新的备考真题,为考生、家长和教师提供有根据的参考,帮助考生对考试形成更明确的认知。

　　最后,我们希望本系列出版物能够帮助广大考生实现更加高效的备考,真正帮助中国青少英语学习者提升综合语言技能。

ETS 中国区总裁

王梦妍

编写说明

TOEFL Junior® 考试是可以测评出考生英语学习能力和进步情况的专业考试，可以全面、真实地反映出考生在生活英语和学术英语两方面的水平。

本书是一本官方备考书，为有兴趣了解 TOEFL Junior® 考试的教师、家长和学生提供针对 TOEFL Junior® 标准考试和 TOEFL Junior® 口语考试的介绍。为了提供有效且实用的信息，本书在撰写时参考了 ETS 公布于官网的信息，并参考了 Practice Test for TOEFL Junior® Standard Test 和 Handbook for TOEFL Junior® Tests。

本书的第 1 章以问答形式解答了教师、家长和学生普遍提出的问题。

第 2 章对 TOEFL Junior® 标准考试进行综述。

第 3 章、第 4 章以及第 5 章着重于具体考试题型的展示，并提供官方真题以及解析等内容，以便教师、家长和学生可以更好地了解考试题型。

第 6 章针对 TOEFL Junior® 标准考试，从听力理解、语言形式与含义、阅读理解三个方面分别提出学习建议，同时给出 TOEFL Junior® 口语考试的学习建议。

第 7 章和第 8 章是两套由 ETS 公布的、完整的 TOEFL Junior® 标准考试真题。

第 9 章是两套真题的详细解析。

第 10 章是两套真题的听力文本。

目 录

附　录 **255**

第①章

关于
TOEFL Junior® 考试

▶▶▶

1. 谁研发了 *TOEFL Junior®* 考试?

Educational Testing Service (ETS),中文名称为美国教育考试服务中心。它是一家非营利性教育机构。

2. 什么是 *TOEFL Junior®* 考试?

TOEFL Junior® 考试考查中学生在以英语为媒介的学习环境中所具备的社交英语和学术英语语言技能的熟练程度。这项考试为学校、教师、家长和考生提供了一个客观的标准来衡量考生的英语语言能力和学习进展,同时也可作为是否让考生参加英语水平提升课程的参考依据。*TOEFL Junior®* 考试包括 *TOEFL Junior®* 标准考试和 *TOEFL Junior®* 口语考试。

3. 谁可以参加 *TOEFL Junior®* 考试?

ETS 为满足 11 至 17 岁学生的英语检测需求研发了 *TOEFL Junior®* 考试。考试可能也适用于其他学生,但其适用性取决于学生的英语水平。这项考试不适用于尚未达到基本熟练水平的学生。

4. *TOEFL Junior®* 标准考试的考试结构是什么?

TOEFL Junior® 标准考试包含三部分——听力理解、语言形式与含义、阅读理解。

听力理解以社会和人际交往(Social and Interpersonal)、教学指导(Navigational)以及学术(Academic)这三个语言领域进行划分,考查考生听和理解英语的能力。语言形式与含义考查考生在关键英语技能方面的熟练程度,比如对学术和非学术语境中的语法和词汇的掌握程度。阅读理解考查考生对英语非学术文本和学术文本的阅读和理解能力。每个部分包含 42 道含有四项选项的选择题,共计 126 道选择题。考试总时长为 1 小时 55 分钟。

下列表格对 *TOEFL Junior®* 标准考试的考试结构进行了总结。

考试模块	题目数量	考试时间
听力理解	42	40 分钟
语言形式与含义	42	25 分钟
阅读理解	42	50 分钟
总计	126	1 小时 55 分钟

5. *TOEFL Junior®* 标准考试的考试内容是什么？

下列表格对 *TOEFL Junior®* 标准考试的三个部分所测试的内容进行了概括。

考试模块	测试内容
听力理解	考查考生在社会和人际交往、教学指导、学术三个方面听英语和理解英语的能力
语言形式与含义	考查考生在关键英语技能方面的熟练程度，比如语法和词汇运用能力
阅读理解	考查考生阅读和理解英语学术和非学术文章的能力

6. *TOEFL Junior®* 标准考试如何计分？

TOEFL Junior® 标准考试的分数是由考生回答正确的题目数量决定的。在所有计分的题目中，每一项正确答案在该部分中所占的分数相等。每部分正确答案的数量会转换成一个 200—300 之间的分数。总分数是三个部分分数之和，因此总分数在 600—900 之间。

下列表格对 *TOEFL Junior®* 标准考试的分数进行了总结。

考试模块	分数范围
听力理解	200—300
语言形式与含义	200—300
阅读理解	200—300
总分	600—900

虽然每次考试所使用的试卷有所不同，但是 *TOEFL Junior®* 标准考试的所有试卷都衡量同一类技能。这就意味着考生在不同试卷之间所得的分数是具有可比性的。另请参考附录 1 "*TOEFL Junior®* 标准考试总分数等级描述"，对处于不同成绩等级的考生能力做进一步了解。

7. *TOEFL Junior®* 口语考试的考试结构是什么？

该口语考试考查考生在课堂内外使用英语进行口头交流的能力。考试包括 4 个语言任务，共计约 18 分钟。

下列表格对 *TOEFL Junior®* 口语考试的考试结构进行了总结。

考试模块	任务数量	考试时间
口语	4	约 18 分钟

在考试过程中，考生将佩戴耳机，通过听录音和看屏幕来获取题目指示。考生的作答将通过麦克风进行录音。

8. *TOEFL Junior*® 口语考试的考试内容是什么？

以下是对 4 个语言任务的描述。

任务一：大声朗读

考生将有 1 分钟的时间先自行默读一小段文字，并在随后的 1 分钟内对着麦克风大声朗读该段文字。

任务二：看图说话

考生将看到 6 幅图片，并根据图片所示内容做出描述。考生将有 1 分钟的时间准备，并在随后的 1 分钟内对着麦克风作答。

任务三：非学术类听说

考生将听到一位老师或几个学生谈论一个与校园相关的话题，并在听后对音频内容进行口头表述。在听录音过程中考生可以做记录。考生将有 45 秒的时间准备，并在随后的 1 分钟内对着麦克风作答。

任务四：学术类听说

考生会听到一位老师谈论一个学术话题。在听录音过程中考生可以做记录。之后考生要对音频内容进行口头表述。考生将有 45 秒的时间准备，并在随后的 1 分钟内对着麦克风作答。

9. *TOEFL Junior*® 口语考试如何计分？

TOEFL Junior® 口语考试所包含的题目须用英语口头作答。考生的回答将由 ETS 评分人员依照标准化评分条例进行打分。口语评分系统实施多重严格措施以保证口语考试分数的可信度，其中包括尝试使用新问题、要求评分人员在进行口语考试打分前通过严格测评、由评审组专家组长实时监测打分质量并评析打分人员工作表现。考试成绩区间为 0—16 分。另请参考附录 3 "*TOEFL Junior*® 口语考试分数等级描述"，对处于不同成绩等级的考生能力做进一步了解。

10. *TOEFL Junior*® 标准考试的有效性如何体现？

ETS 确保 *TOEFL Junior*® 标准考试能够衡量青少年英语学习者在以英语为教学媒介的学术环境中的交流能力。

这项考试是基于语言任务的相关信息而设计的，而这些语言任务是中学生在以英语为学习媒介的学校应该完成的。

这些信息来源广泛，包括：

- 将英语作为一门外语进行教授的国家（如中国、智利、法国、韩国和日本）的英语标准、课程和教科书；
- 美国初中英语学习者的英语水平标准（比如美国加利福尼亚州、科罗拉多州、佛罗里达州、纽约州和得克萨斯州的标准以及世界级教学设计和测试联盟标准）；
- 经验丰富的语言评估专家的建议；
- 关于在学术环境中使用的语言的学术文献。

经过对所搜集的资料的仔细分析，ETS 确定了衡量学生英语语言水平的三个必要领域：

- 社会和人际交往（Social and Interpersonal）——该领域包含用于建立和维持人际关系的语言。比如，考生应当理解朋友在轻松的对话中所讲的内容，或者能够阅读来自朋友或者老师的私人邮件。
- 教学指导（Navigational）——该领域指考生与同伴、老师以及学校其他工作人员就学校和课程相关材料进行交流的语言任务。比如，考生应当理解老师关于家庭作业的口头指令，并能够从学校相关的通知中提取关键信息。
- 学术（Academic）——该领域指考生在学习英文学术内容的过程中开展的语言活动。这一领域语言使用的实例包括理解学术讲座中的观点和理解学术文章。

TOEFL Junior® 标准考试中的听力理解和阅读理解考试旨在综合测量考生在上述三个领域中的英语交流能力。语言形式与含义的题目则旨在评估潜在的语言运用能力。

11. *TOEFL Junior*® 考试成绩的有效期是多久？

TOEFL Junior® 考试成绩有效期为自考试之日起两年以内。

第2章

TOEFL Junior® 标准考试内容综述

▶▶▶

TOEFL Junior® 标准考试包含三个部分——听力理解、语言形式与含义、阅读理解。每部分包含 42 道题目，考试总时长约 2 小时。所有问题都设置在校园环境背景下。

听力理解

听力理解从社会和人际交往（Social and Interpersonal）、教学指导（Navigational）以及学术（Academic）这三个领域考查考生的听力能力。这部分包含三种不同的题目类型：

- 课堂教学：在这类任务中，考生会听到由老师、校长、图书管理员或其他学校工作人员做的简短的讲话。每则讲话持续 20—45 秒。听完后，考生要回答 1 道题目。这道题目可能是让考生找出这则讲话的主旨或目的，或根据说话者所讲的内容做出推断或预测。

- 短对话：在这类任务中，考生将会听到两名学生或学生与学校工作人员（如老师或图书管理员）之间的对话。对话持续 60—90 秒。听完后，考生要回答 3—4 道题目。这些题目可能是让考生找出这段对话的主旨或其中一个重要细节；根据对话内容做出推断或预测；找出说话者谈及某些信息的原因；或者当说话者使用某种语调或强调某些用词的时候，辨别出他 / 她当下的感受或想要表达的意思。

- 学术听力：在这类任务中，考生会听到关于学术主题的课堂讲座或讨论。听完后，考生要回答 4—5 道题目。讲座或讨论持续约 120—210 秒。这些题目可能是让考生找出讲座或讨论的主旨或其中一个重要细节；根据讲座或讨论的内容做出推断或预测；找出说话者谈及某些信息的原因；或者当说话者使用某种语调或强调某些用词的时候，辨别出他 / 她当下的感受或想要表达的意思。

语言形式与含义

语言形式与含义考查考生对英语语法结构和词汇知识的理解程度。这些题目出现在一系列短语篇中，题目要求考生选择正确的单词或短语将句子补充完整。每个语篇都是考生在校园背景下阅读的题材：

- 邮件、便条或公告
- 教科书文章节选

这部分主要包含两种不同类型的题目。语言形式题目考查语法结构知识（如动词时态、关系从句、语序以及形容词或副词的形式）。语言含义题目考查词汇知识。

阅读理解

阅读理解考查考生对学校环境中可能会遇到的非学术和学术文本的阅读和理解能力。非学术文本的例子包括：

- 往来信件（邮件、便条和书信）
- 非线性文本（时间表或海报）
- 新闻文章（如，出现在学校或当地报纸上的文章）

学术文本的例子包括：

- 记叙文
- 历史人物传记
- 出现在教科书上的有关某一学术主题的文章

阅读理解部分考查考生的以下能力：

- 理解文本的主旨
- 找出支持文本主旨的重要事实性信息
- 根据文本对未明确给出的信息做出推断
- 根据语境确定不熟悉的单词或短语的含义
- 找出代词所指代的单词
- 辨别作者的意图

第 3 章

听力理解

　　该部分考试要求考生根据听到的多段语段和对话回答问题。每段对话只播放一遍。共计 42 道题目，题目之间间隔 12 秒，总时长为 40 分钟。该部分考试可以更详细地划分成三个任务类型。

　　任务类型一：课堂教学（Classroom Instruction）。在这类题目中，考生会听到由老师、校长、图书管理员或学校其他工作人员做的简短的讲话。每则讲话持续 20—45 秒。听完后，考生要回答 1 道题目。每题有 4 个选项。听力理解部分通常有 6—10 道课堂教学题目。

　　任务类型二：短对话（Short Conversation）。在这类题目中，考生会听到两名学生或学生与学校工作人员（如老师或图书管理员）之间的对话。对话持续 60—90 秒。听完后，考生要回答 3—4 道题目。每题有 4 个选项。听力理解部分通常有 15—17 道短对话题目。

　　任务类型三：学术听力（Academic Listening）。在这类题目中，考生会听到关于学术主题的课堂讲座或讨论。听完后，考生要回答 4—5 道题目。每题有 4 个选项。听力理解部分通常有 16—17 道学术听力题目。

　　接下来是每个类型的样题。

扫码听样题录音

任务类型一：课堂教学（Classroom Instruction）

样题 1

What will the class probably do next?

(A) Design a poster

(B) Color the leaves

(C) Eat lunch outside

(D) Collect fallen leaves

听力文本

(Narrator): Listen to a science teacher talking to her students.

(Woman): First, we are going to collect some leaves that have fallen from the trees. Then, we will compare the colors of those leaves. After that, we will use the leaves to make a poster about what happens to trees during autumn. OK, now put on your jackets and let's head outside.

(Narrator): What will the class probably do next?

解析： 本题问"学生们接下来会做什么？"。老师告诉学生穿好大衣后"head outside（去外面）"和"collect some leaves that have fallen from the trees（收集一些树上掉落的树叶）"，由此可见选项 (D)"收集落叶"为正确答案。听力材料中提及"use the leaves to make a poster（用这些叶子做海报）"，但是这并不是学生们接下来要做的事，所以选项 (A)"设计一张海报"错误。另外，老师让学生"compare the colors of those leaves（比较叶子的颜色）"，但并没有让学生给叶子涂颜色，所以选项 (B)"给叶子涂颜色"错误。选项 (C)"在外面吃午餐"在听力材料中没有提及，因此错误。

样题 2

What is probably true about the dance?

(A) It is a very popular event.

(B) It is not usually held on a Friday.

(C) It will take place in the cafeteria.

(D) It is the first dance of the school year.

听力文本

(Narrator): Listen to a school principal speaking over the intercom.

(Man): Next Friday is the annual school dance. Tickets go on sale starting today in the school cafeteria during lunch. They will be on sale all week. Make sure you buy a ticket in advance, as we won't be selling them at the door the night of the dance. We only have 150 tickets to sell, and they usually sell out before the day of the dance. You don't want to miss this special event!

(Narrator): What is probably true about the dance?

解析：本题问"关于舞会哪一项可能是正确的？"。听力材料中老师说"We only have 150 tickets to sell, and they usually sell out before the day of the dance.（我们只卖 150 张票，而且通常会在舞会前一天就售光）"，表示这个活动非常受欢迎，所以选项 (A)"这是一场非常受欢迎的活动"为正确答案。另外，听力材料中提到"Tickets go on sale … in the school cafeteria …（票……在学校自助餐厅售卖）"，自助餐厅是售票的地点，并不是活动的举办场所，所以选项 (C)"舞会在自助餐厅举办"是错误的。选项 (B)"舞会通常不在周五举办"和选项 (D)"这是本学年第一场舞会"在听力材料中均未提及，故错误。

任务类型二：短对话（Short Conversation）

样题

1. What does the boy ask the girl to do?

   (A) Join a team

   (B) Help him study

   (C) Eat lunch with him

   (D) Lend him a textbook

2. What subject is the girl interested in?

   (A) Math

   (B) History

   (C) Science

   (D) Geography

3. What does the boy offer to give the girl?

   (A) A library card

   (B) The title of a book

   (C) A list of questions

   (D) The names of students

4. Where will the event be held this year?

   (A) In the gym

   (B) In the library

   (C) In the cafeteria

   (D) In the science room

听力文本

(Narrator): Listen to a conversation between two friends from school.

(Boy): Maria, would you like to be on my team in next week's trivia quiz?

(Girl): Trivia quiz? I've heard about it, but I don't know exactly what it is.

(Boy): It's a general-knowledge contest. All of the teams are given a set of questions to answer—questions on all kinds of topics—and the team that gets the most correct answers wins.

(Girl): Sure, I guess I could play. But why do you want me on your team?

(Boy): Well, our team already has students who are interested in biology, history, and math. But we're not too good at geography. A lot of questions are about various countries, continents, and things like that. We need someone strong in geography—like you!

(Girl): Well, geography is my favorite subject. You can count me in! … Should I study for this?

(Boy): Hmm … It's hard to study for this kind of competition. But if you want, I have examples of questions that were asked in the quizzes in the past. A list like that would give you a general idea of what to expect.

(Girl): That would be great. So will it be held in the library?

(Boy): Not this time. Now we'll be in the gym. A lot more teams are signing up to play this time, so they had to move it to a place with more space. Even the cafeteria wasn't big enough.

(Girl): Wow—the gym is pretty big.

(Boy): Well, that just shows you how popular the trivia quiz has become!

(Narrator): Now answer the questions.

第 1 题解析：本题问"男孩让女孩做什么？"。听力材料第一句男孩就问女孩是否愿意 "be on my team in next week's trivia quiz（在下周的知识问答比赛中跟我一队）"，所以选项 (A)"加入一个团队"为正确答案。选项 (B)"帮助他学习"、选项 (C)"和他一起吃午饭"和选项 (D)"借给他课本"均未在听力材料中提及，故错误。

第 2 题解析：本题问"女孩对哪个科目感兴趣？"。男孩对女孩说自己的队伍中"has students who are interested in biology, history, and math（有喜欢生物、历史和数学的同学）"，但还需要"someone strong in geography（擅长地理的人）"，刚好女孩说自己最喜欢的科目就是地理，由此可以推测出女孩对地理感兴趣，选项 (D)"地理"为正确答案。选项 (A)"数学"和选项 (B)"历史"是队伍中其他成员感兴趣的科目，故错误。选项 (C)"科学"在听力材料中未提及，故错误。

第 3 题解析：本题问"男孩提出要给女孩什么？"。女孩在答应加入以后想为比赛做准备，男孩说自己有"examples of questions（一些例题）"可以给女孩，所以选项 (C)"考题清单"为正确答案。选项 (A)"图书卡"、选项 (B)"书名"和选项 (D)"学生们的名字"均未在听力材料中提及，故错误。

第 4 题解析：本题问"这个活动今年在哪里举行？"。听力材料中，女孩问"… will it be held in the library?（……是在图书馆举行吗？）"，男孩首先进行了否定，然后说是在体育馆举行，因为报名的队伍多了，需要更大的场地，所以选项 (A)"在体育馆"正确，选项 (B)"在图书馆"错误。另外，听力材料中提及"Even the cafeteria wasn't big enough（就连自助餐厅都不够大）"，所以选项 (C)"在自助餐厅"错误。选项 (D)"在科学教室"未在听力材料中提及，故错误。

任务类型三：学术听力（Academic Listening）

样题

1. What are the speakers mainly talking about?

   (A) A new road in their town

   (B) A new way to build roads

   (C) The early history of roads

   (D) The cost of building roads

2. Why does the woman talk about animals?

(A) To explain how the first roads were created

(B) To point out that long ago most people did not travel much

(C) To describe an event that happened on a road nearby

(D) To suggest that traveling on country roads can be dangerous

3. Why did the people in England build ridge ways?

(A) To connect small towns to major cities

(B) To allow cars to drive around small towns

(C) To create roads that water would not wash away

(D) To create a separate road for transporting animals

4. What does the woman say about roads in ancient Greece?

(A) They were constructed on all of Greece's islands.

(B) They were not as good as roads built by the Romans.

(C) They were often washed away in the rain.

(D) They connected Greece to the Roman Empire.

听力文本

(Narrator): Now you will hear part of a radio program.

(Man): Hello, listeners. Today I'll be speaking with Ms. Amanda Jones, the town director of road transportation. Thank you for joining us.

(Woman): It's my pleasure.

(Man): Ms. Jones, it seems like there are always new roads to build or old ones to fix. Let's start with new roads. How do you decide where to put in a new road?

(Woman): Well, that's an interesting question. One way to think about it is to go back in history. You know, people didn't build the first roads. Animals did. These roads were really just tracks—just paths—that animals made in the dirt as they walked to find food or water. Then people started to use them. In fact, some of the roads we drive on today were at one time paths made by wild animals.

(Man): But we humans began making roads for ourselves at some point, right?

(Woman): Yes, of course. We made them when we needed them … which happened when we started to settle in communities, and we wanted to trade with people in other communities. Even then, the roads were pretty simple. Let me ask a question: Why would we need anything more, like paved roads?

(Man): Well, I suppose when we wanted to carry things … when we built vehicles, like carts and wagons.

(Woman): Exactly! And that's when you start to see better roads, roads made with logs or, better yet, stone or brick. And roads made with good drainage—a good road has to have a place for water to go. Rainwater can really damage a road, or even wash it away. In England, thousands of years ago, people made roads on ridges—along the cliffs and hills beside streams and rivers. Why? Because it's drier there. "Ridge ways," they called them. Some ridge ways still exist in England—they're still used today for walking and hiking. Now road building really started to increase when nations began to grow. In ancient India, rulers created big road networks—it helped them to control a lot of land from central cities. And the Romans became excellent road builders. After all, they had a huge empire to connect together. But the roads in ancient Greece were not as good as those of the Romans. They didn't put as much effort into road building. Why? Because Greece is full of islands, and they traveled more by boat.

(Narrator): Now answer the questions.

第 1 题解析：本题问"对话者主要在谈论什么？"。根据听力材料可知，女士在整段采访中提及了三个信息点：人们最初走的路是动物踩出来的、人们开始为自己修路，以及古印度、古罗马和古希腊的路。综上，女士讲的是道路的发展历史。在四个选项中，选项 (C)"道路的早期历史"最合适，为正确答案。选项 (A)"他们城镇中的一条新路"、选项 (B)"一种修路的新方法"和选项 (D)"修路的费用"均不能概括讲话人所讲内容的大意。

第 2 题解析：题目问"为什么女士要谈到动物？"。听力材料中，女士说，道路的最初建造者并不是人类，而是动物们，因为动物会先踩出来小道或是小径，所以选项 (A)"解释最初的道路是如何产生的"是正确的。选项 (B)"指出很久以前大多数人都不怎么出行"、选项 (C)"描述一个发生在附近路上的事件"和选项 (D)"说明在乡村公路上旅行会很危险"在听力材料中均未提及，故错误。

第 3 题解析：本题问"为什么英国人修建山脊公路？"。材料中，女士提及"people made roads on ridges（人们在山脊上修路）"，并解释它的意思是"along the cliffs and hills beside streams and rivers（沿着小溪和河流旁边的悬崖和山丘修路）"，原因是"it's drier there（那里更干燥）"，说的是悬崖和山丘这些地方更干燥，路不会被雨水冲毁，所以选项 (C)"为了修建不会被水冲走的道路"为正确答案。选项 (A)"将大城市与小城镇连起来"、选项 (B)"能让汽车在小镇上到处行驶"和选项 (D)"为运输动物开辟一条单独的道路"在听力材料中并没有提及，故错误。

第 4 题解析：本题问"关于古希腊的路，女士说了些什么？"。女士在听力材料最后提及了古印度、古罗马和古希腊的道路。她说古罗马人是非常优秀的"road builders（修路者）"，而古希腊因为岛屿众多，人们不怎么修路，而是"traveled more by boat（更多地靠船出行）"，所以将两者对比可知选项 (B)"古希腊的路没有罗马人修的路好"为正确答案，同时也可排除选项 (A)"它们被修建在希腊所有岛屿上"。选项 (C)"它们常被雨水冲走"和选项 (D)"它们连接了希腊和罗马帝国"均未在听力材料中提及，故错误。

第4章

语言形式与含义

　　语言形式与含义考查考生在关键英语技能方面的熟练程度，比如语境中的语法和词汇。每一道题目都有一个选项框，其中包含四个可能将句子补充完整的选项。考生须从中选出最佳答案。共计 42 道题目，时长为 25 分钟。一般有 7 个语篇，形式包括公告、邮件、便条和学术文章节选等。

样题 1

Questions 1–4 refer to the following part of a short story.

1. **When Dan knocked on the door of the old gray house, he was a little**

(A) total.

(B) funny.

(C) foreign.

(D) nervous.

解析：本题的选择依据要看后文。后文提到，Dan 的朋友说住在那所房子里的女人很不友好。因此去敲门的 Dan 内心应该是紧张的，所以选项 (D) 是正确答案。同时可判断选项 (A)"完全的"、选项 (B)"滑稽的"和选项 (C)"外来的"均错误。

2. **His friends at school had said that the woman who lived in the house was unfriendly,**

(A) finding the cat

(B) the cat he had found

(C) he had found the cat

(D) the cat had been found

but Dan was sure that _____ **in his yard was hers. He wanted**

to take it to her.

解析："that"引导宾语从句，表示 Dan 确定在他院子里找到的猫是她的。从句缺主语，因此可以排除选项 (C) 和 (D)。以句意上看可以排除选项 (A)，因此选项 (B) 是正确答案。"he had found"用于修饰"the cat"。

3. "Hello," a woman's voice responded to his knock. "Who is it?"

"Hi. I'm your neighbor from down the street," Dan said _____ she opened the

(A) as
(B) that
(C) which
(D) during

door a few centimeters. "Is this cat yours?"

"Oh, my goodness," the woman said with a big smile. She pulled the door open wide.

解析："as" 作为连词，意思是 "当……的时候"。此处意思是 "当她把门打开了几厘米时，Dan 说"。因此选项 (A) 是正确答案。

4. "Yes, this is Daisy, and I've been worried about her! Thank you so much for

(A) bring
(B) brings
(C) brought
(D) bringing

her back!"

解析："for" 作为介词，后面要使用动词的 -ing 形式。因此选项 (D) 是正确答案。

样题 2

Questions 1–9 refer to the following essay.

1. **People's behavior during public events has changed _____ the years,**

(A) by

(B) for

(C) after

(D) over

解析："over" 作为介词，意思是"在……期间"。本句意为"这些年来，人们在公共场合的行为发生了变化"。因此选项 (D) 是正确答案。

2. **perhaps because views on _____ appropriate have changed.**

(A) considering what

(B) they considered it

(C) what is considered

(D) that it is considered

解析："what is considered" 与选项后的"appropriate"构成名词性从句，做介词补足成分。本句意为"可能是因为（人们）对什么是合适的行为的看法改变了"。因此选项 (C) 是正确答案。

3. During a classical music concert, for example, _____ until

- (A) no people to clap
- (B) people do not clap
- (C) clapping people do not
- (D) people are not clapping

the musicians finish playing the composition.

解析："people do not clap" 是一般现在时的主谓结构，表示一种客观事实。本句意为"例如，在一场古典音乐会中，人们在音乐家演奏完乐曲之后才会鼓掌"。因此选项 (B) 是正确答案。

4. It would be hard _____ the audience clapping in the middle of a

- (A) imagines
- (B) imagined
- (C) to imagine
- (D) imagination

performance.

解析：本题考查 "It + be 动词 + 形容词 + to do sth" 的句型。本句意为"很难想象观众会在一场表演的中间鼓掌"。因此选项 (C) 是正确答案。

5. It may come as a surprise to many, however, that long ago, this is exactly

- (A) what people did.
- (B) that people do it.
- (C) people had done it.
- (D) what did people do.

解析："what people did" 是 "is" 的表语从句。本句意为"然而，可能会令很多人感到惊讶的是，在很久之前，人们正是这样做的"。因此选项 (A) 是正确答案。

6. The audience laughed loudly, clapped, and _____ great moments.

(A) cheerful

(B) cheered

(C) cheering

(D) has cheered

解析："cheered" 是 "cheer" 的过去式，在句子中与 "laughed" "clapped" 一起做并列谓语，表示过去的动作。本句意为 "观众们大声地笑、鼓掌，并为伟大的时刻欢呼"，因此选项 (B) 是正确答案。

7. That was _____ people showed their regard for a performer's skills.

(A) why

(B) how

(C) what

(D) which

解析："how" 的意思是 "怎样，如何"，表示方式。本句意为 "那是人们对表演者的技能表达敬意的方式"。因此选项 (B) 为正确答案。

8. One reason that people's behavior was so _____ may be that in the past,

(A) differs

(B) differed

(C) to differ

(D) different

classical music concerts were more like today's pop music shows.

解析："different" 是形容词，表示 "不同的"，在句中做 was 的表语。本句意为 "人们的行为如此不同的原因之一可能是，在过去，古典音乐会更像现在的流行音乐演出"。因此选项 (D) 为正确答案。

9. Long ago, classical music was not thought to be _____ it is now.

(A) more serious since

(B) so serious than

(C) as serious so

(D) as serious as

解析："as + 形容词 + as" 表示 "像……一样"。本句意为 "很久之前，古典音乐没有像现在这样被认为那么严肃"。因此选项 (D) 为正确答案。

第 5 章

阅读理解

阅读理解部分考查考生对英文学术文本和非学术文本的阅读和理解能力。共计 42 道题目，时长为 50 分钟。阅读理解部分通常有 6—7 篇文章。文章形式包括但不限于时间表、广告、公告、邮件、书面留言、故事和学术文章节选。

样题 1

Questions 1–4 are about the following announcement.

Student Volunteers Needed!

On Saturday, December 12th, from 10 A.M. until 4 P.M., Carverton Middle School will be holding a music festival in the school gymnasium. The special event will <u>feature</u> a variety of professional musicians and singers.

We are looking for Carverton students to help with the jobs listed below.

Task	Time	Date
Make posters	1 P.M.–4 P.M.	December 5th
Set up gym	11 A.M.–4 P.M.	December 11th
Help performers	9 A.M.–4 P.M.	December 12th
Welcome guests	10 A.M.–2 P.M.	December 12th
Clean up gym	4 P.M.–7 P.M.	December 12th

Interested students should speak with Ms. Braxton, the music teacher. Students who would like to help at the festival must have written permission from a parent or guardian.

1. What time will the festival begin?

    (A) 10 A.M.

    (B) 11 A.M.

    (C) 1 P.M.

    (D) 2 P.M

> **解析：** 本题问"这个音乐节什么时候开始？"。根据原文"On Saturday, December 12th, from 10 A.M. until 4 P.M., Carverton Middle School will be holding a music festival in the school gymnasium.（12 月 12 日周六上午 10 点至下午 4 点，Carverton 中学将会在校体育馆举办音乐节）"可知，音乐节的开始时间是上午 10 点，因此选项 (A)"上午 10 点"正确。选项 (B)"上午 11 点"、选项 (C)"下午 1 点"和选项 (D)"下午 2 点"均错误。

2. In line 3, the word <u>feature</u> is closest in meaning to _____ .

    (A) look

    (B) keep

    (C) include

    (D) entertain

> **解析：** 本题问"在第 3 行，单词 feature 与_____意思最接近"。包含该词的句子是"The special event will <u>feature</u> a variety of professional musicians and singers.（这个特别活动将_____许多专业音乐家和歌手）"。根据句意推测，该句说的应该是此次活动会有 / 来专业的音乐家和歌手。因此选项 (C)"包括"是正确的。选项 (A)"看"、选项 (B)"保持"和选项 (D)"使娱乐"均错误。

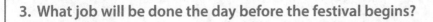

3. **What job will be done the day before the festival begins?**

   (A) Making posters

   (B) Setting up the gym

   (C) Cleaning up the gym

   (D) Helping the performers

解析：本题问"在节日开始的前一天要做好什么工作？"。因为音乐节是 12 月 12 日开始，那么举办的前一天就是 12 月 11 日。在表格内，12 月 11 日对应的 Task 是"Set up gym（布置体育馆）"，因此选项 (B)"布置体育馆"是正确的。选项 (A)"做海报"、选项 (C)"打扫体育馆"和选项 (D)"帮助演出者"均错误。

4. **Who is told to talk to Ms. Braxton?**

   (A) Parents

   (B) Students

   (C) Teachers

   (D) Performers

解析：本题问"谁被告知要和 Braxton 老师沟通？"。在公告的最后一部分提到"Interested students should speak with Ms. Braxton ..."，所以正确答案是选项(B)"学生"。选项(A)"家长"、选项 (C)"老师"和选项 (D)"演出者"均错误。

样题 2

Questions 1–9 are about the following passage.

Line   When another old cave is discovered in the south of France, it is not usually news. Rather, it is an ordinary event. Such discoveries are so frequent these days that hardly anybody pays heed to them. However, when the Lascaux cave complex was discovered in 1940,

5   the world was amazed. Painted directly on its walls were hundreds of scenes showing how people lived thousands of years ago. The scenes show people hunting animals, such as bison or wild cats. Other images depict birds and, most noticeably, horses, which appear in more than

10   300 wall images, by far outnumbering all other animals. Early artists drawing these animals accomplished a monumental and difficult task. They did not limit themselves to the easily accessible walls but carried their painting materials to spaces that required climbing

15   steep walls or crawling into narrow passages in the Lascaux complex.

    Unfortunately, the paintings have been exposed to the destructive action of water and temperature changes, which easily wear the images away. Because the Lascaux caves have

20   many entrances, air movement has also damaged the images inside. Although they are not out in the open air, where natural light would have destroyed them long ago, many of the images have deteriorated and are barely recognizable. To prevent further damage, the site was closed to tourists in 1963, 23 years after it was discovered.

1. Which title best summarizes the main idea of the passage?

    (A) Wild Animals in Art

    (B) Hidden Prehistoric Paintings

    (C) Exploring Caves Respectfully

    (D) Determining the Age of French Caves

解析：本题问"哪个标题最好地总结了文章主旨？"。通读文章可知，该文章主要讲述了 Lascaux 洞穴群中的壁画。文章描述了壁画所绘内容、壁画所在位置以及出现损毁的原因等。综上可以判断选项 (B)"隐秘的史前壁画"最合适，为正确答案。选项 (A)"艺术作品中的野生动物"、选项 (C)"恭敬地探索洞穴"和选项 (D)"确定法国洞穴的年代"均不能概括主旨。

2. In line 3, the words <u>pays heed to</u> are closest in meaning to _____ .

    (A) discovers

    (B) watches

    (C) notices

    (D) buys

解析：本题问"在第 3 行，短语 pays heed to 与_____意思最接近"。文章第 2—3 行的句子说的是"这类发现在这些年如此频繁以至于很少有人_____这些发现"。合理推测该句意思是"这种发现太频繁了，以至于大家都习以为常／很少关注"。因此最为合适的单词是 notices（注意），选项 (C) 是正确答案。选项 (A)"发现"、选项 (B)"看"和选项 (D)"购买"均错误。

3. Based on the passage, what is probably true about the south of France?

    (A) It is home to rare animals.

    (B) It has a large number of caves.

    (C) It is known for horse-racing events.

    (D) It has attracted many famous artists.

解析：本题问"基于文章，关于法国南部哪一项可能是正确的？"。选项 (A)"这里是稀有动物的家园"在文章中并未提及，故排除。文章只在第 9 行提到洞内的壁画上画有马的图案，选项 (C)"这里因赛马活动而闻名"与该意思不符，故错误。选项 (D)"它吸引了很多著名的艺术家"在文章中也未提及，故错误。通过对第 2 题的解析可知，在法国南部，古代洞穴的发现很常见，所以可以合理推测出，法国南部的洞穴一定不少，所以选项 (B) 是正确答案。

4. In line 8, the word <u>depict</u> is closest in meaning to _____ .

    (A) show

    (B) hunt

    (C) count

    (D) draw

解析：本题问"在第 8 行，单词 depict 与_____意思最接近"。文章第 7—8 行的句子说："场景展示了人们狩猎动物，比如野牛和野猫"，紧接着包含 depict 的句子出现："其他一些图案_____鸟以及最引人注目的马……"。我们可以合理推测，这里想要表达的是"其他图上画的是 / 展示的是"等类似的意思。所以选项 (A)"展示"是正确的。选项 (B)"打猎"、选项 (C)"数数"和选项 (D)"画画儿"均错误。

5. According to the passage, which animals appear most often on the cave walls?

(A) Birds

(B) Bison

(C) Horses

(D) Wild cats

解析：本题问"根据文章，哪种动物在洞壁上出现得最多？"。根据文章中第 8—10 行句子的描述可知，壁画上有鸟和马，马在 300 多幅画中出现，数量远超其他种类的动物，因此选项 (C)"马"是正确答案。选项 (A)"鸟"、选项 (B)"野牛"和选项 (D)"野猫"均错误。

6. In line 12, the word <u>They</u> refers to _____ .

(A) walls

(B) artists

(C) animals

(D) materials

解析：本题问"在第 12 行，They 指代的是_____"。代词一般代替之前出现的内容，因此需要从上一句中找答案；且"they"一般指代复数名词，可以进一步缩小范围。前面的句子说："画这些动物的早期艺术家完成了一项重大而又艰巨的任务"。句中符合以上标准的单词有"artists"和"animals"。而包含"They"一词的句子意思是"他们并不把自己局限于容易爬到的墙壁，而是带着他们的绘画材料……"，句中这些动作由"artists"做出最合适。因此选项 (B)"艺术家"是正确答案。选项 (A)"墙"、选项 (C)"动物"和选项 (D)"材料"均错误。

7. Why was painting inside the Lascaux complex a difficult task?

    (A) It was completely dark inside.

    (B) The caves were full of wild animals.

    (C) Painting materials were hard to find.

    (D) Many painting spaces were difficult to reach.

解析：本题问"为什么在 Lascaux 洞穴群中画画儿是一项艰难的任务？"。"difficult task"这个表达出现在文章第 12 行，因此，答案应该在这附近。文章提到，早期的画家要带着绘画材料攀爬陡峭的墙壁或爬进狭窄的通道，而这就是在Lascaux洞穴群中画壁画很难的原因。四个选项中只有选项 (D) "很多画画儿的地方很难到达"符合文义，因此为正确答案。选项 (A) "洞里一片漆黑"、选项 (B) "洞里都是野生动物"和选项 (C) "绘画材料很难找到"均错误。

8. According to the passage, all of the following have caused damage to the paintings EXCEPT _____ .

    (A) temperature changes

    (B) air movement

    (C) water

    (D) light

解析：本题问"根据文章，下列选项都对壁画造成了损坏，除了_____"。题目中"EXCEPT"大写，强调需要选出没有对壁画造成损毁的因素。根据文章第 18 行可知，水和温度变化都对壁画造成了损毁，因此选项 (A) "温度变化"和选项 (C) "水"错误。根据第 20 行内容可知，空气流动也损伤了壁画，因此选项 (B) "空气流动"错误。选项 (D) "光"符合题目要求，为正确答案。

9. **What does the passage say happened at the Lascaux caves in 1963?**

   (A) Visitors were prohibited from entering.

   (B) A new lighting system was installed.

   (C) Another part was discovered.

   (D) A new entrance was created.

解析：本题问"这篇文章提及 1963 年在 Lascaux 洞穴发生了什么？"。"1963"是非常明显的定位词，可以由此定位到文章第 23 行。文中说，为了防止壁画被进一步破坏，在 1963 年，这个地方不许游客进入了。因此选项 (A)"游客被禁止进入"是正确答案。选项 (B)"安装了一个新的照明系统"、选项 (C)"另一部分洞穴被发现了"以及选项 (D)"新建了一个入口"在文章中均没有对应信息，故错误。

第 ❻ 章

TOEFL Junior® 标准考试和口语考试
学习建议

▶▶▶

TOEFL Junior® 考试不是一项通过及格或不及格来界定成绩的考试，也不存在任何帮助考生准备这项考试的最佳学校、教材或学习方法，因为这项考试不基于某一特定的教学课程。只有经过相对较长时间的学习与练习，才能获得较强的语言能力。因此请将 *TOEFL Junior*® 考试当作衡量你是否取得进步的工具。以下提升听力技能、语言形式与含义答题技能和阅读技能的建议都需要持续且频繁地进行。如果在考试前不久才开始学习英语或尝试采取以下建议，那么英语能力很难有显著提升。

以下是一些提升听力技能的建议：

- 观看英语电影和电视节目以及收听英语广播是提高英语听力技能的极好途径。英语音像制品同样有帮助。互联网也是一个很好的资料来源，你可以使用这些资源来提升英语听力技能。
- 仔细听说话者说的内容。
- 通过问自己问题保持主动性。比如，说话者表达的主要观点是什么？
- 想想说话者在干什么。换句话说，这段演讲或对话的目的是什么？比如，说话者是在道歉、抱怨还是给出建议？
- 说话者的声音是冷静的还是激动的？说话者的语气向你表达了什么？
- 注意通过重音和语调来表达含义的方式。
- 思考一段谈话或讨论是如何发生的。听那些表明引言、主要步骤或主要观点、例子以及结论或者总结的标志词。
- 听那些表明观点之间联系和关系的词（如 because、however、therefore 等）。
- 听录音材料，在不同的地方停下来，预测接下来会给出什么信息或者表达什么观点。
- 在听讲座期间或听完讲座之后，写出所谈论内容的大纲。

以下是一些提升语言形式与含义答题技能的建议：

- 首先读懂一篇文本。然后，回顾同一篇文本，这一次注意构成句子的不同方式。
  - 在每个句子中，确定每个单词的词性。试着辨别出名词、动词、形容词、副词、介词、限定词和连词。此外，试着辨别出动词的时态。
  - 通过找到结构线索（如连接词或者标点符号）发现句子的其他部分与主句的关系。

- 找到衔接词（如 because、however、therefore 等），注意这些词是如何衔接观点的。
- 增加你的词汇量，每天学习 6—7 个新单词。不断扩充单词表，不时复习整个单词表，以确保你不会遗忘这些单词的含义。
- 记英语日记。每天花几分钟用英文写日记。
    - 如果你在学校里上英语课且学习语法，当你写日记时，注意使用你新学到的语法结构。
    - 当你完成一篇日记的时候，一定要回顾并重读你写的内容。修改是提升写作能力的关键。改正你发现的任何错误。标出你不确定的地方，并在班级里询问。

以下是一些提升阅读技能的建议：

- 每天阅读几页英文内容。阅读多种体裁的英文文本，包括短篇小说、报纸和杂志文章，以及关于科学、社会学、艺术等学术主题的非虚构文本。很多文本可以在互联网上找到。
- 练习快速地略读一篇文章以获得文章大意。培养快速浏览和辨明主旨的能力。
- 略读完一篇文章后，再仔细地读一遍，把文章主旨、要点和重要事实写下来。
- 当你遇到一个不熟悉的单词时，试着从语境中确定它的含义。如果不能从语境中确定含义的话，去词典中查它的意思。
- 用下划线标出所有的代词（he、him、they、them 等），并指出它们在文章中所指代的名词。

以下是一些提升口语能力的建议：

- 尽量每天学习新的单词。这些单词不一定来自教科书。像英语的新闻、歌曲、电影和电视节目等都是很好的生词来源。
- 看英语电影或电视节目时，注意说话人如何运用抑扬顿挫、缩略形式（如 he's、what's 等）、适当停顿和其他语言特点，然后在自己说英语的时候尽量模仿说话人的这些特点。
- 听英语新闻、广播、纪录片或者播客，以此练习听力理解。把听到的内容用自己的话概括出来讲给朋友听；你也可以把自己说的录下来，然后让你的朋友或者老师给你反馈。
- 和你的朋友练习复述故事。用英语给他们讲你最喜欢的电影或者小说。

- 准备一个连词列表（如 because、but、so 等）。在你说英语的时候尽量使用这些连词来更有效地连接你的想法。
- 练习描述事物。在日常生活中，你会常常描述东西、动作、人物和情景。你需要掌握很多形容词来描述它们。
  - 谈论关于你最喜欢的东西。选择你喜欢的书、电影、歌曲、演员、运动队伍、食谱、城市等，说出至少三个你喜欢的原因。
  - 描述你的学校或房子。它看起来是什么样子的？里面的人们怎么样？这个地方哪里好，哪里需要提升？
  - 描述你最喜欢的一次度假或者你理想中的度假。
- 和你的朋友玩游戏也是提升英语口语的好机会。你们可以玩寻宝游戏，也可以扮演老师来互相布置任务。重要的是，在游戏中，你要练习用英语给你的朋友下达指令。
- 拿漫画书或者绘本的某一页，练习用英语按顺序复述图片中的故事及其细节。和你的朋友一起练习，然后对比你们的复述。重复练习几次，直到你们觉得你们的复述可以非常好地概括图片中的故事。

第 7 章

全真考题一

Test Book
for the
TOEFL Junior®
Standard Test

Do not open until you are told to do so.

YOU CANNOT COPY, DISCUSS, OR SHARE
QUESTIONS OR ANSWERS FROM THIS TEST.

THIS TEST BOOK MUST NOT BE TAKEN FROM THE ROOM.

©2022 Educational Testing Service, Princeton, NJ, USA. All rights reserved.
The ETS logo, TOEFL, and TOEFL Junior are registered trademarks of
Educational Testing Service (ETS) in the United States and other countries.

xxxxxx

In English with Confidence™

Listening Comprehension

The listening section has 42 questions. Follow along as you listen to the directions to the listening section.

Directions

In this section of the test, you will hear a teacher or other school staff member talking to students. Each talk is followed by one question. Choose the best answer to each question and mark the letter of the correct answer on your answer sheet. You will hear each talk only one time.

Here is an example:

What does the teacher want the students to do?

(A) Help a new classmate
(B) Prepare for gym class
(C) Welcome a guest speaker
(D) Return books to the library

The correct answer is (A), "Help a new classmate."

Here is another example:

What will the students probably do next?

(A) Sing a song
(B) Listen to some music
(C) Choose instruments to play
(D) Discuss the life of a musician

The correct answer is (B), "Listen to some music."

Go on to the next page, and the test will begin with question number one.

扫码获取听力录音

1. **What will the students be doing at the aquarium?**

   (A) Helping the aquarium staff

   (B) Attending a show on underwater life

   (C) Learning how new exhibits are made

   (D) Seeing an exhibit on unusual sea creatures

2. **What will the students probably do next?**

   (A) Go to look at animals

   (B) Give notes to the teacher

   (C) Meet at the zoo's entrance

   (D) Talk about an animal they have studied

3. **What does the nurse remind the students to do?**

   (A) Make an appointment with her in her office

   (B) Ask their parents to call her office

   (C) Return the completed medical form to her

   (D) Give the medical form to their parents

4. **What is the purpose of the announcement?**

   (A) To encourage students to participate in after-school activities

   (B) To invite students to the mathematics competition

   (C) To thank students for cooperating with the teachers

   (D) To remind students that they must leave immediately after school

5. **Why is the teacher talking about the visiting students?**

   (A) To explain how to behave when the students arrive

   (B) To encourage everyone to join an exchange program

   (C) To describe the daily life of students in other countries

   (D) To suggest questions to ask the visiting students

6. **What does the teacher imply about the experiment?**

   (A) It can be dangerous.

   (B) It is easy to perform.

   (C) It requires careful planning.

   (D) It takes a long time to set up.

GO ON TO THE NEXT PAGE

7. **What is the purpose of the librarian's talk?**

   (A) To invite students to come to a book fair

   (B) To advertise some new books at the library

   (C) To discuss books that were popular in the winter

   (D) To remind students to return books they borrowed before the vacation

8. **Why is the teacher apologizing?**

   (A) He cannot bring paint to the next class.

   (B) He provided a messy kind of paint.

   (C) He did not realize students did not have paints.

   (D) He did not bring newspaper for the students to use.

9. **What is probably true about last year's poster?**

   (A) The judges found errors in it.

   (B) It won the science competition.

   (C) It earned fewer points than this year's poster.

   (D) It contained more pictures than this year's poster.

GO ON TO THE NEXT PAGE

GO ON TO THE NEXT PAGE

Now you will hear some conversations. Each conversation is followed by three or more questions. Choose the best answer to each question and mark the letter of the correct answer on your answer sheet. You will hear each conversation only one time.

10. **What does the teacher imply when she says, "But I wasn't the only one"?**

   (A) Other people came to the picnic, too.
   (B) Many people enjoyed the boy's cake.
   (C) Many people brought cakes to the picnic.
   (D) She brought additional items to share.

11. **What was the boy's mother afraid of?**

   (A) That people would not like the cake
   (B) That the cake would not be big enough
   (C) That she would not enjoy herself at the picnic
   (D) That she would not have time to make the cake

12. **What does the teacher ask the boy to do?**

   (A) Show her how to bake the cake
   (B) Bring her the recipe for the cake
   (C) Thank his mother for baking the cake
   (D) Invite his mother to the music club picnic

13. **What will the teacher do on Monday?**

   (A) Bake a cake at home
   (B) Visit a bakery
   (C) Bring the boy a piece of her cake
   (D) Teach the boy's class how to bake a cake

14. What is the main topic of the conversation?

(A) A karate coach at school

(B) A new community center

(C) Signing up for a karate class

(D) Winning a championship

15. What caused the boy to be interested in karate?

(A) A movie he recently saw

(B) A video game he recently played

(C) A community center Web site

(D) A friend who recently started karate classes

16. What does the girl imply when she says there might be cancellations after the first class?

(A) The class might interfere with school activities.

(B) The class might be too hard for some students.

(C) She thinks she might not like the class.

(D) The class might be too crowded.

17. Why does the boy mention Coach Peters?

(A) To tell the girl who his volleyball coach was

(B) To give a reason why the girl's friend left the volleyball team

(C) To help explain why he does not mind a demanding instructor

(D) To show that he likes volleyball more than karate

18. What are the speakers mainly discussing?

(A) A trip that the class is planning

(B) A topic for the student's final project

(C) A community event sponsored by the school

(D) Some missed assignments the student needs to complete

19. What subject does the teacher most likely teach?

(A) Art

(B) Science

(C) History

(D) Literature

20. Where is the girl's family originally from?

(A) Egypt

(B) Japan

(C) China

(D) Mexico

21. What does the girl mean when she says, "So I was wondering"?

(A) She wants to change the assignment.

(B) She wants to work with another classmate.

(C) She wants to ask the teacher for an extension.

(D) She wants the teacher to clarify a lesson.

GO ON TO THE NEXT PAGE

22. What did the boy lose?

(A) A folder
(B) A backpack
(C) An important piece of paper
(D) A school project

23. Why didn't the boy turn in his permission slip sooner?

(A) He did not know when it was due.
(B) He forgot to ask his parents to sign it earlier.
(C) He did not think he would want to go on the trip.
(D) He did not think his parents would let him go on the trip.

24. How does the boy probably feel when he says, "I already did that. I can't find it anywhere"?

(A) Jealous
(B) Hopeful
(C) Confident
(D) Frustrated

25. What does the boy imply when he says, "Yeah, I guess that's my only option"?

(A) He will not go on the field trip.
(B) He will ask his parents to call the teacher.
(C) He will ask the teacher for a new permission slip.
(D) He will visit the science museum with his parents.

26. What will the students probably do next?

(A) Call the boy's parents
(B) Look in the boy's backpack
(C) Walk to the science museum
(D) Go to Ms. Gomez' classroom

GO ON TO THE NEXT PAGE

Now you will hear some talks and discussions about academic topics. Each talk or discussion is followed by three or more questions. Choose the best answer to each question and mark the letter of the correct answer on your answer sheet. You will hear each talk or discussion only one time.

27. **What is the speaker mainly talking about?**

    (A) Ways artists make frames for their work
    (B) The importance of frames for works of art
    (C) An unusual frame on a painting in a museum
    (D) Differences between the frames of two paintings

28. **What does the speaker say about the materials used to make frames?**

    (A) Many different kinds of materials are used.
    (B) The materials used in frames are often expensive.
    (C) Most materials used in old frames are no longer available.
    (D) The materials in old frames last longer than newer materials.

29. **What will visitors see at the end of the tour?**

    (A) A film about frames from the nineteenth century
    (B) Several artists making frames for their paintings
    (C) A collection of paintings in their original frames
    (D) People maintaining and repairing frames

30. **What did the museum learn about the painting of the children?**

    (A) It had been moved many times.
    (B) It was no longer in its original frame.
    (C) It was not as old as people had originally thought.
    (D) It was painted by a different artist than most people had thought.

GO ON TO THE NEXT PAGE

31. **Why are the teacher and student talking about cliffs, beaches, and valleys at the beginning of the discussion?**

    (A) To review how these different landforms are created

    (B) To discuss landforms they see every day

    (C) To compare the different qualities of water

    (D) To explain how large bodies of water formed on Earth

32. **Why does the student talk about sand?**

    (A) To introduce a topic related to landforms

    (B) To explain the difference between beaches and valleys

    (C) To give an example of rocks worn away by water

    (D) To describe the type of rock found near the ocean

33. **What is the tool called a water jet used for?**

    (A) Cooling hot objects

    (B) Cutting hard objects

    (C) Cleaning dirty objects

    (D) Filling empty containers

34. **According to the student, what is one problem with the water jet?**

    (A) It works very slowly.

    (B) It makes a lot of noise.

    (C) It uses a lot of water quickly.

    (D) It can only be used in a few locations.

GO ON TO THE NEXT PAGE

35. **What is the main topic of the discussion?**

    (A) A famous archaeological site
    (B) The cost of archaeological artifacts
    (C) A method archaeologists use to tell the age of artifacts
    (D) A method archaeologists use to find artifacts

36. **Why does the teacher talk about balloons and kites?**

    (A) To describe how weather affects aerial photographs
    (B) To describe how archaeologists took aerial photographs in the past
    (C) To explain how ancient artifacts were transported one hundred years ago
    (D) To explain how modern archaeology has improved in the past one hundred years

37. **What can archaeologists learn from some aerial photographs?**

    (A) The types of crops grown in ancient times
    (B) The number of artifacts left by ancient people
    (C) The location of ancient villages
    (D) The time when ancient people left an area

38. **What are crop marks?**

    (A) Patterns in the height and color of crops
    (B) Painted signs marking specific types of crops
    (C) Different kinds of soil used by farmers to grow crops
    (D) Fences or walls built to protect crops

GO ON TO THE NEXT PAGE

39. **What is the teacher mainly talking about?**

    (A) Plants that are eaten by sea animals
    (B) Sea animals that live near the shore
    (C) How sea animals find food in sand
    (D) The main predators of small sea animals

40. **What is mentioned about ocean plants in coastal waters?**

    (A) They have special adaptations.
    (B) They keep coastal waters clean.
    (C) They have difficulty surviving.
    (D) They are dangerous to animals.

41. **Where can masked crabs usually be found?**

    (A) Buried deep under the sand
    (B) Hidden in seaweed near the shore
    (C) Outside of the water on the beach
    (D) Swimming just above the seafloor

42. **Why does the beach hopper only come out at night?**

    (A) It is safe from birds.
    (B) It has less competition for food.
    (C) It cannot tolerate the daytime heat.
    (D) It can hunt animals that are only active at night.

Language Form and Meaning

Directions

In this section of the test, you will answer 42 questions found in several different texts. Within each text are boxes that contain four possible ways to complete a sentence. Choose the word or words in each box that correctly complete each sentence. Mark the letter of the correct answer on your answer sheet.

Here are two sample questions:

1. The idea that rocks last forever and that rocks

(A) still
(B) very
(C) quite
(D) never

change

is not completely true. If you have ever stood next to a rushing river, you

2.

(A) saw
(B) seen
(C) are seeing
(D) may have seen

the water hammering away at the rocks.

The correct answer to **Sample 1** is (D), "never." The correct answer to **Sample 2** is (D), "may have seen."

GO ON TO THE NEXT PAGE

Questions 1–4 refer to the following notice.

The environmental club is holding

1. (A) a bake sale
   (B) a bake sale is
   (C) and a bake sale
   (D) that a bake sale

next Monday at 3 P.M. in the

hallway outside of the cafeteria. All the money

2. (A) raised
   (B) raising
   (C) to raise
   (D) was raised

will go to the

International Nature Foundation,

3. (A) either
   (B) what
   (C) any
   (D) an

organization that protects endangered

animals. The sale will

4. (A) save
   (B) select
   (C) feature
   (D) purchase

delicious cookies, cupcakes, muffins, and more.

Please stop by!

GO ON TO THE NEXT PAGE

Questions 5–8 refer to the following e-mail.

Thanks for your e-mail. I am finally starting

5. (A) to feel better.
   (B) better feeling.
   (C) have felt better.
   (D) feeling is better.

6. (A) Instead,
   (B) However,
   (C) Otherwise,
   (D) As a result,

I will probably miss school again tomorrow since the doctor said I

should rest. Could you please tell me

7. (A) which I missed
   (B) I have missed it
   (C) what I have missed
   (D) those I was missing

in biology class this week

so I can work on our assignments? I would really

8. (A) satisfy
   (B) suggest
   (C) anticipate
   (D) appreciate

it.

Thanks,

Ricardo

GO ON TO THE NEXT PAGE

Questions 9–12 refer to the following announcement.

9. (A) just starts
    (B) just starting
    (C) has just started
    (D) was just started

The French club ⎡ ⎤ a lunch group in the cafeteria. On Tuesdays and

Thursdays during lunch, students who wish to practice their French should

10. (A) hand in
    (B) take after
    (C) give up
    (D) look for

the table with the French flag. All conversations at the French table

11. (A) completely will be held
    (B) will completely held be
    (C) held completely will be
    (D) will be held completely

in French.

12. (A) The Spanish club
    (B) It is the Spanish club
    (C) While the Spanish club
    (D) Because the Spanish club

will be

starting a similar group next month.

GO ON TO THE NEXT PAGE

Questions 13–18 refer to the following article from a magazine about technology.

Some people depend on clothing

13. (A) their keeping
    (B) they are kept
    (C) to keep them
    (D) it keeps them

safe while they are working.

Astronauts

14. (A) by working
    (B) they work
    (C) who work
    (D) are working

outside of a spacecraft must wear special space suits to

protect their bodies.

15. (A) Even a tiny hole in the space suit
    (B) The space suit has even a tiny hole in it
    (C) There is even a tiny hole in the space suit
    (D) Whether in the space suit, even a tiny hole

could create a loss

of pressure and cause a dangerous situation. In recent years scientists

16. (A) develop
    (B) developing
    (C) are developed
    (D) have developed

space suits made of high-tech fabrics and gel. If the space suit gets a

small hole in it, the gel quickly spreads into

17. (A) a
    (B) the
    (C) any
    (D) some

hole and closes it up. These space

suits also have tiny computers in

18. (A) it.
    (B) this.
    (C) they.
    (D) them.

If a large hole is made in the suit, the tiny

computer sends a warning to the astronaut to move to safety quickly.

GO ON TO THE NEXT PAGE

Questions 19–26 refer to the following student essay.

The onion is a well-known ingredient

19. (A) found
    (B) finding
    (C) to find it
    (D) that found

in many national cuisines.

20. (A) It also
    (B) Is also
    (C) It is also
    (D) Also, despite its

among the oldest foods known to have been eaten by humans.

21. (A) Sometimes
    (B) Whenever
    (C) However
    (D) During

archaeologists manage to collect bits of food from prehistoric objects,

tiny pieces of onion have often been found. Determined to be

22. (A) many
    (B) more of
    (C) much as
    (D) more than

5,000 years

old, these first onions were probably wild plants

23. (A) instead
    (B) whether
    (C) although
    (D) rather than

vegetables grown by

farmers. There are two reasons

24. (A) for
    (B) how
    (C) why
    (D) it was

the onion has been so popular throughout

GO ON TO THE NEXT PAGE

history: it is easy to grow and it

25. (A) can store it
    (B) to be stored
    (C) able to store
    (D) can be stored

for long periods of time without

spoiling. Thanks to the protection provided by the onion's dry outer layer, the inside can remain

26. (A) fresh
    (B) recent
    (C) passive
    (D) harmless

for many months.

Questions 27–34 refer to the following passage from a history book.

We do not know exactly when or how people first built ships. However,

27. (A) that we imagine
    (B) we imagine what
    (C) it is easy to imagine
    (D) to imagine it is easy

that people long ago may have tried using floating objects, such

as pieces of wood,

28. (A) things transport
    (B) to transport things
    (C) things are transported
    (D) transportation of things

over water. They may then have realized

that by tying many floating objects together, even heavier items

29. (A) to
    (B) are
    (C) will
    (D) could

be carried

across water. Most probably, people at first built very simple boats

30. (A) that made pieces of wood
    (B) pieces of wood to be made
    (C) and pieces of wood were made
    (D) that were made of pieces of wood

tied together.

31. (A) Each
    (B) Such
    (C) Either
    (D) Another

boats were

probably moved by people sitting on them and paddling with their hands. The next step may have

GO ON TO THE NEXT PAGE

32. (A) flat objects using
    (B) flat objects to use
    (C) to use flat objects
    (D) it used flat objects

been ___ to row the boat. As we know, the use of sails eventually

would allow boats to be moved by wind power.

33. (A) The early boats pictured
    (B) Picturing the early boats
    (C) They pictured the early boats
    (D) The early boats were pictured

on

ancient objects such as vases or wall paintings were thus not the result of a single invention.

Rather, they were created gradually through a process in which each step represented

34. (A) an improvement
    (B) an institution
    (C) a production
    (D) a creation

over the previous attempt.

Questions 35–42 refer to the following passage from a book about birds.

Although birds like ducks and geese are excellent fliers,

35. (A) and spend
    (B) they spend
    (C) spend them
    (D) they spend it

most of their

time in water. All year round, these birds can be seen floating on lakes and rivers, even when it is

36. (A) It keeps these birds
    (B) These birds are kept
    (C) What keeps these birds
    (D) To have kept these birds

very cold.

from getting wet and cold is the natural oil on

their feathers. The oil simply stops water

37. (A) at
    (B) to
    (C) from
    (D) during

penetrating their feathers.

Additionally,

38. (A) underneath their oily feathers,
    (B) underneath are their oily feathers,
    (C) underneath their feathers are oily,
    (D) their oily feathers are underneath them,

birds have another layer of

very soft feathers called down.

39. (A) Primarily
    (B) It is primarily
    (C) What is primarily
    (D) Its being primarily

this soft, lightweight down that

GO ON TO THE NEXT PAGE

helps the bird stay warm

40. (A) even it dives when
    (B) when even dives it
    (C) even when it dives
    (D) it even dives when

into freezing water. In fact, down is so

good at

41. (A) doing
    (B) having
    (C) adding
    (D) keeping

things warm that people also use it for this purpose. All around the

world, down is used to stuff coats, blankets, and other articles, making them

42. (A) but
    (B) both
    (C) either
    (D) they are

lightweight and warm.

GO ON TO THE NEXT PAGE

NO TEST MATERIAL ON THIS PAGE

Reading Comprehension

Directions

In this section of the test, you will read several texts and answer 42 questions. Choose the correct answer to each question and mark the letter of the correct answer on your answer sheet.

Before you start, read the sample text and the questions below.

Sample Text

The Golden Gate Bridge is a famous bridge in San Francisco. The bridge has a red color, but gray clouds often surround it. On clear days people come to take pictures of the bridge. The pictures show the green hills next to the bridge and the blue water under it.

Sample Question 1

What is the text mostly about?

(A) Gray clouds
(B) San Francisco
(C) A famous bridge
(D) Taking photographs

The correct answer is (C), "A famous bridge."

Sample Question 2

What color is the Golden Gate Bridge?

(A) Red
(B) Green
(C) Blue
(D) Gray

The correct answer is (A), "Red."

Questions 1–4 are about the following e-mail.

To: The Student Science Institute info@ssi.org
From: Ben Mason bmason@starnet.com
Date: March 12

I am a student at Avon Middle School. A friend of mine told me about the
Student Science Institute and your summer classes for students. I am interested in
studying the ocean. When I go to university, I plan to learn all about the animals and
Line plants that live in the sea. Every year, my family goes to <u>visit</u> my grandparents. Their
  5 house is very close to the seashore. When I am there, I like to take walks with my
grandparents along the beach. I try to identify seashells and seaweed. My parents
gave me a book that helps me learn about the different kinds of plants and animals I
find. If you have summer classes that teach students about ocean life, please send me
some information about them.

Sincerely,

Ben Mason

GO ON TO THE NEXT PAGE

1. **Why is Ben writing to the Student Science Institute?**

   (A) He wants directions to the institute.
   (B) He wants help identifying a sea animal.
   (C) He wants to know the author of a book.
   (D) He wants information about summer classes.

2. **What detail about his university plans does Ben mention?**

   (A) What subject he wants to study
   (B) When he will be ready to attend
   (C) How his parents will help him
   (D) Which university he hopes to go to

3. **In line 4, the word <u>visit</u> is closest in meaning to _____.**

   (A) find out
   (B) help with
   (C) stay with
   (D) watch over

4. **What does Ben do with his grandparents?**

   (A) Go fishing
   (B) Take walks
   (C) Read stories
   (D) Help make dinner

Questions 5–8 are about the following advertisement.

Summer Work for Students

Carson Middle School has made arrangements with local organizations to create summer work/learning opportunities for students. For more details and an application, call Mr. Dyson, the school administrator, at 555-6532.

Opportunity 1	Do you love animals? The Bartlett Horse Farm needs two students to help with feeding and grooming chores. We have 16 friendly horses and an experienced full-time staff to train student workers. You must be able to commit to four mornings per week from 7:30–11:30 A.M.
Opportunity 2	Tutors are needed to help elementary school students in basic math, reading, and writing. Applicants must have excellent grades. Scheduling is flexible.
Opportunity 3	A young artist is needed at the Cherry Hill Summer Day Camp for children who are 5–10 years old. You will work as an assistant art teacher, helping campers with drawing and painting projects. This is a great opportunity to learn about teaching art. The camps are for the month of July only, from 10:00 A.M.–2:00 P.M., Monday–Friday.
Opportunity 4	Learn the secrets of gardening! Five to seven young people are needed to help at a new community vegetable garden. No experience is necessary—just an interest in learning how to grow fresh vegetables. Participants will get to take home some of what they grow.

Check our Web site each week for additional openings: www.carson.edu/summer—jobs

GO ON TO THE NEXT PAGE

5. How many jobs require the student to teach?

(A) One
(B) Two
(C) Three
(D) Four

6. Which opportunity is for only one student?

(A) Opportunity 1
(B) Opportunity 2
(C) Opportunity 3
(D) Opportunity 4

7. The description for which opportunity does NOT provide information about the work hours?

(A) Opportunity 1
(B) Opportunity 2
(C) Opportunity 3
(D) Opportunity 4

8. What are students instructed to do in order to apply for one of the jobs?

(A) Visit a Web site
(B) Call a school employee
(C) Attend a special meeting
(D) Contact a local organization

GO ON TO THE NEXT PAGE

Questions 9–12 are about the following story.

When I opened my eyes, Miranda was already awake. To my disappointment, she was wearing a blue shirt. Miranda and I have an agreement. Since it is so difficult for people to tell us apart, we have agreed not to dress alike.

Line

5 "I was going to wear blue today," I said.

"You should have gotten out of bed earlier," Miranda replied. "Then you could have been the first dressed." She looked tired, and I could tell she was grumpy and did not want to be bothered this morning.

"Maybe I'll wear blue anyway," I said.

But Miranda knew that I didn't mean it. We both knew that dressing in the same color 10 would confuse people. When we were little, Miranda and I thought it was funny when people mixed us up. We would <u>giggle</u> when someone called me by her name or referred to her as Diana.

In the past, we had even tried to mislead people as a joke, like in our dance class when we were six years old. For several classes, we had convinced the teacher that I was 15 Miranda. Just when the poor teacher thought she knew who was who, Miranda and I had switched back to our real names.

What was funny when we were six years old was annoying now. I was tired of <u>politely correcting teachers</u> who called me Miranda. And at least once a day, Miranda's best friend, Tanya, would rush over and start to talk to me, even though we don't know 20 each other well. Sometimes even our own father looked and waited a moment before talking to one of us.

I turned to look at Miranda as I got out of bed. She still looked tired as she slowly brushed her hair. Then, she sat back down on her bed, putting her hand to her head. "Actually, I don't feel well," she said.

25 "Are you sick?" I asked with concern.

"I think it's just a cold," Miranda answered. "But my head does ache. I think you'll be going to school without me today. It looks like you can wear your blue shirt after all."

My clothes didn't matter to me that much, however. I thought about the day ahead at school without Miranda. I knew that when everyone learned that she was at home sick, 30 nobody would mistake me for her. Strangely, I also knew that I would miss being called by her name.

GO ON TO THE NEXT PAGE

9. Which title best summarizes the story?

   (A) Miranda's Mistake
   (B) Fooling Friends at School
   (C) The Battle over the Blue Shirt
   (D) Twin Sisters and Close Friends

10. In line 11, the word <u>giggle</u> is closest in meaning to _____.

   (A) mistake
   (B) explain
   (C) appear
   (D) laugh

11. In line 18, how does the narrator probably feel when talking about "politely correcting teachers"?

   (A) Frustrated that they often call her by the wrong name
   (B) Disappointed that she looks so much like Miranda
   (C) Angry that they do not think she is funny anymore
   (D) Afraid that she often annoys them

12. What will most likely happen next in the story?

   (A) The narrator will go to school alone.
   (B) The narrator will go to dance class with her sister.
   (C) Both girls will wear the same color shirt to school.
   (D) The narrator will stay home to take care of her sister.

GO ON TO THE NEXT PAGE

Questions 13–18 are about the following passage.

Video games can be found practically everywhere. We see them on the Internet and TV. Most people have played a video
Line game at least once in their lives.
5   The first video games were manufactured in the 1970s. However, they were much different from the ones we see now. They were less colorful and lacked music, and they were not played by people
10   at home. The first video games were played on large machines that stood in public places and were started by players inserting coins into <u>them</u>. They were so immensely popular that their creators
15   decided that customers would be willing to buy home versions of video games. Soon

portable game computers became available, allowing people to play video games at home. Many of the first game computers still exist today in the private collections of gaming enthusiasts.

20   Over the years, video games have become more interesting and complex. While the first games were designed by computer programmers working alone, video game companies were soon <u>assembling</u> large teams of people to design graphics and to write music for games. Thanks to these large teams, today's video games look very realistic, and the images they show are as detailed as photographs.

25   Creating a new video game today is a very time-consuming task, however. The whole team often works together for many years to produce a game that eventually becomes available for sale. Many people are surprised to learn that work on designing their favorite game started years before it arrived on store shelves.

GO ON TO THE NEXT PAGE

13. **What question does the passage answer?**

    (A) Which video games are most popular?
    (B) Who invented the first video game?
    (C) How have video games changed over time?
    (D) Why do people enjoy playing video games?

14. **In line 13, the word them refers to _____.**

    (A) coins
    (B) places
    (C) creators
    (D) machines

15. **What point does the author make about old game computers?**

    (A) They are difficult to repair.
    (B) They can be purchased for little money.
    (C) They can be used to play new video games.
    (D) They are collected by people who like video games.

16. **What does the passage say about the first video game designers?**

    (A) They worked alone.
    (B) They were well paid.
    (C) They played many games.
    (D) They often listened to music.

17. **In line 22, the word assembling is closest in meaning to _____.**

    (A) saving up
    (B) taking apart
    (C) working against
    (D) bringing together

18. **According to the author, what are people surprised to learn?**

    (A) How expensive some video games are
    (B) Where most video games are made
    (C) How long it takes to create a video game
    (D) How long ago the first video games were created

GO ON TO THE NEXT PAGE

Questions 19–26 are about the following passage.

Free diving is a sport in which participants
remain underwater while holding their breath for
several minutes. In one free-diving event, athletes
Line compete to see who can dive deepest without
5 using an oxygen tank, the equipment normally
used by professional divers who spend long
periods underwater. The only equipment used by
free divers is vests to keep them warm, very
long lines to help lower themselves, and weights
10 to help them sink faster.

Free diving as we know it today would have been hard to imagine a century ago.
Scientists had long believed that it was impossible for humans to <u>descend</u> more than
50 meters below the water's surface. Depths below that level were thought to be safe
only for animals used to the high pressure felt at great depths. That belief has been
15 clearly proven wrong by the many divers who have long since broken the 50-meter
mark. Nowadays, many free divers can dive to depths of more than 200 meters. To
appreciate this <u>staggering</u> distance, imagine a 60-story-high building. Reaching a depth
of 200 meters is like traveling in an elevator from the top floor of that building to the
first floor, except that the entire journey takes place underwater. Although free diving to
20 such extreme depths is relatively new in the world of sports competitions, free diving
itself has been practiced since ancient times. For centuries, fishermen have been free
diving to catch fish or collect edible plants growing at the bottom of the sea.

Reaching such great depths and remaining
there for periods of time is possible because the
25 divers have mastered apnea, the technique of
forgoing breathing. Most untrained people can
maintain apnea for around a minute. Experienced
free divers can remain in apnea for ten times that
long. To become free divers, beginners must first
30 practice this skill. To their surprise, they discover
that this first stage of practice does not happen
underwater. Apnea is first practiced by free divers
not by swimming but by walking without
breathing. Learning this first step is only the
35 beginning. True masters of free diving spend long
years before they have the ability to lower
themselves to extreme depths.

GO ON TO THE NEXT PAGE

19. **Which title best summarizes the passage?**

    (A) Deep Divers Study Strange Fish
    (B) Extreme Competitors Dive Deep
    (C) Learning to Breathe Deeply
    (D) Looking for Fun on the Ocean Floor

20. **Which of the following are participants in free-diving competitions NOT allowed to use?**

    (A) Long lines
    (B) Warm vests
    (C) Oxygen tanks
    (D) Heavy weights

21. **According to the passage, what were scientists wrong about?**

    (A) How deep humans are able to dive
    (B) Which animals can dive deepest
    (C) Which types of fish need the least amount of oxygen
    (D) How much oxygen is contained in seawater

22. **In line 12, the word descend is closest in meaning to _____.**

    (A) sit by
    (B) use up
    (C) go down
    (D) move from

23. **What does the author imply about free diving in ancient times?**

    (A) It was a well-paid profession.
    (B) It was a practical skill used in finding food.
    (C) It was more competitive then than it is today.
    (D) It was a skill passed on from parents to children.

24. **In line 17, the word staggering is closest in meaning to _____.**

    (A) heavy
    (B) available
    (C) important
    (D) incredible

25. **Why does the author mention a 60-story building?**

    (A) To explain how free divers practice
    (B) To argue that free diving can be dangerous
    (C) To illustrate how some divers jump into water
    (D) To describe how deep some free divers can go

26. **What is "apnea"?**

    (A) The ability to hold one's breath
    (B) A sea animal found at great depths
    (C) The greatest depth reached by divers
    (D) A piece of equipment used by divers

Questions 27–34 are about the following article.

On Friday night, Downtown Café hosted an exhibit for the students in Mr. Romano's advanced drawing class. The art exhibit was part of the café's *Line* efforts to hold more special events for the
5 community.

Mr. Romano's class had been working on a project that involved drawing buildings in town. When the owner of Downtown Café, Lisa Greenwald, heard about <u>it</u>, she knew it was
10 something the café should be involved in.

"We've been trying to create events that everyone in town can come to and enjoy," said Ms. Greenwald. "When I heard some of the students at the café talking about this project, I
15 thought it would be perfect for us."

The eighth-graders in Mr. Romano's advanced art class have spent the last month walking to different buildings around the downtown area and drawing them. "We're <u>fortunate</u> that the middle
20 school is within walking distance of so many impressive buildings," Mr. Romano said. The drawings include images of First Safety Bank, the library, City Hall, and other local buildings.

Each student selected their two best drawings, 25 and on Friday afternoon they took their pictures over to the café to set them up for display. The show opened to the public at 7 P.M.

All ten of the class's students were present at the exhibit, as was Mr. Romano. Dozens of community
30 members came to the café throughout the evening to admire the students' work.

"These kids are really talented," said Pauline Kirchner, who was walking by the café when she noticed a poster advertising the art show.
35 "And it's wonderful to have an event like this where the whole community can come out to recognize the accomplishments of our students."

In order to take the advanced art class, students must submit a portfolio of their previous work and
40 have taken two years of art class.

"While I always enjoy working with the advanced art class, we have an especially great group of kids this year," Mr. Romano said. "They are each very gifted. So when Ms. Greenwald
45 approached me about having an art show at the café, I thought it would be a good way to share their talents with the whole town."

GO ON TO THE NEXT PAGE

27. Which headline best summarizes the article?

(A) Students Find Jobs at Downtown Café

(B) Students Present Art at Downtown Café

(C) Teacher Encourages Student Art

(D) Students Donate Drawings to Library

28. Why did Ms. Greenwald want to host the art show at the café?

(A) She wanted to do a favor for Mr. Romano.

(B) She wanted to hold more events for the community.

(C) Her daughter was in Mr. Romano's advanced art class.

(D) She heard the students had no other place to exhibit their art.

29. In line 9, the word it refers to _____.

(A) café

(B) class

(C) project

(D) drawing

30. What project have the students been working on all month?

(A) Drawing buildings around town

(B) Painting the walls of the new café

(C) Making new coffee cups for the café

(D) Helping Mr. Romano set up his art studio

31. In line 19, the word fortunate is closest in meaning to _____.

(A) bored

(B) lucky

(C) worried

(D) surprised

32. What is probably true about the middle school?

(A) It is an older building.

(B) It has a large art program.

(C) The students have drawn it in class.

(D) It is located near the downtown area.

33. Why did Pauline Kirchner decide to go to the art exhibit?

(A) She was already inside the café.

(B) She had a drawing at the exhibit.

(C) She thought there would be free coffee.

(D) She was interested by a sign she saw.

34. Why are there only ten students in the advanced art class?

(A) Only ten students were interested in taking it.

(B) Only the most talented students are invited to take it.

(C) The classroom only has enough space for ten students.

(D) The class used to be larger, but many students dropped out.

Questions 35–42 refer to the following letter.

Dear Editor:

I read the article in last week's school newspaper about the new science textbooks the school purchased this year. It seemed <u>bizarre</u> to me that some people apparently do not
Line like the new books because they think the books have too many pictures and graphics.
5 These people would prefer that books include just words and a lot fewer charts and tables. I disagree that there are too many pictures and graphics in the new books, and I want to explain why.

I am not saying that I think reading is not important; of course it is. But when some ideas are just described in sentences and paragraphs, <u>they</u> are not always easy to
10 understand. This is especially true when the ideas are very new to students or really complicated. That is when pictures can really help. They do not replace the words, but they make what the words are saying a lot clearer sometimes. There's a famous saying: "A picture is worth a thousand words." I think that makes sense because sometimes I understand scientific information more quickly once I see a picture of what
15 is going on. But if I only read about the same idea, I might read a lot and still be confused. Many students agree that it is important to get information <u>in visual form</u> rather than simply read it.

Also, pictures, charts, and graphs not only help us while we are students but also to be successful in our jobs when we are adults. Scientists use charts and graphs all the time.
20 Business people do, too, as do people who have to operate machines and follow patterns or maps.

When I took a chemistry class last year, I really appreciated the different diagrams and charts in the textbooks. For example, I learned that water can exist as a solid, liquid, or gas. A chart in the textbook we were using explained this with pictures of water in
25 different forms, like liquid water in a river, solid water in an ice cube, and water that becomes part of the air, like the steam that rises from hot water. The new textbooks have a similar chart about water, and they also have many new diagrams and charts that I think chemistry students will benefit from.

Sincerely,

Ellen Lee

GO ON TO THE NEXT PAGE

35. Why did Ellen probably write the letter?

(A) To disagree with an opinion she read in the newspaper

(B) To explain why some books do not need to include charts and graphs

(C) To express her disappointment about the school's selection of new textbooks

(D) To encourage other students to write to the newspaper

36. In line 3, the word <u>bizarre</u> is closest in meaning to _____ .

(A) encouraging

(B) strange

(C) exciting

(D) correct

37. What do some people dislike about the new textbooks?

(A) The poor quality of the printing

(B) The amount of money they cost

(C) The way they present some information

(D) The range of topics they include

38. In line 9, the word <u>they</u> refers to _____ .

(A) ideas

(B) students

(C) sentences

(D) paragraphs

39. In line 16, the phrase <u>in visual form</u> is closest in meaning to _____ .

(A) during class

(B) outside in nature

(C) as a picture or another graphic

(D) through an experiment or research

40. What does Ellen NOT say about charts and graphs to support her argument?

(A) They are used by people in many jobs.

(B) They make some ideas easier to understand.

(C) They make textbooks less expensive to buy.

(D) They are helpful to chemistry students.

41. Why does Ellen mention a river in her letter?

(A) To share what she learned on a recent field trip

(B) To describe a photograph on the cover of a science book

(C) To suggest that charts and graphs are not always appropriate

(D) To give an example of a chart she found useful in a book

42. According to Ellen, what do the old and new science books have in common?

(A) They include a similar number of diagrams.

(B) They were chosen by the same teachers.

(C) They were written by the same author.

(D) They include a chart about water.

NO TEST MATERIAL ON THIS PAGE

第 8 章

全真考题二

▶▶▶

Form Code
4RTJPT2

Test Book
for the
TOEFL Junior®
Standard Test

Do not open until you are told to do so.

YOU CANNOT COPY, DISCUSS, OR SHARE
QUESTIONS OR ANSWERS FROM THIS TEST.

THIS TEST BOOK MUST NOT BE TAKEN FROM THE ROOM.

©2022 Educational Testing Service, Princeton, NJ, USA. All rights reserved.
The ETS logo, TOEFL, and TOEFL Junior are registered trademarks of
Educational Testing Service (ETS) in the United States and other countries.

xxxxxx

In English with Confidence™

Listening Comprehension

The listening section has 42 questions. Follow along as you listen to the directions to the listening section.

Directions

In this section of the test, you will hear a teacher or other school staff member talking to students. Each talk is followed by one question. Choose the best answer to each question and mark the letter of the correct answer on your answer sheet. You will hear each talk only one time.

Here is an example:

What does the teacher want the students to do?

(A) Help a new classmate
(B) Prepare for gym class
(C) Welcome a guest speaker
(D) Return books to the library

The correct answer is (A), "Help a new classmate."

Here is another example:

What will the students probably do next?

(A) Sing a song
(B) Listen to some music
(C) Choose instruments to play
(D) Discuss the life of a musician

The correct answer is (B), "Listen to some music."

Go on to the next page, and the test will begin with question number one.

扫码获取听力录音

1. **What is the purpose of the talk?**

   (A) To promote a new book
   (B) To locate a missing item
   (C) To explain a new library policy
   (D) To announce a schedule change

2. **What does the teacher request that the students do?**

   (A) Prepare paper material for an art class
   (B) Organize an after-school meeting
   (C) Submit completed projects
   (D) Clean the classroom

3. **What will the students probably do next?**

   (A) Learn to pass the ball
   (B) Separate into two teams
   (C) Practice shooting the ball
   (D) Begin stretching exercises

4. **What is the purpose of the announcement?**

   (A) To apologize for interrupting a class
   (B) To ask all students to go to the main office as soon as possible
   (C) To create a list of students in a class
   (D) To remind students to return the contact information form

5. **What is probably true about the video?**

   (A) It is very old.
   (B) It is very long.
   (C) It talks about cats in ancient Egypt.
   (D) It shows how animals survive in the desert.

6. **What does the speaker imply about most students?**

   (A) They usually visit the library after school hours.
   (B) They do not know that the library provides a lot of resources.
   (C) They do not receive a tour of the library their first year.
   (D) They come to the school library for most of their research.

GO ON TO THE NEXT PAGE

7. **What is the purpose of the talk?**

   (A) To remind students about the review sessions before an exam
   (B) To tell students the location of the final exam
   (C) To outline for students what will be discussed in class
   (D) To inform students of the results of an exam

8. **Why is the principal apologizing?**

   (A) A basketball game has been rescheduled.
   (B) The cafeteria has been closed.
   (C) The location of the science fair has been changed.
   (D) A science lecture has been cancelled.

9. **What is probably true about the ceramic bowl?**

   (A) It is very rare.
   (B) It is very small.
   (C) It is similar to modern bowls.
   (D) It is borrowed from another museum.

10. **What is the teacher explaining?**

   (A) New facts about birds
   (B) The previous test the class took
   (C) Why they are studying about birds
   (D) Information about tomorrow's test

GO ON TO THE NEXT PAGE

Now you will hear some conversations. Each conversation is followed by three or more questions. Choose the best answer to each question and mark the letter of the correct answer on your answer sheet. You will hear each conversation only one time.

11. **Where does the conversation probably take place?**

(A) In a hallway
(B) In the schoolyard
(C) In the gymnasium
(D) In the school cafeteria

12. **What is the girl's problem?**

(A) She cannot find her teacher.
(B) She is late for her gym class.
(C) She cannot find a drink she wants.
(D) She does not like lemonade at school.

13. **How does the girl probably feel when she says, "I did, and she told me she doesn't know"?**

(A) Frustrated
(B) Surprised
(C) Relieved
(D) Proud

14. **What will the girl probably do next?**

(A) Go to gym class
(B) Look for a teacher
(C) Buy a bottle of lemonade
(D) Speak with another student

GO ON TO THE NEXT PAGE

15. **What must the students do for their history projects?**

    (A) Research one method of studying history
    (B) Report on a historical event in their town
    (C) Write to newspapers and magazines
    (D) Compare historical information in personal letters and newspapers

16. **Why does the boy mention his teacher, Ms. Wilson?**

    (A) To explain the topic he has been working on
    (B) To suggest that Ms. Wilson is one of his favorite teachers
    (C) To inform the girl that he saw Ms. Wilson at the library
    (D) To describe the book he was looking for

17. **What does the girl suggest that the boy do regarding the book?**

    (A) Ask Jason where he found it
    (B) See if the teacher has another copy
    (C) Borrow it from Jason for a few hours
    (D) Look for it at the library in a few weeks

18. **What will the boy and girl probably do later?**

    (A) Read each other's history projects
    (B) Trade library books with each other
    (C) Return their books to the library together
    (D) Look together for historical letters and newspapers

19. **What is being celebrated?**

    (A) A student's birthday
    (B) A student's award
    (C) A student's return to class
    (D) The end of the school year

20. **Where is the party being held?**

    (A) In a classroom
    (B) In the cafeteria
    (C) At a student's home
    (D) At the teacher's home

21. **What is the teacher doing when she says, "All right, let's see. The decorations are up—they look great—and we've put a tablecloth on the table. We have cups, napkins, paper plates"?**

    (A) Telling the student what to go ask for
    (B) Noting things that she and the student have accomplished
    (C) Suggesting a way to make the room look nicer
    (D) Making a list of things she needs to buy

22. **What is the teacher going to do next?**

    (A) Look for cups
    (B) Pick up the cake
    (C) Get some ice cream
    (D) Call a student's parent

23. **Why does the girl not want to miss the choir concert?**

    (A) She loves to sing.
    (B) Her brother is in the concert.
    (C) She is playing the piano with the choir.
    (D) Her mother told her to be there.

24. **Why is the girl worried about canceling her piano lesson?**

    (A) She is afraid her teacher will be angry with her.
    (B) She will be behind schedule.
    (C) Her mother does not allow canceling lessons.
    (D) She does not want to waste money.

25. **What does the boy suggest that the girl should do?**

    (A) Find out if her mother is coming
    (B) Perform in the concert
    (C) Miss the choir practice once
    (D) Move the piano lesson to another day

26. **What does the girl mean when she says, "What would I do if you weren't here to remind me of everything"?**

    (A) She is grateful the boy helped her.
    (B) She is worried that she has forgotten something.
    (C) She wants to know how she could help the boy.
    (D) She does not know what she should do next.

GO ON TO THE NEXT PAGE

Now you will hear some talks and discussions about academic topics. Each talk or discussion is followed by three or more questions. Choose the best answer to each question and mark the letter of the correct answer on your answer sheet. You will hear each talk or discussion only one time.

27. What are the teacher and students mainly talking about?

(A) How bees teach one another to dance
(B) How bees warn one another of danger
(C) How bees share information with one another
(D) How bees tell one another about other beehives

28. To communicate "stop," what will a honeybee do?

(A) Give a vibrating signal
(B) Steal food from the dancing bee
(C) Dance around the other dancing bee
(D) Bump its tail into that of the dancing bee

29. What do honeybees use to communicate about the location for a new hive?

(A) A movement of the head
(B) A tail-wagging dance
(C) A vibrating signal
(D) A round dance

30. What will the students probably do next?

(A) Take a quiz
(B) Turn in their homework
(C) Look for beehives outside
(D) Watch a movie about bees

31. **What is the main topic of the talk?**

    (A) Why telegraph systems are no longer used

    (B) How telegraph systems have changed over time

    (C) Why the first telegraph systems were difficult to use

    (D) Why Samuel Morse became interested in telegraphs

32. **Why does the teacher talk about televisions?**

    (A) To explain why telegraphs are no longer used

    (B) To explain the meaning of the word "telegraph"

    (C) To show another way electricity can be used for communication

    (D) To point out that early televisions were similar to telegraph machines

33. **What does the teacher think is surprising about Samuel Morse?**

    (A) He was not a professional scientist.

    (B) He did not like using telegraph machines.

    (C) He did not earn much money from inventing the telegraph.

    (D) He thought of the telegraph many years before he invented it.

34. **What point does the teacher make about telegraphers?**

    (A) Their work was very important.

    (B) Most of them were also inventors.

    (C) It was very difficult to become one.

    (D) There were only a few of them.

GO ON TO THE NEXT PAGE

35. What is the teacher mainly talking about?

(A) A new discovery about the Sun
(B) Changes in the brightness of the Sun
(C) Equipment used to study the Sun
(D) A part of the Sun's atmosphere

36. Why does the teacher first talk about a fire in a fireplace?

(A) To illustrate how the Sun produces energy
(B) To compare the Sun to other stars
(C) To describe the color of the corona
(D) To discuss the corona's temperature

37. Why is the Sun's corona dim?

(A) Its particles are spread out.
(B) It is partly liquid.
(C) It is not very hot.
(D) It does not have much energy.

38. Why is the corona easy to see during an eclipse?

(A) The Sun appears bigger.
(B) The Moon blocks the Sun's light.
(C) The corona changes color.
(D) Earth gets closer to the Sun.

GO ON TO THE NEXT PAGE

39. Where did the student see the plant she describes?

(A) In a textbook
(B) On a Web site
(C) On a class trip
(D) On a family vacation

40. According to the teacher, how have succulents adapted in order to survive?

(A) They can store water.
(B) They need little light.
(C) They taste bad to animals.
(D) They blend in with their environment.

41. According to the teacher, what does the word "succulent" refer to?

(A) How the plant tastes
(B) Where the plant grows
(C) What the plant looks like
(D) The person who first named the plant

42. What does the girl imply when she says, "Now I know what I'll be doing my next science report on"?

(A) She has gotten a late start on a science report.
(B) She is interested in learning more about succulent plants.
(C) She did not know that she had so much science homework.
(D) She will decide on the topic of her report later.

Language Form and Meaning

Directions

In this section of the test, you will answer 42 questions found in several different texts. Within each text are boxes that contain four possible ways to complete a sentence. Choose the word or words in each box that correctly complete each sentence. Mark the letter of the correct answer on your answer sheet.

Here are two sample questions:

1. The idea that rocks last forever and that rocks

(A) still
(B) very
(C) quite
(D) never

change

is not completely true. If you have ever stood next to a rushing river, you

2.

(A) saw
(B) seen
(C) are seeing
(D) may have seen

the water hammering away at the rocks.

The correct answer to **Sample 1** is (D), "never." The correct answer to **Sample 2** is (D), "may have seen."

Questions 1–4 refer to the following announcement.

Next Saturday at 8 P.M., Denville Township Public Library

1. (A) hosted
   (B) to host
   (C) hosting
   (D) will host

a talk for

middle school students about

2. (A) improve
   (B) improving
   (C) it improves
   (D) the improvement

study skills. Emily Walters, the

guidance counselor at Denville High School, will discuss ways that students can use their study

time more

3. (A) safely
   (B) instantly
   (C) efficiently
   (D) wonderfully

and become better students. Ms. Walters will also be on

hand afterward to answer any questions

4. (A) may students have
   (B) that students may have
   (C) students may have them
   (D) they may be had by students

regarding the

the transition from middle school to high school.

GO ON TO THE NEXT PAGE

Questions 5–8 refer to the following notice.

5. (A) Will be
   (B) That there is
   (C) There will be
   (D) Because there will be

a group of foreign exchange students from our sister city of

Avignon, France, visiting the school next month. There are approximately 20 students coming, and

6. (A) need they all places
   (B) places all need they
   (C) all places they need
   (D) they all need places

to stay. If you can host an exchange student in your home,

please

7. (A) ask
   (B) tell
   (C) say
   (D) speak

to Ms. Duchamp. Students studying French are especially encouraged

to host, as this is a great opportunity for students

8. (A) practiced
   (B) to practice
   (C) are practicing
   (D) they practiced

their language

skills!

GO ON TO THE NEXT PAGE

Questions 9–12 refer to the following notice on a bulletin board.

Yesterday I found a wristwatch

9. (A) someone left it
   (B) someone leaving
   (C) that someone left
   (D) was left by someone

in the library. If you think this

watch might be yours, you should go to the school administrator's office. Tell Mr. Bryson you lost

your watch and describe

10. (A) like it looks
    (B) looking like
    (C) that it looks like
    (D) what it looks like

so he can make sure the watch I found

GO ON TO THE NEXT PAGE

belongs to you. Also, even if you haven't lost a watch, please

11. (A) tell
(B) hear
(C) share
(D) control

other students

about the watch I found. It's a nice watch, and I'm sure the owner would like

12. (A) it getting back.
(B) to get it back.
(C) back to get it.
(D) it got back.

GO ON TO THE NEXT PAGE

Questions 13–18 refer to the following passage from a history book.

The bookmarks we use today are often just narrow strips of thick paper that we insert between the

pages of a book

13. (A) helps
    (B) to help
    (C) but help
    (D) they help

us return to the place where we stopped reading. It is

perhaps surprising that bookmarks have existed for as

14. (A) long
    (B) long as
    (C) longingly
    (D) longer than

people have had

books. Over time, bookmarks

15. (A) changes
    (B) to change
    (C) have changed
    (D) to have changed

considerably. Nowadays,

16. (A) they have
    (B) they are
    (C) it does
    (D) it is

usually made from inexpensive paper. Bookmarks in the past were often

expensive items

17. (A) made
    (B) making
    (C) that made
    (D) were made

of fine fabric or leather that was often richly decorated.

GO ON TO THE NEXT PAGE

Perhaps one reason bookmarks were relatively precious objects is

18. (A) of their quality
    (B) they had quality
    (C) that their quality
    (D) they were of quality

had to suit the books they marked. Some early books were so

expensive and finely made that it would have been unthinkable for a reader to mark them using an

ordinary piece of cloth or other material that might damage the pages.

Questions 19–26 refer to the following article from a science magazine.

Scientists

19. (A) estimates
(B) estimating
(C) estimate
(D) to estimate

that every month more than a dozen plant and animal species

become extinct. In some cases, human activity is

20. (A) failed
(B) scored
(C) caused
(D) blamed

for the disappearance of a

species. However, extinction occurs naturally as well. It is a process that

21. (A) it took
(B) to have taken
(C) has to be taken
(D) has been taking

place throughout Earth's history. Long before humans existed, some

plant and animal species disappeared.

22. (A) When occasional,
(B) Occasionally,
(C) An occasion,
(D) Occasion,

however, scientists

discover that some species

23. (A) they thought it
(B) thinking it had
(C) thought to have
(D) having thought it

disappeared are not really extinct.

GO ON TO THE NEXT PAGE

24. (A) It was a live animal discovered
    (B) The discovery of a live animal
    (C) They discovered a live animal
    (D) A live animal was discovered

previously considered extinct is known as the

Lazarus effect. A recent example of the Lazarus effect occurred in Laos, where explorers found

25. (A) a mouse-sized animal
    (B) that was a mouse-sized animal
    (C) an animal that the size a mouse
    (D) out an animal the size of a mouse

called *Laonastes aenigmamus*. Before its

26. (A) in
    (B) for
    (C) since
    (D) near to

discovery, this animal was thought to have been extinct

eleven million years!

Questions 27–34 refer to the following passage from a history textbook.

27. (A) Because languages
    (B) There languages
    (C) It is a language
    (D) Languages

with very few speakers are commonly referred to as small

languages. Though

28. (A) spoken
    (B) that spoke
    (C) it had spoken
    (D) they were speaking

by only a few people, these languages can

still have a great impact historically. In North America there are some languages

29. (A) quite
    (B) very
    (C) too
    (D) so

small that their names are known to few people besides experts who study

languages.

30. (A) One
    (B) Any
    (C) Some
    (D) Another

such language, Laurentian, was spoken in a few dozen villages

in eastern parts of North America. By the end of the 1500s, the language died out; today

GO ON TO THE NEXT PAGE

31. (A) are there no speakers
    (B) there are no speakers
    (C) no speakers are there
    (D) are no speakers there

of Laurentian. However, even though it is no longer used,

Laurentian has left

32. (A) a mark lasted
    (B) to last a mark
    (C) a lasting mark
    (D) was a lasting mark

on all of today's languages. When the French

explorer Jacques Cartier came into contact with Laurentian speakers in the mid-1500s, they taught

33. (A) it
    (B) that
    (C) him
    (D) them

the word "kanata," meaning "village." The word "kanata" gave rise to the

name of the country

34. (A) today we call it
    (B) it is called today
    (C) that today we call
    (D) our calling it today

Canada.

Questions 35–42 refer to the following passage from a science textbook.

When we pick up a rock and

35. (A) it held
    (B) hold it
    (C) holding it
    (D) to have held it

in our hands, it feels hard and solid.

Some rocks are so hard that we may have

36. (A) imagined it difficult
    (B) imagining difficulty
    (C) difficulty imagining
    (D) to imagine difficulty

how anything could

destroy them.

37. (A) Even the hardest rocks,
    (B) Even rocks are the hardest,
    (C) The hardest rocks even though,
    (D) There are even the hardest rocks,

however, no matter how large they

are, can be worn away.

38. (A) Little
    (B) As little
    (C) Little as
    (D) As little as

a drop of water falling on a rock is enough

39. (A) tiny bits removed
    (B) removing tiny bits
    (C) to remove tiny bits
    (D) tiny bits are removed

from it. Of course, the effects of a single drop of water falling

on a hard rock are

40. (A) too
    (B) that
    (C) ever
    (D) how

small for us to see. However, when even seemingly gentle

GO ON TO THE NEXT PAGE

forces act on hard rocks

41. (A) at
    (B) over
    (C) to
    (D) from

millions of years, the resulting changes are incredible.

In fact, the deep caves and tunnels

42. (A) now found
    (B) to find now
    (C) finding now
    (D) that now find

in some of the world's hardest

rocks are the result of millions of years of falling rain and flowing streams.

NO TEST MATERIAL ON THIS PAGE

Reading Comprehension

Directions

In this section of the test, you will read several texts and answer 42 questions. Choose the correct answer to each question and mark the letter of the correct answer on your answer sheet.

Before you start, read the sample text and the questions below.

Sample Text

> The Golden Gate Bridge is a famous bridge in San Francisco. The bridge has a red color, but gray clouds often surround it. On clear days people come to take pictures of the bridge. The pictures show the green hills next to the bridge and the blue water under it.

Sample Question 1

What is the text mostly about?

(A) Gray clouds
(B) San Francisco
(C) A famous bridge
(D) Taking photographs

The correct answer is (C), "A famous bridge."

Sample Question 2

What color is the Golden Gate Bridge?

(A) Red
(B) Green
(C) Blue
(D) Gray

The correct answer is (A), "Red."

GO ON TO THE NEXT PAGE

Questions 1–4 are about the following schedule.

Berkfield Community Center

Summer Art Classes

Photography Basics

Section 1

Monday, Wednesday, Friday: 10 A.M.–12 P.M.
Instructor: visiting artist Mr. Stefan Hendershot

Section 2

Monday, Thursday: 6:30 P.M.–8:30 P.M.
Instructor: Ms. Beth Beranski

Photographing Nature

Tuesday, Thursday: 7 P.M.–9 P.M. and Saturday: 10 A.M.–12 P.M.
Instructor: Ms. Sheila Jackson

Beginning Drawing

Monday, Thursday: 6:30 P.M.–8:30 P.M.
Instructor: Mr. Arthur Bellini

Advanced Drawing

Wednesday, Friday: 2 P.M.–5 P.M.
Instructor: visiting artist Mr. Stefan Hendershot

Oil Painting Weekend Workshop*

Saturday, July 12, and Sunday, July 13
Instructors: Mr. Arthur Bellini and Ms. Beili Zheng

Sculpting with Clay**

Saturday: 1 P.M.–5 P.M.
Instructor: (to be determined)

*   *limited to 12 students*

** *students must be 14 or older*

To find out more: Visit our Web site at www.berkfieldcc.org.

1. **How many instructors teach photography classes?**

   (A) One
   (B) Two
   (C) Three
   (D) Four

2. **Which class meets at the same times as Ms. Beth Beranski's class?**

   (A) Oil Painting
   (B) Advanced Drawing
   (C) Beginning Drawing
   (D) Photographing Nature

3. **Which instructor most likely does NOT teach regularly at the center?**

   (A) Ms. Beili Zheng
   (B) Mr. Arthur Bellini
   (C) Ms. Sheila Jackson
   (D) Mr. Stefan Hendershot

4. **Which class has an age requirement for students?**

   (A) Oil Painting
   (B) Sculpting with Clay
   (C) Advanced Drawing
   (D) Photographing Nature

GO ON TO THE NEXT PAGE

Questions 5–7 are about the following advertisement.

School World

Back-to-School Supply Sale!

It's time to get ready for another school year! Here at School World, we've got all the school supplies students will need to have a great school year. All our school supplies are sorted by section to make it easier for you to find everything you need. We've also listed which grades need what supplies to make it easier for you to find everything. Our employees are always available if you need help finding your supplies, so please feel free to ask any of them if you need help.

Supplies	Store Section	Needed by Grades
Pens, pencils, erasers	1	1–8
Paper, notebooks	2	1–8
Calculators, rulers, protractors	3	6–8
Crayons, paints, brushes, sketchbooks	4	1–8
Backpacks, book bags	5	1–8

Students with current school ID cards are eligible for a 10 percent discount on their purchases. Don't forget to show us your school ID card when you come up to pay for your supplies so that you can receive this discount.

GO ON TO THE NEXT PAGE

5. In which section of the store would a student find art supplies?

   (A) One
   (B) Two
   (C) Three
   (D) Four

6. The supplies in section three would most likely be used in which of the following classes?

   (A) Fourth-grade English
   (B) Fifth-grade social studies
   (C) Seventh-grade math
   (D) Eighth-grade music

7. What should students do to take advantage of the discount?

   (A) Present a student identification card
   (B) Ask a store employee for help
   (C) Visit all sections of the store
   (D) Bring a school-supplies list

GO ON TO THE NEXT PAGE

Questions 8–11 are about the following announcement.

We need your help!

The Community Library is holding a used book sale to raise money for our new weekly program, Children's Story Hour. Last year we held a similar sale because we wanted to try something new that might provide the extra funding needed for special
Line events. That sale was so successful that we're doing it again! But we need everyone's
5 help. The library has a few used books to sell, but we need many more. We're asking members of the community to give us books they no longer need. Practically anything you have we will take, including novels, nonfiction books, picture books, and even cookbooks. It doesn't matter how old your books are, as long as they are in good condition. Drop-off dates are this Monday through Wednesday. The following Thursday, Friday, and Saturday are the sale dates.

GO ON TO THE NEXT PAGE

8. How many book sales has the library held in the past?

   (A) None
   (B) One
   (C) Two
   (D) Three

9. What does the writer want people to do?

   (A) Donate money
   (B) Work at the sale
   (C) Read to children
   (D) Provide used books

10. Based on the information in the notice, what will probably NOT be for sale?

    (A) Cookbooks
    (B) Very old books
    (C) Damaged books
    (D) Children's books

11. On what day does the sale begin?

    (A) Monday
    (B) Wednesday
    (C) Thursday
    (D) Saturday

GO ON TO THE NEXT PAGE

Questions 12–18 are about the following story.

Four classmates, David, Anna, Maria, and John, were sitting together in the kitchen of David's house.

"Doesn't that soup look delicious?" asked Anna as she looked through the pages of
Line the cookbook. The cookbook had large, colorful pictures of soups and other dishes.
5 "It does! Let's look up the recipe so we can make it for the picnic," suggested David.

Maria and John nodded their heads in agreement. The students had been asked to make a special dish for the upcoming school picnic. But after reading the list of ingredients, David sighed. "I don't think we have corn or potatoes here," he said, frowning. "Maybe we should make something else instead."

10 "Hey, I think we have some corn at my house!" exclaimed Anna. "I'll go get it right now."

"And my mother just bought a big bag of potatoes," added John. "I'll ask her if we can use some. Could you boil some water while Anna and I go get the vegetables?"

"That's a great idea," said Maria. She looked at the recipe. "Do you have carrots,
15 David?"

"Yes. I just picked some from our garden in the back of the house," he replied, nodding. "Once we have the corn and potatoes, we'll be ready to make the soup!"

David filled a pot with water and washed and cut the carrots. Maria used a spoon to measure out the spices and salt that they needed to put in the soup. Anna and John came
20 back in less than ten minutes with the corn and potatoes.

"That was quick!" remarked David. "It's nice that your houses are so close to mine. Now the soup will be done in no time. We'll hardly have to wait!"

The soup was finished cooking in just half an hour and had such a nice aroma that David's mother came into the kitchen, saying, "Mmm. Something smells delicious! I
25 could tell from the other room that someone must be cooking something wonderful in here."

"It's soup we're making for the picnic!" said David excitedly. "I couldn't have made it alone, and with everyone's help, it was easy. And it's just about ready!"

GO ON TO THE NEXT PAGE

12. What is the best title for the story?

(A) David's Shopping List
(B) Choosing the Best Vegetables
(C) Friends Cook a Dish Together
(D) Students Write Their Own Recipe

13. In line 5, the word <u>it</u> refers to _____.

(A) page
(B) soup
(C) book
(D) recipe

14. Why are the students cooking?

(A) They were hungry.
(B) They were asked to make a dish for a picnic.
(C) They wanted to test their cooking skills.
(D) They wanted to cook a special dinner for their parents.

15. Who has a garden at home?

(A) John
(B) Anna
(C) Maria
(D) David

16. Where do Anna and John go during the story?

(A) To a farm
(B) To a grocery store
(C) To their own homes
(D) To a teacher's house

17. In line 22, the phrase <u>in no time</u> is closest in meaning to _____.

(A) while away
(B) very quickly
(C) without help
(D) with no effort

18. In line 23, the word <u>aroma</u> is closest in meaning to _____.

(A) smell
(B) color
(C) taste
(D) smoothness

GO ON TO THE NEXT PAGE

Questions 19–27 are about the following passage.

When we look at the night sky, we see the Moon, bright stars, and occasionally a meteor shooting across the sky. What we do *not* notice is space junk, including items lost by astronauts and thousands of pieces of broken rockets and satellites, objects now *Line* circling the Earth.

5   These unwanted objects made by humans, often referred to as orbital debris, do not fall to Earth. Instead, they circle the planet and make the region of space surrounding the Earth a huge junkyard. Space junk is a serious problem because such objects move at speeds that are dangerous to astronauts who work in space. Moving faster than airplanes, these objects must be avoided because <u>they</u> can injure astronauts or damage the 10   equipment they use.

Because more and more orbital debris <u>accumulates</u> every year, astronauts must be increasingly careful when they work in space. Space agency scientists on Earth watch the sky to determine the locations of these dangerous objects both at the moment of observation and the time when astronauts will be in space. These scientists record the 15   size, the speed, and the direction of movement of these objects. They then use this information to calculate where the debris will be when astronauts are scheduled to work in space.

For now, this strategy is sufficient to help astronauts <u>dodge</u> trouble. With time, though, there will be too many objects to keep track of. Officials in many countries are now 20   considering other solutions to this problem. They agree that too much debris could one day make future research in space impossible. They also believe that steps must be taken soon not only to clean up the existing orbital debris but also to keep more from entering space.

GO ON TO THE NEXT PAGE

19. **Which title best summarizes the passage?**

    (A) Bright Stars Light the Night Sky
    (B) Space Flights Available to Tourists
    (C) Faster Rockets Make Space Research Easier
    (D) Mess in Space Creates Problems for Scientists

20. **What is orbital debris?**

    (A) Garbage that circles Earth
    (B) Planes that are used to carry astronauts
    (C) Distant stars that can be seen from Earth
    (D) Meteors that can be seen from Earth

21. **In line 9, the word they refers to _____.**

    (A) tools
    (B) objects
    (C) scientists
    (D) astronauts

22. **In line 11, the word accumulates is closest in meaning to _____.**

    (A) opens
    (B) collects
    (C) prepares
    (D) repairs

23. **What is the goal of the space agency scientists mentioned in the passage who observe objects in space?**

    (A) To reduce the weight of the objects
    (B) To increase the speed of the objects
    (C) To predict the locations of the objects
    (D) To determine where the objects came from

24. **According to the passage, what is a growing problem for astronauts in space?**

    (A) The length of time they are away from home
    (B) The unsafe working conditions as they do their jobs
    (C) The many international regulations they must follow
    (D) The amount of technical knowledge they need to have

25. **What does the author say about the speed at which orbital debris moves?**

    (A) It is extremely fast.
    (B) It is difficult to measure.
    (C) It is affected by Earth's weather.
    (D) It is slower than that of airplanes.

26. **In line 18, the word dodge is closest in meaning to _____.**

    (A) hide
    (B) repair
    (C) avoid
    (D) doubt

27. **According to the passage, what do some officials hope to do in the future?**

    (A) Build stronger rockets
    (B) Send more astronauts into space
    (C) Increase funding for space research
    (D) Remove unwanted objects from space

129

Questions 28–34 are about the following passage.

Ibadan is one of the largest cities in Nigeria. It began in the nineteenth century as a small settlement consisting only of a small number of families living in a few mud houses. At first the people there lived in compounds, neighborhoods of houses
Line surrounded by walls. Each compound was occupied by an extended family with many
5 relatives living in neighboring houses, all protected by the surrounding wall. With time, more and more compounds were built. At the same time, other areas of the city also grew.

Today Ibadan is an <u>enormous</u> city with its own university and national airport. The city also has a railway line that connects it to Nigeria's port city Lagos and to
10 neighboring countries. As the city grew, however, people decided to tear down the walls around the compounds, eventually connecting the neighborhoods with nearby farming areas, winding roads, and large markets.

In today's Ibadan many more houses have been <u>erected</u>. However, the city's newer houses are made of brick instead of mud. Most are covered with tin roofs. Given
15 Ibadan's weather throughout most of the year, tin is an ideal material. It is durable, so residents can go many years without worrying about leaks during the region's heavy rains.

GO ON TO THE NEXT PAGE

28. **What is the passage mainly about?**

   (A) The development of a city
   (B) Trade in an African region
   (C) The life of a farming family
   (D) The history of a small country

29. **According to the passage, what is a compound?**

   (A) A group of houses
   (B) The founder of a city
   (C) A meeting of farmers
   (D) A line of railway tracks

30. **What did people in Ibadan remove from the city?**

   (A) Food markets
   (B) Old railroad lines
   (C) The farms within its borders
   (D) The walls around neighborhoods

31. **In line 8, the word _enormous_ is closest in meaning to _____.**

   (A) famous
   (B) serious
   (C) empty
   (D) large

32. **In line 13, the word _erected_ is closest in meaning to _____.**

   (A) entered
   (B) filled
   (C) built
   (D) met

33. **What does the passage suggest is often true of the weather in Ibadan?**

   (A) It is cold.
   (B) It is rainy.
   (C) It is foggy.
   (D) It is windy.

34. **What advantage of tin is mentioned in the passage?**

   (A) It is lightweight.
   (B) It lasts a long time.
   (C) It keeps a house cool.
   (D) It does not cost much.

GO ON TO THE NEXT PAGE

Questions 35–42 are about the following passage.

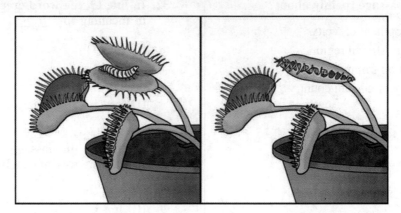

The Venus flytrap has long fascinated plant enthusiasts. The Venus flytrap has amazing leaves that are able to suddenly snap shut when an insect crawls on <u>them</u>. The Venus flytrap is a carnivorous plant, and like all carnivores, it eats meat. In the case of *Line* the Venus flytrap, the meat comes in the form of insects and other very small animals.

5   There are other kinds of carnivorous plants besides the Venus flytrap. However, most of them have sticky leaves to capture insects. The insect, once caught, is then slowly <u>consumed</u> by the plant. The Venus flytrap, though, is not very sticky. Instead, to trap insects, it moves its leaves with incredible speed. The leaves of a Venus flytrap can shut in less than a second, which makes them the fastest moving part of any known plant.

10 Compare this leaf movement with that of the leaves or flowers of other plants, which require the stimulation of light and may take hours or days to open.

Furthermore, the Venus flytrap does not simply close up every time it is touched. Researchers who study the plant have found that its leaves are actually covered with tiny hairs. It is these hairs that <u>trigger</u> the shutting of the trap. Only when at least two of these

15 hairs are disturbed will the Venus flytrap snap shut. Thanks to this adaptation, the plant is likely to shut only when it feels an insect moving and not for other reasons, like when it is hit with a raindrop or blown by the wind.

GO ON TO THE NEXT PAGE

35. **What is the passage mainly about?**

   (A) An unusual kind of plant
   (B) A newly discovered insect
   (C) A harmful species of insect
   (D) A plant created by scientists

36. **In line 2, the word <u>them</u> refers to _____.**

   (A) leaves
   (B) insects
   (C) carnivores
   (D) enthusiasts

37. **What is a carnivore?**

   (A) An insect that feeds on plants
   (B) The sticky surface of a leaf
   (C) A plant that can trap water
   (D) A species that eats meat

38. **In line 7, the word <u>consumed</u> is closest in meaning to _____.**

   (A) smelled
   (B) saved
   (C) eaten
   (D) felt

39. **What record does the Venus flytrap hold among plants?**

   (A) It is the world's largest.
   (B) It drinks the most water.
   (C) Its smell is the strongest.
   (D) Its leaves move the fastest.

40. **What did researchers learn about the leaves of the Venus flytrap?**

   (A) They reflect light.
   (B) They absorb water.
   (C) They contain tiny hairs.
   (D) They are coated with a sticky substance.

41. **In line 14, the word <u>trigger</u> is closest in meaning to _____.**

   (A) cause
   (B) avoid
   (C) guard
   (D) locate

42. **According to the passage, what determines whether an insect will be trapped by a Venus flytrap?**

   (A) How large the insect is
   (B) Whether the wind is blowing
   (C) The manner in which the insect moves on a leaf
   (D) What time of day it is when the insect lands on the plant

STOP

NO TEST MATERIAL ON THIS PAGE

第9章

答案详解

全真考题一

Part 1 – Listening

Answer Key			
Question Number	**Answer**	**Question Number**	**Answer**
1.（例题）	A	21.	A
2.（例题）	B	22.	C
1.	A	23.	B
2.	A	24.	D
3.	C	25.	C
4.	D	26.	D
5.	A	27.	B
6.	B	28.	A
7.	A	29.	D
8.	B	30.	C
9.	B	31.	A
10.	B	32.	C
11.	A	33.	B
12.	B	34.	B
13.	C	35.	D
14.	C	36.	B
15.	A	37.	C
16.	B	38.	A
17.	C	39.	B
18.	B	40.	C
19.	C	41.	A
20.	D	42.	A

Answer Explanation

1. （例题）**(A)**。本题为说话者意图题。听力材料大意为老师让同学们友好对待新同学 Sarita。本题问"老师想让学生们做什么？"。根据听力材料中老师说的"Today we have a new student joining our class.（今天我们班来了一名新同学）"，"showing her around the school（带她参观学校）"和"so please be friendly（请表现得友善些）"，可知选项 (A)"Help a new classmate（帮助一名新同学）"为正确答案。选项 (B)"Prepare for gym class（为体育课做准备）"是错误的，因为听力材料提到的是"explaining how to find gym（说明如何找到体育馆）"。选项 (C)"Welcome a guest speaker（欢迎一位演讲嘉宾）"和选项 (D)"Return books to the library（把书还给图书馆）"在听力材料中均未提及，为错误选项。

2. （例题）**(B)**。本题为预测题。听力材料大意为音乐老师让学生们听歌曲中有哪些乐器。本题问"学生们接下来可能会做什么？"。根据关键短语"enjoy the music（欣赏音乐）"可以推测学生们接下来会听老师播放的音乐，因此选项 (B)"Listen to some music（听音乐）"为正确答案。选项 (A)"Sing a song（唱一首歌）"是错误的，因为听力材料中提及"The next song I will play …（接下来我要播放的歌曲……）"，可见老师接下来会播放歌曲而不是让学生们唱歌。选项 (C)"Choose instruments to play（挑选乐器来演奏）"和选项 (D)"Discuss the life of a musician（讨论一位音乐家的一生）"在听力材料中均未提及，因此为错误选项。

1. **(A)**。本题为主旨题。听力材料大意为学生们马上要在海洋水族馆参加一项特殊活动，水族馆工作人员正在做讲解。本题问"学生们将会在水族馆做什么？"。听力材料中提到"… we've planned a special activity for you. Today you'll be working with our staff members.（……我们为你们策划了一次特殊的活动。今天你们将和我们的工作人员一起工作）"，可知选项 (A)"Helping the aquarium staff（帮助水族馆的工作人员）"为正确答案。选项 (B)"Attending a show on underwater life（看一场海洋生物的表演）"和选项 (D)"Seeing an exhibit on unusual sea creatures（看一场有关罕见水下生物的展览）"均是错误的，因为听力材料中提到"Instead of visiting our regular exhibits or attending one of our shows on underwater life …（既不参观我们的常规展览也不看我们其中一个水下生物的表演……）"。选项 (C)"Learning how new exhibits are made（了解新展品是怎么制作的）"在听力材料中并未提及，为错误选项。

2. **(A)**。本题为预测题。听力材料大意为老师带学生们去动物园并要求学生们每人选一种动物做记录。本题问"学生们接下来可能会做什么？"。根据听力材料中的关键句"… I'd like each of you to pick out one animal and write down some notes about what makes it special.（……我希望你们每个人都选一种动物并写一些关于它的特别之处的笔记）"可以推断出接下来学生们会去挑选动物，观察并做记录，因此选项 (A) "Go to look at animals（去看动物）"是正确答案。选项 (B) "Give notes to the teacher（把笔记给老师）"在听力材料中并未提及，因此为错误选项。选项 (C) "Meet at the zoo's entrance（在动物园入口集合）"是错误的，因为听力材料中提到"We will meet at the zoo's entrance in one hour.（一小时后我们在动物园门口集合）"，这发生在观察和做记录以后，并不是学生们接下来要做的事情。选项 (D) "Talk about an animal they have studied（谈论一种他们研究过的动物）"是错误的，因为听力材料中提到"Once we get back to the classroom, you're going to tell the rest of the class why you think the animal is interesting.（我们一回到教室，你们就要告诉其他同学为什么你们认为这种动物很有趣）"，也就是说学生们会谈论他们在动物园看到的动物，但是这件事要在回教室以后再做。

3. **(C)**。本题为主旨题。听力材料大意为学校护士提醒学生们将填好的健康档案表带给她。本题问"护士提醒学生们做什么？"。根据关键句"Please talk to your parents tonight and come in tomorrow with the form all filled out.（请今晚和你们的父母讲一下，然后明天带着填好的表过来）"可以推断出选项 (C) "Return the completed medical form to her（将填好的健康档案表交给她）"是正确答案。选项 (A) "Make an appointment with her in her office（和她在办公室预约个时间）"和选项 (B) "Ask their parents to call her office（让他们的父母打电话到她办公室）"并没有在听力材料中提及，因此错误。选项 (D) "Give the medical form to their parents（把健康档案表给他们的父母）"是错误的，因为听力材料中提到"We sent them to your home address …（我们把表邮寄到了你们家……）"，所以不用学生们拿表给他们的父母。

4. **(D)**。本题为说话者意图题。听力材料大意为校长广播通知学生们放学后立即离开。本题问"通知的目的是什么？"。根据关键句"… there will be no after-school activities and all students must leave the school building immediately after their last lesson.（……没有课后活动了，所有学生必须在最后一节课后立刻离开教学楼）"可以判断选项 (D) "To remind students that they must leave immediately after school（提醒学生们放学后必须立即离开）"为正确答案。同时可以判断选项 (A) "To encourage students to participate in after-school activities（鼓励学生们参加课后活动）"是错误的。选项 (B) "To invite students to the mathematics competition（邀请学

生们参加数学竞赛）"是错误的，因为听力材料中校长说"The only students who may stay in the building are the students in the Mathematics Club. They will be attending a competition later this afternoon.（可以留在大楼里的学生只有数学俱乐部的学生。他们将在今天下午晚些时候参加一个竞赛）"，由此可见校长并不是邀请学生们参加数学竞赛，只是说参加数学竞赛的学生可以不离校。选项 (C)"To thank students for cooperating with the teachers（感谢学生们配合老师）"是错误的，虽然听力材料提到"Thank you all for your cooperation.（谢谢你们配合）"，但这并不是通知的目的，而是礼貌的结束语，让学生们好好配合安排。

5. **(A)**。本题为说话者意图题。听力材料大意为老师交代学生们要如何对待 20 名交换生。本题问"老师为什么要提及来访的学生们？"。根据关键句"You should always be polite and helpful to our guests.（你们对我们的客人应该总是彬彬有礼而且乐于帮助）"，这是在讲待人接物的方式，因此选项 (A)"To explain how to behave when the students arrive（阐述在交换生们到来后要如何表现）"为正确答案。选项 (B)"To encourage everyone to join an exchange program（鼓励所有学生加入交换生项目）"是错误的，听力材料中只提及"exchange students visiting our school（交换生造访我们学校）"，并未鼓励学生们参加交换生项目。选项 (C)"To describe the daily life of students in other countries（描述别国学生的日常生活）"是错误的，因为听力材料中老师并没有进行描述，只是鼓励学生们"talk to them about life in their countries（和他们谈谈他们国家的生活）"。选项 (D)"To suggest questions to ask the visiting students（建议学生们可以向交换生提出的问题）"是错误的，因为听力材料中老师只是提醒本校学生"they may ask some surprising questions（交换生可能会问一些奇怪的问题）"。

6. **(B)**。本题为推断题。听力材料大意为老师向学生们展示盐晶及其获取方法。本题问"关于该实验，老师暗示了什么？"。根据关键句"But in fact, all you need to do is hang a piece of thread over a glass of salt water and wait a few days!（但是事实上，你要做的只是在一杯盐水上方悬挂一根绳，然后等上几天！）"可以看出制作盐晶并不是难事，因此选项 (B)"It is easy to perform.（它容易操作）"是正确答案。选项 (A)"It can be dangerous.（它可能很危险）"、选项 (C)"It requires careful planning.（它需要详细的计划）"以及选项 (D)"It takes a long time to set up.（它需要准备很长时间）"均是错误的。

7. **(A)**。本题为说话者意图题。听力材料大意为图书管理员邀请学生们参加书展。本题问"图书管理员讲话的目的是什么？"。根据关键句"… I've decided to hold a book fair at the library

today. I'd like to invite each of you to come to the fair after lunch.（……我决定今天在图书馆办一场书展。我想邀请你们每个人午饭后来参加书展）"可以确定选项 (A)"To invite students to come to a book fair（邀请学生们来书展）"为正确答案。选项 (B)"To advertise some new books at the library（在图书馆为一些新书做广告）"是错误的，因为听力材料中并未提及。选项 (C)"To discuss books that were popular in the winter（讨论冬季的流行书）"是错误的，因为图书管理员只说"If you want, you can borrow some of the year's best books for all of winter vacation.（如果你们愿意，你们可以借一些年度好书来度过整个寒假）"。选项 (D)"To remind students to return books they borrowed before the vacation（提醒学生们在放假之前归还借的书）"在听力材料中并未提及，因此为错误选项。

8. **(B)**。本题为主旨题。听力材料大意为美术老师对学生们表示歉意。本题问"老师为什么道歉？"。根据关键句"I'm sorry that I didn't realize it would take so long for this paint to dry.（我很抱歉我没意识到这种颜料变干会花这么长时间）"和"I know these paints have been sloppy …（我知道这些颜料很稀……）"判断出，选项 (B)"He provided a messy kind of paint.（他提供了一种很难用的颜料）"是正确的。选项 (A)"He cannot bring paint to the next class.（他下节课不能带来颜料了）"是错误的，因为听力材料中提到"… so next time we'll use different ones.（……所以下次我们会用些别的颜料）"，这表明老师会在下次提供新的颜料。选项 (C)"He did not realize students did not have paints.（他没有意识到学生们没有颜料）"是错误的，因为听力材料中说的是老师没意识到提供的颜料不好用，而不是学生们没有颜料用。选项 (D)"He did not bring newspaper for the students to use.（他没有带报纸给学生们用）"是错误的，因为听力材料中提到"… I've put newspaper on the ground to avoid making a mess.（……我在地上铺了报纸以避免弄得一团糟）"，由此可知老师已经拿报纸过来铺地了，不需要因为没带报纸而向学生们道歉。

9. **(B)**。本题为推断题。听力材料大意为今年的海报没能得奖，老师希望学生们可以学习一下去年得奖的海报。本题问"关于去年的海报，以下哪项可能是正确的？"。选项 (A)"The judges found errors in it.（裁判发现上面有错）"是错误的，因为听力材料中未提及。选项 (B)"It won the science competition.（它赢下了科学比赛）"是正确的，因为听力材料中提到，"We need to concentrate more on these posters if we want to start winning competitions again. To start, we can look at last year's poster as an example.（如果我们想要再次赢得比赛，我们就得更注重海报的制作。首先，我们可以看看去年的海报，将其作为范例）"，由此可以合理推测去年的海报得奖了，不然老师也不会用去年的海报作为范例。选项 (C) "It earned fewer points than this year's poster.（它的得分比今年的海报少）"是错误的。虽然文中没有提及去年的海报得多少分，但可知是得奖的，再加上听力材料提及今年的海报"earned half the points possible for the competition（只获得了比赛的一半分数）"，可以合理推测去年的海报得分应该比今年的高。选项 (D) "It contained more pictures than this year's poster.（它包含的图片比今年的海报要多）"是错误的。今年海报没有得奖的重要原因之一是"had too many pictures（有太多的图片）"，而且老师让学生们参照去年的海报，所以可以合理推测去年得奖的海报必然不会有这个问题。

Questions 10–13

该听力材料讲的是一个老师夸奖男孩妈妈做的蛋糕很美味，并希望拿到食谱。

10. **(B)**。本题为语用意义题。本题问"老师说'但我不是唯一一个'的时候暗示了什么？"。老师提问"Did you bake it yourself?（是你自己烘焙的吗？）"，男孩回答"My mother did. I'm glad you enjoyed it.（我母亲做的。我很高兴您喜欢它）"，紧接着老师又说"Oh, I did. But I wasn't the only one!（哦，我很喜欢。但我并不是唯一一个喜欢这个蛋糕的人！）"从上面的信息可以合理推测男孩或老师把蛋糕还分享给了其他人，他们也很喜欢这个蛋糕，所以选项 (B) "Many people enjoyed the boy's cake.（许多人喜欢男孩的蛋糕）"为正确答案。选项 (A) "Other people came to the picnic, too.（其他人也来野餐了）"、选项 (C) "Many people brought cakes to the picnic.（许多人带了蛋糕来野餐）"和选项 (D) "She brought additional items to share.（她带来了其他东西跟大家分享）"均不能从这句话中推测出来，所以为错误选项。

11. **(A)**。本题为细节题。本题问"男孩的妈妈担心什么？"。根据对话中男孩所说"… but she was afraid people might not like it.（……但她担心人们可能会不喜欢这个蛋糕）"可以判断选项 (A) "That people would not like the cake（担心人们不喜欢蛋糕）"是正确的。选项 (B) "That the cake would not be big enough（担心蛋糕不够大）"是错误的，因为听力材料中未提及。选项 (C) "That she would not enjoy herself at the picnic（担心她在野餐中玩得不开心）"是错误的，因为听力材料中并没有提及妈妈是否参加了野餐。选项 (D) "That she would not have time to make the cake（担心她没有时间做蛋糕）"是错误的，因为听力材料中未提及时间方面的问题。

12. **(B)**。本题为细节题。本题问"老师让男孩做什么？"。根据老师所说"Could you ask your mother to write down the recipe and bring it to me tomorrow?（你能让你妈妈把食谱写下来，然后明天带给我吗？）"可以判断选项 (B)"Bring her the recipe for the cake（把蛋糕的食谱拿给她）"是正确答案。同时可以判断选项 (A)"Show her how to bake the cake（教她怎么烤蛋糕）"、选项 (C)"Thank his mother for baking the cake（感谢他妈妈烤了蛋糕）"和选项 (D)"Invite his mother to the music club picnic（邀请他妈妈去音乐俱乐部野餐）"均为错误选项。

13. **(C)**。本题为预测题。本题问"老师在周一会做什么？"。根据对话中关键句"If you bring the recipe, I'll bake it this weekend and bring a piece for you and your mother on Monday.（如果你带给我食谱，我会在周末烤这种蛋糕并在周一给你和你妈妈带一块儿）"可以判断选项 (C)"Bring the boy a piece of her cake（给男孩带一块儿她烤的蛋糕）"是正确的。同时可以判断选项 (A)"Bake a cake at home（在家烤蛋糕）"、选项 (B)"Visit a bakery（去面包店）"以及选项 (D)"Teach the boy's class how to bake a cake（教男孩所在班级烘焙蛋糕）"均为错误选项。

Questions 14–17

该听力材料讲的是一个男孩和一个女孩在谈论空手道课程。

14. **(C)**。本题为主旨题。本题问"该对话的主要话题是什么？"。整个听力材料中男孩和女孩都在就空手道课程进行谈论。男生没有第一时间报名，因此女孩帮他想办法；两人还谈到空手道课的教练很严格。由此可以判断选项 (C)"Signing up for a karate class（报名空手道课程）"是正确答案。选项 (A)"A karate coach at school（学校的空手道教练）"和选项 (B)"A new community center（一个新的社区中心）"在听力材料中未提及。选项 (D)"Winning a championship（赢得冠军）"不能对听力材料进行概括，为错误选项。

15. **(A)**。本题为细节题。本题问"是什么引发了男孩对空手道的兴趣？"。根据男孩所说"I'd love to learn karate, especially after just seeing that movie about the kid who learns to defend himself.（我很想学空手道，尤其是在看了那部有关一个孩子学习保护自己的电影之后）"，由此可以判断选项 (A)"A movie he recently saw（他最近看的一部电影）"是正确答案。同时可以判断选项 (B)"A video game he recently played（他最近玩的一款电子游戏）"、选项 (C)"A community center Web site（一个社区中心网站）"以及选项 (D)"A friend who recently started karate classes（一位最近开始上空手道课的朋友）"均为错误选项。

16. (B)。 本题为推断题。本题问"当女孩说第一节课后可能会有人退课时，她暗示了什么？"。根据关键句"Because the instructor is very demanding—he makes you work and wants you to be 100 percent committed to the class. （因为指导老师要求很严格——他要求你努力练习并希望你百分之百地投入课程）"。由此可以判断选项 (B) "The class might be too hard for some students. （这门课对一些学生来说可能太难）"是正确答案。选项 (A) "The class might interfere with school activities. （空手道课可能会影响学校活动）"并未在听力材料中提及，因此是错误的。选项 (C) "She thinks she might not like the class. （她觉得她可能不喜欢这门课）"是错误的，因为听力材料中女孩说"So, I'm glad I signed up on the first day the class was announced. （所以，我很高兴我在课程通知的第一天就报名了）"。选项 (D) "The class might be too crowded. （上空手道课的人可能太多了）"在听力材料中未提及，为错误选项。

17. (C)。 本题为修辞结构题。本题问"男孩为什么要提起教练 Peters?"。提及教练 Peters 时女孩说"He was tough—he wouldn't let my friend stay on the team after he missed just one practice! （他很严格——他把我只是错过一次训练的朋友开除出队了）"，然后男孩说"But it was worth it for those willing to work hard ... （但是对于那些愿意努力的人来说是值得的……）"，由此可以判断选项 (C) "To help explain why he does not mind a demanding instructor （解释为什么他不介意教练严厉）"是正确答案。同时可以判断选项 (A) "To tell the girl who his volleyball coach was （告诉女孩他的排球教练是谁）"是错误的，因为男孩并不是想介绍他的教练，而是想说教练很严格。选项 (B) "To give a reason why the girl's friend left the volleyball team （给出女孩的朋友离开排球队的原因）"是女孩提到的内容，并不是男孩提及 Peters 教练的原因。选项 (D) "To show that he likes volleyball more than karate （表明他更喜欢排球而不是空手道）"在听力材料中并未提及，因此为错误选项。

Questions 18–21

该听力材料讲的是女生向老师提出自己对于结课作业选题的想法，并得到了认可。

18. B。 本题为主旨题。本题问"说话者主要在讨论什么？"。整篇对话都围绕女生选择的结课作业的主题而展开。老师提出可以对埃及、美索不达米亚和中国的古代文明进行研究，但是女生想选择玛雅文明，因此可以判断选项 (B) "A topic for the student's final project （该学生结课作业的一个选题）"为正确答案。选项 (A) "A trip that the class is planning （班级正在计划的旅行）"是错误的，因为对话中并没有提及班级有任何旅行计划，而是提问题的女孩和她的家人要去墨西哥探亲旅行。选项 (C)"A community event sponsored by the school（一个由学校赞助的社区活动）"以及选项 (D)"Some missed assignments the student needs to complete（一些该学生需要完成的未写作业）"在听力材料中均未提及，为错误选项。

19. (C)。本题为推断题。本题问"这位老师最有可能教什么科目？"。根据对话的关键词"ancient civilizations（古代文明）""the ancient Mayan culture（古代玛雅文化）"以及"Mayan history（玛雅历史）"可以推测老师所教科目是历史，因此选项 (C)"History（历史）"正确。选项 (A)"Art（美术）"、选项 (B)"Science（科学）"以及选项 (D)"Literature（文学）"均错误。

20. (D)。本题为细节题。本题问"女孩一家最初来自哪里？"。根据关键句"You see, my parents are from Yucatán, Mexico, and my grandparents still live there.（您知道的，我的父母来自墨西哥的尤卡坦州，而且我的祖父母还住在那儿）"可以判断选项 (D)"Mexico（墨西哥）"为正确答案。同时判断选项 (A)"Egypt（埃及）"、选项 (B)"Japan（日本）"以及选项 (C)"China（中国）"均错误。

21. (A)。本题为语用意义题。本题问"当女孩说'所以我想知道……'时，她想表达什么？"。女孩在说出该句子前表达了她对玛雅文明很感兴趣并说她研究该主题有优势——家人来自墨西哥的尤卡坦州；在这句话之后老师接着说"OK, I get it. You'd like to know if you could do your project on Mayan history …（好的，我明白了。你想知道你是否能以玛雅历史为主题写你的作业……）"，由此可以判断选项 (A)"She wants to change the assignment.（她想改变作业）"是正确的。选项 (B)"She wants to work with another classmate.（她想和另一个同学合作）"、选项 (C)"She wants to ask the teacher for an extension.（她想向老师请求延期）"以及选项 (D)"She wants the teacher to clarify a lesson.（她想让老师讲清楚一节课）"均错误。

Questions 22–26

该听力材料讲的是一个男孩弄丢了自己去博物馆实地考察的许可单，女孩向他建议该如何做。

22. (C)。本题为细节题。本题问"男孩丢了什么？"。根据听力材料中的关键句"I can't find my permission slip for the field trip to the science museum tomorrow!（我找不到明天去科学博物馆实地考察的许可单了！）"可以判断选项 (C)"An important piece of paper（一张重要的纸）"是正确答案。选项 (A)"A folder（一个文件夹）"、选项 (B)"A bag（一个背包）"以及选项 (D)"A school project（一份学校作业）"均错误。

23. (B)。本题为推断题。本题问"为什么男孩不早点儿上交他的许可单？"。根据听力材料中的关键句"I kept forgetting to give the permission slip to my mom to sign …（我一直没想起来把实地考察的许可单给我妈妈让她签字……）"可以判断选项 (B)"He forgot to ask his parents to sign it earlier.（他忘了让他父母早些签字）"是正确的。选项 (A)"He did not know when it was due.（他不知道交单子的截止日期）"是错误的，因为听力材料中男孩说"But she said the permission slip is due today.（但是老师说今天应该交单子了）"，可见他是知道截止日期的。选项 (C)"He did not think he would want to go on the trip.（他觉得他不会想参加这次旅行）"是错误的，因为听力材料中男孩说"I really want to go on that trip …（我真的很想参加这次旅行……）"。选项 (D)"He did not think his parents would let him go on the trip.（他觉得他的父母不会让他去这次旅行）"在听力材料中并未提及，为错误选项。

24. (D)。本题为语用意义题。本题问"当男孩说'我已经找过了。可我到处都找不到它'时，男孩可能会是什么感受？"。通过以上题目的分析可知男孩非常想参加这次博物馆之旅，又把许可单丢了，所以心情应该是不开心的或者沮丧的。因此选项 (D)"Frustrated（沮丧的）"最合适。选项 (A)"Jealous（嫉妒的）、选项 (B)"Hopeful（充满希望的）"以及选项 (C)"Confident（有信心的）"均错误。

25. (C)。本题为语用意义题。本题问"当男孩说'是呀，我猜那是我唯一的选择'时，他在暗示什么？"。在男孩说这句话之前，女孩提出了建议："I'm sure Ms. Gomez will give you another copy of the permission slip if you ask her for one. You can have your parents sign it tonight and turn it in tomorrow.（如果你向 Gomez 老师再要一张许可单，她肯定会再给你一份。你可以让你父母今晚签字，明天把单子交上去）"以及"Ms. Gomez is really nice. If you ask her, maybe you can turn it in tomorrow and still come on the trip.（Gomez 老师人很好。如果你跟她要，或许你可以明天交单子，然后照样去这次旅行）"。然后男孩说出这句话，表示他会按照女孩说的试试，也就是跟 Gomez 老师要一张新的许可单，今天回去签字，明天交给 Gomez 老师的同时也去博物馆。因此选项 (C)"He will ask the teacher for a new permission slip.（他会向老师要一张新的许可单）"为正确答案。选项 (A)"He will not go on the field trip.（他不会参加参加博物馆之旅了）"、选项 (B)"He will ask his parents to call the teacher.（他会让他的父母给老师打电话）"以及选项 (D)"He will visit the science museum with his parents.（他将会和他的父母一起参观科学博物馆）"均为错误选项。

26. **(D)**。本题为预测题。本题问"两名学生接下来可能会做什么？"。女孩提议"If you want, I'll go with you. I'm going to her classroom now to hand in my permission slip anyway.（如果你愿意，我陪你一起去。反正我现在也要去她的教室上交我的许可单）"，然后男孩回答"Yeah, that'd be great, thanks!（好，这太好了，谢谢！）"。由此可以判断选项 (D) "Go to Ms. Gomez' classroom（去 Gomez 老师的教室）"为正确答案。而选项 (A) "Call the boy's parents（给男孩的父母打电话）"、选项 (B) "Look in the boy's backpack（翻找男孩的背包）"以及选项 (C) "Walk to the science museum（走着去科学博物馆）"均为错误选项。

Questions 27–30

该听力材料讲的是一位导游阐述艺术作品的外框的重要性。

27. **(B)**。本题为主旨题。本题问"说话者主要讲了什么？"。根据听力材料中提到的"This exhibition … is a little different. All you will see are the frames themselves.（这次的展览有些不同。你只会看到外框本身）"，以及对外框的评价，如"have a practical function（有实用性）""has an artistic value in itself（本身具有艺术价值）"以及"can be helpful when you're trying to learn the history of a work of art（有助于研究艺术作品的历史）"，可以总结出说话者旨在强调艺术品外框的重要性，因此选项 (B) "The importance of frames for works of art（外框对艺术作品的重要性）"最为合适，为正确答案。选项 (A) "Ways artists make frames for their work（艺术家为他们的作品制作外框的方法）"在听力材料中未提及，因此错误。选项 (C) "An unusual frame on a painting in a museum（博物馆一幅画作上的独特画框）"是错误的，因为听力材料中提到"You'll see from our collection that the frames vary widely in style and materials used …（你会发现我们收藏的这些画框在款式和所用材料上非常多样……）"，也就是说，说话者所讲的内容并不针对某个画框。同理，可以判断选项 (D) "Differences between the frames of two paintings（两幅画的画框的不同之处）"也是错误的。

28. **(A)**。本题为细节题。本题问"说话者对制作画框的材料是怎么说的？"。根据听力材料中对画框的描述"… the frames vary widely in style and materials used, in size and in weight …（……这些画框在款式、所用材料、大小和重量上都有很大不同……）"可以判断选项 (A) "Many different kinds of materials are used.（使用了多种不同的材料）"是正确的。选项 (B) "The materials used in frames are often expensive.（制作画框使用的材料通常很昂贵）"、选项 (C) "Most materials used in old frames are no longer available.（旧画框中使用的多数材料已不

再可用）"以及选项 (D) "The materials in old frames last longer than newer materials.（旧画框所使用的材料比新材料更持久）"均未在材料中提及，为错误选项。

29. (D)。本题为细节题。本题问"参观结束时游客会看到什么？"。根据听力材料中的关键句 "After you see the collection … you'll see some of our experts at work. Part of their job is to maintain and repair frames from paintings …（看完收藏品后……你会看到一些我们这儿正在工作的专家。他们工作的一部分就是维护和修理画框……）"，可以判断选项 (D) "People maintaining and repairing frames（维护和修理画框的人）"是正确答案。选项 (A) "A film about frames from the nineteenth century（一部关于 19 世纪的画框的电影）"、选项 (B) "Several artists making frames for their paintings（几位为他们的画作制作画框的艺术家）"以及选项 (C) "A collection of paintings in their original frames（一批放置在原画框内的画儿）"在听力材料中均未提及，为错误选项。

30. (C)。本题为细节题。本题问"博物馆从一幅儿童绘画中得知了什么？"。根据听力材料中的关键句 "People thought it was painted before 1850 …（人们认为它是在 1850 年之前画成的 ……）" 和 "They discovered that the frame was in fact the original frame—it was as old as the painting. And they were able to determine its age: it was made after 1900, not in the 1850s.（他们发现那个画框实际上是原装的——它与这幅画一样古老。他们能够确定它的年代：制作于 1900 年之后，而非 1850 年代。）"，可以判断选项 (C) "It was not as old as people had originally thought.（它并不像人们最初以为的那样年代久远）"为正确答案。同时也可判断选项 (B) "It was no longer in its original frame.（它的画框不是原装的）"是错误的。选项 (A) "It had been moved many times.（它被转移了很多次）"和选项 (D) "It was painted by a different artist than most people had thought.（它的作者与大多数人所想的不同）"在听力材料中均未提及，因此为错误选项。

Questions 31–34

该听力材料讲的是科学课上老师和学生谈论水如何促成了一些地貌的形成，以及人们如何用水来切割金属。

31. (A)。本题为说话人意图题。本题问"为什么老师和学生在讨论开始时谈论悬崖、海滩和山谷？"。根据听力材料中的关键句 "We've been learning about land … things like cliffs, beaches, valleys … and how some of these landforms have mostly been created by—what?（我们一直

在学习陆地……比如悬崖、海滩、山谷……以及其中的一些地貌一般是怎么形成的？）"可以看出，悬崖、海滩和山谷是一些例子，老师用来帮助学生们进行回忆，因此选项 (A) "To review how these different landforms are created（回顾这些不同地貌是如何形成的）"是正确答案。选项 (B) "To discuss landforms they see every day（讨论他们每天看到的地貌）"、选项 (C) "To compare the different qualities of water（比较不同质量的水）"和选项 (D) "To explain how large bodies of water formed on Earth（解释地球上大片的水域是如何形成的）"在听力材料中均未提及，为错误答案。

32. **(C)**。本题为修辞结构题。本题问"学生为什么要谈到沙子？"。听力材料中老师问"Can you give us a few quick examples to review?（你能给我们举几个简单的例子回顾一下吗？）"，接着学生回答"Well, beaches are made of sand, and sand is just bits of rock and shells and things that have been worn away by water.（好吧，海滩是由沙子组成的，而沙子只是岩石、贝壳的碎片以及其他物体被水侵蚀后所留下的东西）"，也就是说海滩的形成是因为水对岩石的侵蚀。由此可以判断选项 (C) "To give an example of rocks worn away by water（为了举一个岩石被水侵蚀的例子）"是正确答案。选项 (A) "To introduce a topic related to landforms（为了引出一个与地貌有关的话题）"、选项 (B) "To explain the difference between beaches and valleys（为了解释沙滩和山谷之间的区别）"以及选项 (D) "To describe the type of rock found near the ocean（为了描述在海附近发现的岩石的种类）"均为错误选项。

33. **(B)**。本题为细节题。本题问"被称为水流喷射器的工具是用来做什么的？"。根据关键句"It's like a hose, but the water comes out really, really fast and hard—hard enough to cut right through metal.（它就像一根胶管，但是水流出的速度非常快、非常猛，猛到可以完全切开金属）"可以判断选项 (B) "Cutting hard objects（切割硬物）"为正确答案。同时可以判断选项 (A) "Cooling hot objects（冷却热物体）"、选项 (C) "Cleaning dirty objects（清洁脏东西）"以及选项 (D) "Filling empty containers（填充空容器）"均为错误选项。

34. **(B)**。本题为细节题。本题问"据学生所说，水流喷射器的一个问题是什么？"。根据关键句"The article made the point that it's loud—so loud that workers using it have to wear things over their ears to protect them!（那篇文章指出，它的声音太大了——大到使用它的工人必须戴上护耳的东西来保护耳朵！）"可以判断选项 (B) "It makes a lot of noise.（它发出很大噪声）"是正确答案。选项 (A) "It works very slowly.（它运转很慢）"、选项 (C) "It uses a lot of water

quickly.（它快速消耗大量的水）"以及选项 (D)"It can only be used in a few locations.（它只能在少数几个地方使用）"在听力材料中均未提及，因此为错误选项。

Questions 35–38

该听力材料主要讨论了考古学家定位古代文物遗址的方法之——航拍摄影。

35. **(D)**。本题为主旨题。本题问"这次讨论的主题是什么？"。根据关键句"And how do they find those artifacts and ruins?（他们是如何找到那些文物和废墟的？）"以及通篇三人都在讨论"get information from aerial photography（从航拍摄影中获得信息）"可以判断选项 (D)"A method archaeologists use to find artifacts（一种考古学家用来寻找文物的方法）"为正确答案。选项 (A)"A famous archaeological site（一个著名的考古遗址）"、选项 (B)"The cost of archaeological artifacts（文物考古的成本）"以及选项 (C)"A method archaeologists use to tell the age of artifacts（一种考古学家用来判断文物年代的方法）"在听力材料中均未提及，为错误选项。

36. **(B)**。本题为修辞结构题。本题问"老师为什么要提及气球和风筝？"。根据听力材料中的关键句"Aerial photography has been used by archaeologists for over a hundred years, even just by attaching cameras to balloons or a kite.（航拍摄影已被考古学家使用一百多年了，甚至只是把相机安装到气球或风筝上）"，可以看出航拍摄影的历史悠久，以及旧时的方法是什么。因此选项 (B)"To describe how archaeologists took aerial photographs in the past（描述考古学家在过去是如何航拍的）"为正确答案。同时可以判断选项 (A)"To describe how weather affects aerial photographs（描述天气如何影响航拍照片）"、选项 (C)"To explain how ancient artifacts were transported one hundred years ago（解释一百年前古文物是如何被运输的）"以及选项 (D)"To explain how modern archaeology has improved in the past one hundred years（解释现代考古学在过去一百年中是如何进步的）"在听力材料中均未提及，为错误选项。

37. **(C)**。本题为细节题。本题问"考古学家可以从一些航拍照片中得知什么？"。根据听力材料中的关键句"And you could see the pattern of greener plants and taller plants. So the plants would kinda be like a map of the ancient village underneath.（你可以看到更绿、更高的植物形成的图案。所以这些植物有点儿像是地下古村落的地图）"可以判断选项 (C)"The location of ancient villages（古村落的位置）"是正确的。选项 (A)"The types of crops grown in ancient

times（古代种植的农作物种类）"是错误的，因为虽然听力材料中提及了农作物，但是老师提及农作物的目的是引导学生理解航拍图像的意义，而并非告诉学生们古代农作物的种类。选项 (B)"The number of artifacts left by ancient people（古人留下的文物数量）"以及选项 (D)"The time when ancient people left an area（古代人离开一个地方的时间）"在听力材料中均未提及，所以为错误选项。

38. **(A)**。本题为细节题。本题问"什么是作物标记？"。最先出现"crop marks"的句子是 "Those kinds of patterns are called crop marks.（这种图案就被称作作物标记）"。这是老师总结女孩发言而提出的概念，所以需要看一下女孩说了什么。女孩说"And you could see the pattern of greener plants and taller plants. So the plants would kinda be like a map of the ancient village underneath.（你可以看到更绿、更高的植物形成的图案。所以这些植物有点儿像是地下古村落的地图）"。也就是说，作物会长得或高或矮，或浅绿或深绿，从而形成某种图案。由此可以判断选项 (A)"Patterns in the height and color of crops（作物高度和颜色所形成的图案）"是正确的。选项 (B)"Painted signs marking specific types of crops（标记特定作物种类的涂色标志）"、选项 (C)"Different kinds of soil used by farmers to grow crops（农民用来种植农作物的不同的土壤种类）"以及选项 (D)"Fences or walls built to protect crops（用于保护农作物而建的篱笆和围墙）"在听力材料中均未提及，为错误选项。

Questions 39–42

该听力材料主要讲了海岸附近生活的海洋动物。

39. **(B)**。本题为主旨题。本题问"老师主要在讲什么？"。整个听力材料中多次提及"sea animals（海洋动物）"，并介绍了为什么沿海水域生活着更少的海洋动物，以及部分这类动物的生存方式。因此可以判断选项 (B)"Sea animals that live near the shore（生活在海岸附近的海洋动物）"为正确答案。选项 (A)"Plants that are eaten by sea animals（被海洋动物吃掉的植物）"、选项 (C)"How sea animals find food in sand（海洋动物如何在沙子中寻找食物）"以及选项 (D)"The main predators of small sea animals（小型海洋动物的主要天敌）"均不能概括听力材料中的信息，为错误选项。

40. **(C)**。本题为细节题。本题问"关于沿海水域的海洋植物，材料中提到了什么？"。根据听力材料中的关键句"The problem is that the waves make it hard for plants to grow near the shore.

The plants would be easily uprooted and washed away. （问题是海浪使植物难以在近岸生长。植物很容易被连根拔起并冲走）"，可以得出沿海水域海洋植物的生长特点，由此可以判断选项 (C) "They have difficulty surviving. （它们难以生存）"为正确答案。选项 (A) "They have special adaptations. （它们有特殊的适应能力）"是错误的，因为听力材料中说"But some creatures, like crabs, clams, sea snails, and sea worms, have adapted to life near the beach. （但是一些生物，如螃蟹、蛤蜊、海蜗牛和海虫，已经适应了近岸的生活）"，可见是一些海洋动物产生了适应性，而不是海洋植物。选项 (B) "They keep coastal waters clean. （它们使沿海水域保持干净）"并未在听力材料中提及，为错误选项。选项 (D) "They are dangerous to animals. （它们对动物来说很危险）"是错误的，因为听力材料提到"Without ocean plants on the seafloor to hide in, small animals are more exposed to the predators that hunt them for food. （没有海底的海洋植物来藏身，小型动物更容易被暴露在以它们为食的捕食者面前）"，所以对动物来说，海洋植物并不危险。

41. **(A)**。本题为细节题。本题问"通常在哪里可以找到面具蟹？"。根据关键句"To find a masked crab, you'd have to dig down deep in the sand at low tide … （要找到一只面具蟹，你必须在退潮时去深挖沙子……）"可以判断选项 (A) "Buried deep under the sand（深埋在沙子下面）"是正确答案。同时可以判断选项 (B) "Hidden in seaweed near the shore（藏在近岸的海藻中）"、选项 (C) "Outside of the water on the beach（在海滩上的水面之外）"以及选项 (D) "Swimming just above the seafloor（在海床上方游来游去）"均为错误选项。

42. **(A)**。本题为推断题。本题问"为什么沙蚤（一种夜行甲壳动物）只在晚上出来？"。根据关键句"Because birds like to eat them, though, the beach hoppers only come out at night … （因为鸟类喜欢吃它们，所以沙蚤只在晚上出来……）"可以判断选项 (A) "It is safe from birds. （可以安全躲开鸟类）"是正确答案。选项 (B) "It has less competition for food. （食物竞争较小）"和选项 (C) "It cannot tolerate the daytime heat. （不能承受白天的高温）"在听力材料中均未提及，为错误选项。选项 (D) "It can hunt animals that are only active at night. （可以捕食只在夜间活动的动物）"是错误的，因为听力材料中说的是"… when they feed on seaweed that has been left on the beach by the tide. （……当它们吃被潮水留在沙滩上的海藻时）"，可见，沙蚤吃的是海藻而不是动物。

Part 2 – Language Form and Meaning

Answer Key			
Question Number	**Answer**	**Question Number**	**Answer**
1.（例题）	D	21.	B
2.（例题）	D	22.	D
1.	A	23.	D
2.	A	24.	C
3.	D	25.	D
4.	C	26.	A
5.	A	27.	C
6.	B	28.	B
7.	C	29.	D
8.	D	30.	D
9.	C	31.	B
10.	D	32.	C
11.	D	33.	A
12.	A	34.	A
13.	C	35.	B
14.	C	36.	C
15.	A	37.	C
16.	D	38.	A
17.	B	39.	B
18.	D	40.	C
19.	A	41.	D
20.	C	42.	B

Answer Explanation

1. (例题) (D)。本题考查的是副词的含义。此句意为"认为岩石永存并且岩石_____改变的观点不完全正确"。选项处需要选择合适的副词修饰"change（改变）"。选项 (A)"still"表示"仍然"，选项 (B)"very"表示"非常"，选项 (C)"quite"表示"相当"，选项 (D)"never"表示"永不"。第一个同位语从句说"岩石永存"，然后用 and 连接另一个同位语从句，两个同位语从句意思应该一致，推测为"岩石永不改变"最合适。因此选项 (D) 为正确答案。

2. (例题) (D)。本题考查的是表达推测含义的谓语动词。此句意为"如果你曾经站在一条湍急的河边，那么你_____流水击打岩石"。很明显选项处缺少谓语。首先可以判断选项 (B)"seen"错误，因为 seen 是 see 的过去分词，不可以充当句子的谓语。通过分析句意可知，"看到流水击打岩石"的场面不一定人人都会经历，因此句子中要有表达推测含义的情态动词。符合这一要求的是选项 (D)"may have seen"，因此为正确答案。另外，该句中主句的时态要与从句的时态保持一致，都使用现在完成时，而选项 (A)"saw"是一般过去时，选项 (C)"are seeing"是现在进行时，均不符合，为错误选项。

Questions 1–4

该语篇主要讲了要举办一场烘焙义卖，筹到的钱用于保护濒危动物。

1. (A)。本题考查的是名词短语做宾语。此句意为"环保俱乐部将于下周一下午三点在食堂外面的走廊举行_____"。通过分析句子结构可知，"is holding"是句子的谓语，选项处为宾语。四个选项中只有选项 (A)"a bake sale（一场烘焙义卖）"符合语法规则，因此为正确答案。选项 (B)"a bake sale is"中"is"多余，选项 (C)"and a bake sale"中"and"多余，选项 (D)"that a bake sale"中"that"多余，均为错误选项。

2. (A)。本题考查的是过去分词的用法。此句意为"所有_____钱都会交给国际自然基金会……"。选项处是一个用来修饰"money（钱）"的成分。"money"与"raise（筹集）"之间是被动关系，钱是被筹集而来的，应该使用过去分词"raised"，所以选项 (A)"raised"为正确答案。选项 (B)"raising"是"raise"的现在分词形式，选项 (C)"to raise"是不定式，二者表达的都是主动的含义，故错误。选项 (D)"was raised"是谓语成分，该句中已有谓语"will

go"，故错误。

3. **(D)**。本题考查的是限定词的含义。结合上题可知，此句意为"所有筹集到的钱都会交给国际自然基金会，_____保护濒危动物的组织"。这里明显是在对"国际自然基金会"做解释说明，需要一个合适的限定词来修饰"organization（组织）"。四个选项中，选项 (A) "either"表示"（两者中的）任何一个"，选项 (B) "what"表示"什么"，选项 (C) "any"表示"任何的，任一的"，选项 (D) "an"表示"一（个）"。分别代入原文，发现意为"一个保护濒危动物的组织"最为合适，所以选项 (D) 为正确答案。

4. **(C)**。本题考查动词的含义。此句意为"这场义卖将_____美味的曲奇饼干、纸杯蛋糕、松饼和更多烘焙食品"。四个选项中，选项 (A) "save"表示"节约"，选项 (B) "select"表示"挑选"，选项 (C) "feature"表示"以……为特色"，选项 (D) "purchase"表示"购买"。将四个选项分别代入原文，发现意为"这场义卖将以美味的曲奇饼干、纸杯蛋糕、松饼和更多烘焙食品为特色"最为合适，因此选项 (C) 为正确答案。

Questions 5–8

该语篇是生病在家休息的 Ricardo 给朋友回复的一封邮件。

5. **(A)**。本题考查的是 start to do sth 的用法。此句意为"我终于开始_____"。关于"start"的用法有两种，其一是"start to do sth"，表示开始做以前未进行的事情，强调一种转变；其二是"start doing sth"，表示开始一项长期活动或经常性的活动。此句想表达的是"身体状况开始好转"，符合"start to do sth"的用法，所以选项 (A) "to feel better（感觉好些了）"为正确答案。选项 (B)、选项 (C) 和选项 (D) 均不满足"start to do sth"的语法要求，为错误选项。

6. **(B)**。本题考查的是副词的含义。此句的意思是"_____，明天我可能还是不能上学，因为医生说我应该休息"。很明显，该句子和前面的句子之间是转折关系——虽然感觉好些了，但还是无法上学。因此选项 (B) "However（然而）"为正确答案。选项 (A) "Instead（相反地）"、选项 (C) "Otherwise（否则）"和选项 (D) "As a result（结果）"均无法构成转折关系，为错误选项。

7. **(C)**。本题考查的是宾语从句。此句意为"你能告诉我这周的生物课上_____吗？这样我就可以做咱们的作业了"。通过看选项可知，这里想表达的是"你可以告诉我这周的生物课上我错过了什么吗？"。这个"什么"应该用"what"表示，并构成宾语从句："关系代词（what）+ 主语 + 谓语动词"，因此选项 (C)"what I have missed"为正确答案。其中"me"是"tell"的宾语，"what I have missed"是"tell"的另一个宾语，因为"tell"后可以接双宾语，即"tell sb sth（告诉某人某事）"。其他选项均不符合语法结构，为错误选项。

8. **(D)**。本题考查动词的含义。此句意为"我会非常_____"。上一句中，Ricardo 问同学课上讲了什么内容，此句来表达感激。四个选项中，选项 (A)"satisfy"意为"使满意"，选项 (B)"suggest"意为"建议"，选项 (C)"anticipate"意为"预料"，选项 (D)"appreciate"意为"感激"。将四个选项分别代入原文，发现意为"我会非常感激"最合适，因此选项 (D) 为正确答案。

Questions 9–12

该语篇主要讲的是法语俱乐部（French club）开展了一项新活动，本文介绍了该活动的地点、规则和时间。

9. **(C)**。本题考查的是谓语动词的使用。此句意为"法语俱乐部在食堂_____一个午餐小组"。通过分析句子结构可知，选项处缺少谓语，由此直接排除非谓语形式的选项 (B)"just starting"。"The French club（法语俱乐部）"与"start（开办）"之间是主动关系，而选项 (D)"was just started"表被动关系，所以选项 (D) 错误。通过句意可知，法语俱乐部开办午餐小组的这一行为发生在过去，所以表示一般现在时的选项 (A)"just starts"错误。选项 (C)"has just started"为现在完成时，强调过去的行为对现在造成的结果或影响，符合语法规则，为正确答案。

10. **(D)**。本题考查动词短语的含义。此句意为"在周二和周四的午餐时间，想要练习法语的学生应该_____带有法国旗帜的餐桌"。四个选项中，选项 (A)"hand in"意为"上交"，选项 (B)"take after"意为"像"，选项 (C)"give up"意为"放弃"，选项 (D)"look for"意为"寻找"。分别代入后，发现意为"应该找带有法国旗帜的餐桌"最为合适，因此选项 (D) 为正确答案。

11. **(D)**。本题考查的是被动语态的使用和副词的位置。此句意为"在法语餐桌上的所有对话_____用法语"。通过分析句子结构可知，"conversations（对话）"和"hold（进行）"之间是被动关系，正确选项应满足"be done"的结构，所以选项 (B)"will completely

held be" 和选项 (C) "held completely will be" 为错误选项。另外，副词 "completely（全部）" 修饰 "in French（用法语）"，应放在 "in French" 的前面，因此选项 (D) "will be held completely" 为正确答案。

12. (A)。本题考查的是名词短语做主语。此句意为 "_____ 也将在下个月组织一个类似的小组"。通过分析句子结构可知，句子缺少主语，而选项 (B) "It is the Spanish club" 是完整句子，所以为错误选项。另外，选项 (C) "While the Spanish club" 和选项 (D) "Because the Spanish club" 分别包含连词 "While" 和 "Because"，使句子变成了不完整的复合句，所以为错误选项。只有选项 (A) "The Spanish club（西班牙语俱乐部）" 是名词短语，可做句子的主语，意为 "西班牙语俱乐部也将在下个月组织一个类似的小组"，因此为正确答案。

Questions 13–18

该语篇主要讲的是一些人需要身穿特制的衣服来确保工作安全，比如宇航员。

13. (C)。本题考查的是不定式结构。此句意为 "一些人在工作的时候依靠衣服 _____ 安全"。通过分析句子结构可知，"some people" 是主语，"depend on" 是谓语，这里不需要另一套主谓结构，因此选项 (B) "they are kept" 和选项 (D) "it keeps them" 可以排除。另外，直接宾语 "clothing" 和 "keep them safe" 是目的关系，表示 "衣服是用来确保安全的"，故选项 (C) "to keep them" 用不定式说明衣服的作用——保护人们的安全，为正确答案。

14. (C)。本题考查的是定语从句。此句意为 "在航天器外 _____ 宇航员必须穿特殊的太空服来保护他们的身体"。通过分析句子结构可知，选项处是修饰 "Astronauts（宇航员）" 的定语从句，需要关系代词 "who" 或 "that" 引导，只有选项 (C) "who work" 符合语法规则，为正确答案，意为 "在航天器外工作的宇航员"。其他选项均不符合语法结构，为错误选项。

15. (A)。本题考查的是名词短语做主语。此句意为 "_____ 会造成失压并导致危险情况"。通过分析句子结构可知，选项处应为句子的主语。选项 (B) "The space suit has even a tiny hole in it" 和选项 (C) "There is even a tiny hole in the space suit" 是完整句子，不能充当句子的主语，因此排除。另外，选项 (D) "Whether in the space suit, even a tiny hole" 中有连词 "Whether" 和逗号，将句子变成了复合句，代入后句意为 "无论是否穿宇航服，即使是一个小洞都会造成失压并导致危险情况"，前后意思不通顺，因此选项 (D) 错误。选项 (A) "Even a tiny hole in the

space suit（即使是宇航服里的一个小洞）"是名词短语，可做句子的主语，且符合句意，为正确答案。

16. **(D)**。本题考查的是谓语动词的使用。此句意为"近年来，科学家们_____由高科技布料和凝胶制成的宇航服"。通过分析句子结构可知，选项处为句子谓语，而选项 (B) "developing" 不能充当句子谓语，故排除。"scientists（科学家们）"与"develop（研发）"之间是主动的关系，而选项 (C) "are developed" 是被动语态，故排除。另外，通过标志性时间状语"In recent years（近年来）"可知研发已经持续了一段时间，因此选项 (D) "have developed" 更合适。

17. **(B)**。本题考查的是限定词的含义和用法。此句的意思是"如果宇航服破了一个小洞，凝胶就会快速扩散到_____小洞并黏合它"。可见，选项处应是一个用来修饰"hole（洞）"的限定词。四个选项中，选项 (A) "a" 表示"一（个）"；选项 (B) "the" 是定冠词，指已提到的人或事物；选项 (C) "any" 表示"任何的，任一的"；选项 (D) "some" 表示"某个"，是指未知的或未确指的人或事物。在此句中已经提到了"a small hole"，后面明显说的是补上"这个洞"，因此应该用"the"来对"hole"进行限定，所以选项 (B) "the" 为正确答案。

18. **(D)**。本题考查的是代词的使用。句意为"这些宇航服也会有微型电脑在_____"。通过分析句意可知，应该是在宇航服里有微型电脑，因此所选代词要能指代"These space suits"。由于"These space suits"是名词复数，而选项 (A) "it" 和选项 (B) "this" 都只能指代名词单数，故排除；选项 (C) "they" 可以指代名词复数，但只能做句子的主语，而此处为宾语，故排除。选项 (D) "them" 可以指代名词复数，且可以做宾语，因此选项 (D) 为正确答案。

Questions 19–26

该语篇主要讲的是洋葱作为知名的烹饪原料有着长久的历史。

19. **(A)**。本题考查的是动词的过去分词。此句意为"洋葱是一种知名的、在许多国家菜肴中都能_____的食材"。通过分析句意可知，选项处是"ingredient（食材）"的修饰成分，"ingredient（食材）"与"find（发现）"之间是被动关系，所以应该使用"find"的过去分词形式，即 found，所以选项 (A) 为正确答案。

20. **(C)**。本题考查的是主语和谓语动词的使用。句意为"_____已知的人类食用的最古老的食物之一"。"It"在这里指"洋葱"。通过分析句子结构可知，句子缺少主语和谓语。在选项 (C)"It is also"中，"It"是主语，"is"是谓语，成分齐全，为正确答案。选项 (A)"It also"中缺少谓语，选项 (B)"Is also"中缺少主语，选项 (D)"Also, despite its"中既没有主语也没有谓语，均为错误选项。

21. **(B)**。本题考查的是连词和副词的含义。前面提到洋葱是一种由来已久的食物，此句继续说 "_____考古学家们设法从史前物品上收集食物残渣，经常发现洋葱碎"。四个选项中，选项 (A)"Sometimes"意为"有时候"，选项 (B)"Whenever"意为"每当"，选项 (C)"However"意为"然而"，选项 (D)"During"意为"在……期间"。分别代入后，发现意为"每当考古学家们设法从史前物品上收集食物残渣，经常发现洋葱碎"最为合适，因此选项 (B) 为正确答案。

22. **(D)**。本题考查的是 more than 的含义和用法。选项所在句子意为"确定已有_____ 5000 年，首批洋葱……"。经分析可知，选项处应为用于修饰"5000 年"的成分。选项 (A)"many（许多）"通常与名词复数连用，后面不直接跟具体数字，故排除。选项 (B)"more of"表示"更多的"，后面通常跟名词而非数字，故排除。选项 (C)"much as"表示"尽管，虽然"，后面需要跟句子，故排除。选项 (D)"more than"意为"超过"，通常与数量连用，在此处表示"超过 5000 年"，符合题意，因此选项 (D) 为正确答案。

23. **(D)**。本题考查的是单词或词组的含义和用法。句意为"确定已超过 5000 年，首次出现的洋葱很可能是野生植物_____农民种植的蔬菜"。选项 (A)"instead"是副词，意为"反而"；选项 (B)"whether"是连词，意为"是否"；选项 (C)"although"是连词，意为"虽然"；选项 (D)"rather than"是并列连词，意为"而不是"。根据句意可知，洋葱出现得很早，它最初很可能是一种野生植物而不是种植出来的蔬菜。四个选项中只有"rather than"的含义最为符合，因此选项 (D) 为正确答案。

24. **(C)**。本题考查的是 why 作为关系副词引导定语从句的用法。选项所在句子意为"洋葱在历史上能一直受欢迎有两个原因……"。该句使用了"there be"句型。选项后是一个从句，其主语是"the onion"，谓语是"has been so popular"，因此选项处应该选择一个可以引导句子的成分。其中"why"作为关系副词可以引导定语从句，意为"洋葱在历史上能一直受欢迎有两个原因"，因此选项 (C) 为正确答案。

25. (D)。本题考查的是谓语动词的使用。此句接上一句继续阐述洋葱一直受欢迎的原因。句子意为"它容易生长，并且_____很长时间都不变质"。通过分析句子结构可知，"and"前后是并列的两个句子，因此选项处应该是句子的谓语，而选项(B)"to be stored"是不定式，选项(C)"able to store"是形容词短语，都不能充当谓语动词，故排除。另外，"it"（洋葱）与"store（贮存）"之间是被动关系，而选项(A)"can store it"表达的是主动关系，故排除；选项(D)"can be stored"既可以充当谓语，又能表达被动关系，意为"并且可以被贮存很久都不变质"，因此选项(D)为正确答案。

26. (A)。本题考查形容词的含义。此句意为"由于洋葱外面那层干皮的保护，里面可以保持_____数月"。"remain"是动词，意为"保持不变"，后面通常接形容词。在四个选项中，选项(A)"fresh"意为"新鲜的"，选项(B)"recent"意为"近来的"，选项(C)"passive"意为"被动的"，选项(D)"harmless"意为"无害的"。根据上下文意思，"保持新鲜"最符合语境，因此选项(A)为正确答案。

Questions 27–34

该语篇主要讲的是船的建成是一个逐步的过程，每个新的步骤都是对前一步骤的改进。

27. (C)。本题考查的是"it is + 形容词 + to do sth"句型。文章首句意为"我们并不确切地知晓人们是何时或如何开始造船的"。紧接着用"However（然而）"表示转折，句子意为"然而，_____人们很久之前可能试着用漂浮的物体，比如木头，……"。通过分析句子结构可知，"that"引导的是"imagine"的宾语从句，那么选项处应该包含主句的主语和谓语。很明显，选项(A)"that we imagine"和选项(D)"to imagine it is easy"不能充当句子的主语和谓语，故排除。选项(B)"we imagine what"中的"what"不能和后面的"that"连用，故排除。选项(C)"it is easy to imagine"使用了"it is + 形容词 + to do sth"句型，表示"做某事是……的"，其中包含了主语"it"和谓语"is"，句意为"然而，不难想象，人们很久之前就试着用漂浮的东西，比如木头……"。因此选项(C)为正确答案。

28. (B)。本题考查的是"use sth to do sth"的用法。由第27题的分析可知，这句话意为"人们很久之前就试着用漂浮的东西，比如木头，在水上_____"。"such as pieces of wood"短语前后有逗号，是插入语，即使去掉也不影响句子结构。由此，我们得到了"have tried using floating objects to transport things"这个表达，其中"try doing"表示"尝试做某事"，use sth to do sth 表示"使用某物做某事"。根据这一动词短语可以判断选项 (B)"to transport things"为正确答案，本句意为"……人们很久之前就试着用漂浮的物体在水上运送东西"。

29. (D)。本题考查的是情态动词"could"的用法。句意为"他们那时可能意识到通过把许多可以漂浮的东西捆在一起，即使较重的物品也_____被运过河"。通过分析句子结构可知，"that"引导的是一个宾语从句，"by tying many floating objects together"是方式状语，"heavier items（较重的物品）"是宾语从句的主语，选项处需要与"be carried"一起构成宾语从句的谓语。四个选项中，只有选项 (C)"will"和选项 (D)"could"是情态动词，可以与"be carried"构成谓语。但是 will 的语气过于肯定，而 could 意为"可能"，表示"即使较重的物品也可能被运过河"，更加符合原文的语境，因此选项 (D) 为正确答案。

30. (D)。本题考查的是定语从句的结构。此句意为"很有可能，人们最初建造了非常简易的船，_____绑在一起"。从句子结构来看，"people（人们）"是主语，"built（建造）"是谓语，"boats"是宾语，已经构成完整的句子，因此选项处应为一个修饰"boats"的定语从句，故排除选项 (B) 和选项 (C)。由于"boats（船）"和"make（制作）"之间是被动关系，因此选项 (D)"that were made of pieces of wood"为正确答案，表示"这些船是由捆绑在一起的木块儿制作而成的"。另外，"tied"是"tie（捆，系）"的过去分词，用于修饰"pieces of wood"。

31. (B)。本题考查的是限定词的含义。此句意为"_____船很可能是由坐在上面的人用手划水来移动的"。四个选项中，选项 (A)"Each"意为"每个"，选项 (B)"Such"意为"这样的"，选项 (C)"Either"意为"（两者中的）任何一个"，选项 (D)"Another"意为"另一"。"Each""Either"或"Another"只能修饰名词的单数形式，而句中"boats"是复数，因此选项 (A)、(C) 和 (D) 都可以排除。将选项 (B) 代入原文，句意为"这样的船可能是由坐在上面的人用手划水来移动的"，符合题意，因此选项 (B) 为正确答案。

32. (C)。本题考查的是不定式做表语的用法。"The next step（下一步）"承接上文，将继续讲在人们用手划船之后，又有了什么新进步。该句意为"下一步可能是_____划船"。通过分析句子结构可知，主语为"The next step"，谓语动词为"may have been"，因此句子缺少表语，而选项 (D)"it used flat objects"包含主语、谓语和宾语，不符合此处成分需求，故排除。通过观察四个选项，可以知道句意为"用扁平的物体来划船"，其中能和"have been"连用的

只有选项 (C)"to use flat objects",表示"下一步可能是用扁平的物体来划船",因此选项 (C) 为正确答案。

33. **(A)**。本题考查的是名词短语做主语的用法。本题的前一句说,"正如我们所知,帆的使用最终使得船能够利用风能移动"。然后本题所在的句子意为"古代物件上_____,例如花瓶和壁画上,并不只是一次发明的产物"。通过分析句子结构可知,句子的谓语动词是"were","the result of a single invention"是表语,所以句子缺少主语。四个选项中,选项 (C)"They pictured the early boats"和选项 (D)"The early boats were pictured"是完整句子,不能充当句子的主语,故排除。选项 (B)"Picturing the early boats"是动名词短语,在语法上可以充当句子的主语,但选项 (B) 做主语时,谓语动词应为单数形式,而此句的谓语动词"were"是复数形式,故选项 (B) 错误。选项 (A)"The early boats pictured"是名词短语,可充当句子的主语,且"boats"为复数,能与此句的谓语动词"were"保持一致,为正确答案。该句子意为"画在古代物件(如花瓶和壁画)上的早期的船不只是一次发明的产物"。

34. **(A)**。本题考查的是名词的含义。此句意为"相反,它们是在一个过程中被逐步创造出来的,在这个过程中,每一步都代表着对之前尝试的_____"。四个选项中,选项 (A)"an improvement"意为"一次改进",选项 (B)"an institution"意为"一个机构",选项 (C)"a production"意为"一场演出"(这里 production 为可数名词),选项 (D)"a creation"意为"一个作品"。这个句子是在对语篇进行总结,说明船不是由一次发明而来,而是通过不断改进而来——从用手划船,到用桨,再到用帆,每一次改变都是一次进步,因此选项 (A)"an improvement"符合题意,为正确答案。

Questions 35–42

该语篇主要讲的是在水中度过大多数时间的鸟类是怎么保暖的。

(注意:鸭和鹅属于鸟类。)

35. **(B)**。本题考查的是主语和谓语的使用。此句意为"虽然像鸭子和鹅这样的鸟儿是非常优秀的飞行者,但_____大部分时间都待在水中"。通过分析句子结构可知,这是一个由连词"although(虽然)"引导的复合句,前面是让步状语从句,后面是主句,主句缺少主语和谓语,宾语是"most of their time"。由于本句已经判定为 although 引导的复合句,因此选项 (A)"and spend"排除。选项 (C)"spend them"缺少主语且包含多余的宾语"them",故排除。

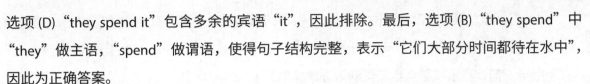

选项 (D)"they spend it"包含多余的宾语"it",因此排除。最后,选项 (B)"they spend"中"they"做主语,"spend"做谓语,使得句子结构完整,表示"它们大部分时间都待在水中",因此为正确答案。

36. (C)。本题考查的是主语从句的结构。本句的前一句说,"一年四季,即使天气很冷,也能看到这些鸟儿浮在湖面和河面上"。第 36 题所在的句子意为"_____避免变得湿冷的是它们羽毛上的天然油脂"。通过分析句子结构可知,选项处应为句子的主语,且根据选项可以看出这里需要的是主语从句。由于从句中未提及不让它们感到湿冷的物质是什么,所以需要使用"what"来指代这个东西,那么此处主语从句的结构为"what(关系代词)+ 谓语动词 + 宾语"。因此选项 (C)"What keeps these birds"为正确答案。"keep sb from doing sth"的意思是"使某人免于做某事",该句意为"使这些鸟儿免受湿冷的是它们羽毛上的天然油脂"。

37. (C)。本题考查的是"stop sb/sth from doing sth"的用法。此句意为"这种油脂能阻止水渗透进它们的羽毛"。通过分析句意可知,选项处需使用"stop sb/sth from doing sth"表达"阻止某人 / 某物做某事"的含义,因此选项 (C)"from"为正确答案。

38. (A)。本题考查介词短语的用法。此句意为"此外,_____,鸟类还有另外一层非常柔软的羽毛,叫作羽绒"。通过分析句子结构可知,本题选项处前后有逗号,它只作为句子中的一个成分,不能包含谓语,因此包含 be 动词"are"的选项 (B)、(C) 和 (D) 都排除。选项 (A)"underneath their oily feathers"意为"在它们的油性羽毛下",符合介词用法,也符合句意,因此为正确答案。

39. (B)。本题考查的是强调句型"it is + 被强调部分 + that + 其他部分"。此句意为"_____这种柔软、轻盈的羽绒帮助鸟类保持温暖"。首先注意句中有"that",表明此句不是简单句。"that"前面应该为主句,主句中应该有主谓,所以选项 (A)"Primarily"和选项 (D)"Its being primarily"可以排除。继续观察选项和句子结构可知,此句是强调句型,且强调部分为句子的主语。强调句型的结构为"it is + 主语 + that + 其他部分",选项中只有选项 (B)"It is primarily"符合语法结构,其中"primarily"是表达程度的副词,不影响句子的整体结构。句意为"主要是这种柔软、轻盈的羽绒帮助鸟类保持温暖",因此选项 (B) 为正确答案。

40. (C)。本题考查连词的用法。根据对第 39 题的分析可知,该句的意思是"主要是这种柔软、轻盈的羽绒帮助鸟类_____冰水中保持温暖"。通过观察发现,四个选项中都有连词

"when"，即本题所在部分是由"when"引导的时间状语从句，其结构是"when + 主语 + 谓语"。因此只有选项 (C)"even when it dives"符合，其中"even"作为副词表程度，可以置于引导词前，表示"甚至当鸟类潜入冰水中时"。

41. **(D)**。本题考查动词的辨析。此句意为"事实上，羽绒非常有利于保暖，以至于人们也因此使用羽绒"。该句中有"so ... that ..."表示"如此……以至于……"。另外，"at"是介词，其后的动词必须使用 -ing 形式。四个选项中，选项 (A)"doing"是"do"的现在分词，意为"做"；选项 (B)"having"是"have"的现在分词，意为"有"；选项 (C)"adding"是"add"的现在分词，意为"增加"；选项 (D)"keeping"是"keep"的现在分词，意为"保持"。将四个选项代入原文中，会发现"保持温暖"最合适，也符合"keep sth + 形容词"的用法，因此选项 D 为正确答案。

42. **(B)**。本题考查"both ... and ..."的用法。此句意为"在全世界，羽绒被用于填充外套、毯子和其他物品，让它们_____轻便又暖和"。通过分析句意可知，"lightweight"和"warm"都用来形容外套、毯子等物品，二者是并列关系。选项 (B)"both"可以与选项后的"and"组成"both ... and ..."结构，表示"既……又……"，即"让这些物品既轻便又暖和"，因此选项 (B) 为正确答案。选项 (A)"but"意为"但是"，表转折，不符合语境，故排除。选项 (C)"either"意为"（两者中的）任何一个"，通常用"either ... or ..."表示"要么……要么……"，表示选择关系，代入原句意为"这些物品要么轻便要么暖和"，不符合语境，故排除。选项 (D)"they are"既不符合语法规则也不符合语境，故排除。

Part 3 – Reading

Answer Key			
Question Number	Answer	Question Number	Answer
1.（例题）	C	21.	A
2.（例题）	A	22.	C
1.	D	23.	B
2.	A	24.	D
3.	C	25.	D
4.	B	26.	A
5.	B	27.	B
6.	C	28.	B
7.	D	29.	C
8.	B	30.	A
9.	D	31.	B
10.	D	32.	D
11.	A	33.	D
12.	A	34.	B
13.	C	35.	A
14.	D	36.	B
15.	D	37.	C
16.	A	38.	A
17.	D	39.	C
18.	C	40.	C
19.	B	41.	D
20.	C	42.	D

Answer Explanation

（例题）Questions 1–2

该语篇主要描述了金门大桥以及其周围的风景。

1. **（例题）(C)**。本题为主旨题。本题问"文本主要讲的是什么？"。语篇中第一句是"The Golden Gate Bridge is a famous bridge in San Francisco.（金门大桥是一座位于旧金山的著名大桥）"，接着具体介绍了金门大桥周围的风景以及人们在此的活动。由此可以判断选项 (C) "A famous bridge（一座著名的桥）"为正确答案。选项 (A) "Gray clouds（灰色的云）"、选项 (B) "San Francisco（旧金山）"以及选项 (D) "Taking photographs（拍照）"均是错误的，因为它们只是在描述金门大桥过程中所提及的片面信息。

2. **（例题）(A)**。本题为细节题。本题问"金门大桥是什么颜色的？"。根据文中句子"The bridge has a red color …（桥身是红色的……）"可以判断选项 (A) "Red（红色）"为正确答案。选项 (B) "Green（绿色）"、选项 (C) "Blue（蓝色）"以及选项 (D) "Gray（灰色）"均为错误选项。

Questions 1–4

该语篇中 Ben Mason 给学生科学研究院写了一封邮件，表达了对海洋研究的兴趣，同时询问了暑假课程。

1. **(D)**。本题为作者意图题。本题问"Ben 为什么写邮件给学生科学研究院？"。根据语篇中最后一句"If you have summer classes that teach students about ocean life, please send me some information about them.（如果你们有面向学生的关于海洋生物的暑期课程，请发给我一些相关的课程信息）"可以判断选项 (D) "He wants information about summer classes.（他想要关于暑期课程的信息）"为正确答案。选项 (A) "He wants directions to the institute.（他想知道去研究院的路）"在语篇中并未提及，为错误选项。选项 (B) "He wants help identifying a sea animal.（他想要别人帮忙辨认一种海洋生物）"是错误的，因为语篇中说的是"I try to identify seashells and seaweed.（我试图分辨贝壳和海藻）"，这是他自己做的事情，并不是在请研究院帮忙。选项 (C)"He wants to know the author of a book.（他想知道一本书的作者）"在语篇中并未提及，为错误选项。

2. **(A)**。本题为细节题。本题问"Ben 提到了他的大学计划中的什么细节？"。根据语篇中的关键句"When I go to university, I plan to learn all about the animals and plants that live in the sea.（我上大学后，我计划学习所有生活在海里的动物和植物）"可以推断选项 (A)"What subject he wants to study（他想学什么科目）"为正确答案。选项 (B)"When he will be ready to attend（他什么时候准备好入学）"、选项 (C)"How his parents will help him（他的父母将如何帮他）"以及选项 (D)"Which university he hopes to go to（他希望去哪所大学）"在语篇中均未提及，为错误选项。

3. **(C)**。本题为词汇题。本题问"第 4 行中的'visit'与_____意思最接近"。包含该词的句子是"Every year, my family goes to visit my grandparents.（每年，我的家人都会_____我的祖父母）"。选项 (A)"find out"意思是"查明，弄清"，选项 (B)"help with"意思是"帮助"，选项 (C)"stay with"意思是"同……待在一起"，选项 (D)"watch over"意思是"看守，监视"。根据语篇中"When I am there …（当我在那里的时候……）"可知，我去祖父母家，相当于去看望、拜访或是同他们待在一起。因此选项 (C) 意思最接近，为正确答案。

4. **(B)**。本题为细节题。本题问"Ben 和他的祖父母一起做什么？"。根据语篇中的关键句"When I am there, I like to take walks with my grandparents …（当我在祖父母那里时，我喜欢和他们一起散步……）"可以判断出选项 (B)"Take walks（散步）"为正确答案。选项 (A)"Go fishing（钓鱼）、选项 (C)"Read stories（读故事）"以及选项 (D)"Help make dinner（帮忙做饭）"在语篇中均未提及，因此为错误选项。

Questions 5–8

该语篇是某中学为学生提供的四个暑期工作的机会，说明了工作地点、时间等信息。

5. **(B)**。本题为细节题。本题问"有几份工作需要学生教课？"。整体阅读表格发现 Opportunity 2 中有一句描述"help elementary school students in basic math（帮助小学生学基础数学）"，同时 Opportunity 3 中有一句描述"You will work as an assistant art teacher, helping campers with drawing and painting projects.（你会作为美术老师助理，帮助参营者进行绘画项目）"。因此，

一共有两份工作涉及教课，所以选项 (B)"Two（两个）"是正确答案。

6. **(C)**。本题为细节题。本题问"哪个工作机会只要一名学生？"。在 Opportunity 3 中发现信息 "A young artist is needed at the Cherry Hill Summer Day Camp …（Cherry Hill 夏令营需要一名年轻的艺术家……）"，由此可以判断选项 (C)"Opportunity 3（第 3 个机会）"为正确答案。而 Opportunity 1 提到的是"The Bartlett Horse Farm needs two students …（Bartlett 马场需要两名学生……）"，所以选项 (A)"Opportunity 1（第 1 个机会）"错误。Opportunity 2 中提到"Tutors are needed to …（需要多名助教做……）"，这里使用的是名词复数，也就是说需要多名助教，所以选项 (B)"Opportunity 2（第 2 个机会）"错误。Opportunity 4 中提到"Five to seven young people are needed …（需要 5—7 名年轻人……）"，所以选项 (D)"Opportunity 4（第 4 个机会）"错误。

7. **(D)**。本题为否定事实题。本题问"哪个机会未提供有关工作时长的信息？"。根据Opportunity 1 中的关键句"You must be able to commit to four mornings per week from 7:30–11:30 A.M.（你必须保证每周有四个上午的时间，从上午 7：30 至上午 11：30）"排除选项 (A)"Opportunity 1"。根据 Opportunity 2 中的关键句"Scheduling is flexible.（时间安排灵活）"排除选项 (B)"Opportunity 2"。根据 Opportunity 3 中的关键句"The camps are for the month of July only, from 10:00 A.M.–2:00 P.M., Monday–Friday.（夏令营只在 7 月进行，周一至周五上午 10：00 至下午 2：00）"排除选项 (C)"Opportunity 3"。Opportunity 4 中并没有出现时间相关信息，故选项 (D)"Opportunity 4"为正确答案。

8. **(B)**。本题为细节题。本题问"为了申请其中一份工作，学生们被指示要怎么做？"。根据关键句"For more details and an application, call Mr. Dyson, the school administrator …（如需更多详细信息以及申请，请致电学校管理员 Dyson 先生……）"可以判断出选项 (B)"Call a school employee（给一位学校工作人员打电话）"是正确答案，同时可以判断选项 (D)"Contact a local organization（联系一个当地组织）"是错误的。选项 (A)"Visit a Web site（浏览网站）"是错误的，因为根据关键句"Check our Web site each week for additional openings …（每周查看我们的网站以便了解更多职位空缺……）"可知，查网站能获得更多职位信息，但并不能进行申请。选项 (C)"Attend a special meeting（参加一个特别的会议）"在语篇中未提及，为错误选项。

Questions 9–12

该语篇主要讲述了一对双胞胎姐妹在早上讨论穿什么颜色衣服的问题，继而回忆了以前这对双胞胎被人认错的情况。

9. **(D)**。本题为主旨题。本题问"哪个标题能最好地概括这个故事？"。通读语篇可知 Miranda 和 Diana 是双胞胎，为了不被认错要穿不同的衣服。这一天 Miranda 先穿了蓝色的衬衫，而 Diana 也想穿，但在得知 Miranda 因头疼不能去上学后，Diana 想的却是"My clothes didn't matter to me that much, however. I thought about the day ahead at school without Miranda.（我穿什么对我来说没那么重要了。我想的是这一天在学校里都将没有 Miranda）"。由此可以判断出两姐妹感情很好，选项 (D)"Twin Sisters and Close Friends（双胞胎姐妹和亲密朋友）"最合适，为正确答案。同时可以判断选项 (C)"The Battle over the Blue Shirt（蓝衬衫之战）"是错误的，因为两人没有因此起争执。选项 (A)"Miranda's Mistake（Miranda 的错误）"在语篇中未提及，为错误选项。选项 (B)"Fooling Friends at School（在学校愚弄朋友）"是错误的，因为根据"In the past, we had even tried to mislead people as a joke …（过去，我们甚至把误导他人当作开玩笑……）"可知，这是她们小时候的行为，并不能概括全篇主旨。

10. **(D)**。本题为词汇题。本题问"第 11 行的'giggle'与_____意思最接近"。包含该词的句子是"When we were little, Miranda and I thought it was funny when people mixed us up. We would giggle when someone called me by her name or referred to her as Diana.（在我们小的时候，Miranda 和我觉得让人们把我们弄混很有趣。当有人叫我她的名字或称她为 Diana 时，我们会_____）"。句中用"funny（有趣的）"来形容该事，那么两人被认错的时候应该是会笑的，所以选项 (D)"laugh（笑）"最合适，为正确答案。选项 (A)"mistake（误解）"、选项 (B)"explain（解释）"以及选项 (C)"appear（出现）"均为错误选项。

11. **(A)**。本题为推断题。本题问"在第 18 行，叙述者（Diana）在谈到'礼貌地纠正老师'时，大概是什么感受？"。说这句话之前，Diana 一直在讲述她们两人小时候愚弄他人的经历，紧接着说了关键句"What was funny when we were six years old was annoying now.（对于六岁的我们来说很逗趣的事情现在却很恼人）"。由"annoying（令人烦恼的）"可以推测她在"礼貌地纠正老师们"的时候态度应该是消极的，因此选项 (A)"Frustrated that they often call her by the wrong name（对经常被叫错名字而苦恼）"是最合适的，所以是正确答案。选项 (B)"Disappointed that she looks so much like Miranda（因她长得这么像 Miranda 而感到失望）"、选项 (C)"Angry that they do not think she is funny anymore（为他们不再认为她有趣而生气）"以及选项 (D)"Afraid that she often annoys them（因经常惹他们生气而感到害怕）"在语篇中都不能推测出来，为错误选项。

12. (A)。本题为推断题。本题问"接下来最有可能发生什么？"。故事的最后 Miranda 说"I think you'll be going to school without me today.（我想你今天要没有我陪着自己去上学了）"，可以合理推测出选项 (A)"The narrator will go to school alone.（叙述者，即 Diana，将独自去学校）"为正确答案。同时可以判断选项 (B)"The narrator will go to dance class with her sister.（叙述者将和她的姐姐 / 妹妹一起去上舞蹈课）"、选项 (C)"Both girls will wear the same color shirt to school.（两个女孩会穿相同颜色的衬衫去学校）"以及选项 (D)"The narrator will stay home to take care of her sister.（叙述者会待在家里照顾她的姐姐 / 妹妹）"均为错误选项。

Questions 13–18

该语篇主要讲述了电子游戏的发展变化。

13. (C)。本题为主旨题。本题问"该语篇对什么问题做出了回答？"。根据该语篇第 2—4 段的段首句"The first video games were manufactured in the 1970s.（最早的电子游戏诞生于 20 世纪 70 年代）"，"Over the years, video games have become more interesting and complex.（多年来，电子游戏变得更有趣、更复杂了）"，以及"Creating a new video game today is a very time-consuming task, however.（然而，如今创作一款新的电子游戏是一件非常耗时的工作）"可知该语篇讲的是电子游戏从 20 世纪 70 年代至今的发展变化。因此选项 (C)"How have video games changed over time?（随着时间的推移电子游戏是如何变化的？）"为正确答案。选项 (A)"Which video games are most popular?（哪些电子游戏最受欢迎？）"、选项 (B)"Who invented the first video game?（谁发明了第一款电子游戏？）"以及选项 (D)"Why do people enjoy playing video games?（为什么人们喜欢玩电子游戏？）"均为错误选项。

14. (D)。本题为代词指代题。本题问"第 13 行中的'them'指的是_____"。该词所在句子是"The first video games were played on large machines that stood in public places and were started by players inserting coins into them.（最早的电子游戏是在大型机器上玩的，这些大型机器被放置在公共场所，玩家通过往_____里塞硬币启动游戏）"。"them"是代词，一般指代前文中出现的事物，且指代的事物一定是复数。加上对句子的理解，可以合理判断

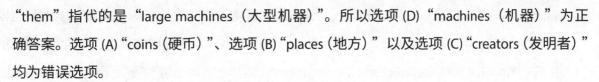

"them"指代的是"large machines（大型机器）"。所以选项 (D)"machines（机器）"为正确答案。选项 (A)"coins（硬币）"、选项 (B)"places（地方）"以及选项 (C)"creators（发明者）"均为错误选项。

15. **(D)**。本题为细节题。本题问"作者对于旧的游戏机持什么观点？"。根据关键句"Many of the first game computers still exist today in the private collections of gaming enthusiasts.（许多最初的游戏机如今仍然存在于游戏爱好者的私人收藏中）"可以判断出选项 (D)"They are collected by people who like video games.（它们被喜欢电子游戏的人收藏了）"是正确答案。选项 (A)"They are difficult to repair.（它们难以维修）"、选项 (B)"They can be purchased for little money.（花很少钱就可以买到它们）"以及选项 (C)"They can be used to play new video games.（它们可用来玩新的电子游戏）"在语篇中均未提及，为错误选项。

16. **(A)**。本题为细节题。本题问"关于首批电子游戏设计师，语篇中讲了什么？"。根据语篇中的关键句"While the first games were designed by computer programmers working alone …（虽然最初的游戏是由独自工作的电脑程序员设计的……）"可以判断选项 (A)"They worked alone.（他们独自工作）"是正确答案。选项 (B)"They were well paid.（他们的薪水很高）"、选项 (C)"They played many games.（他们玩过很多游戏）"以及选项 (D)"They often listened to music.（他们经常听音乐）"在语篇中均未提及，为错误选项。

17. **(D)**。本题为词汇题。本题问"第 22 行中的'assembling'一词与_____意思最接近"。该词所在句子是"While the first games were designed by computer programmers working alone, video game companies were soon assembling large teams of people to design graphics and to write music for games.（虽然最初的游戏是由独自工作的电脑程序员设计的，但电子游戏公司很快就_____庞大的团队来设计图形并为游戏编写音乐）"。句中"while"为连词，将前后两部分做了对比，那么"独自工作"的反义就是"团队合作"。空格处的动词应与"团队"构成搭配，如"组建""召集""雇用"等。在选项 (A)"saving up（保存）"、选项 (B)"taking apart（拆开）"、选项 (C)"working against（违背）"和选项 (D)"bringing together（集合，聚集）"中，选项 (D) 最合适，表示"游戏公司召集团队"。

18. **(C)**。本题为细节题。本题问"根据作者所述，让人们感到惊讶的是什么？"。根据语篇中的关键句"Many people are surprised to learn that work on designing their favorite game started

years before it arrived on store shelves.（许多人惊讶地发现，他们最喜欢的游戏的设计工作早在游戏上架数年前就开始了）"可以判断人们惊讶于创作游戏需要如此之久的时间，因此选项 (C)"How long it takes to create a video game（创作一款电子游戏需要花多长时间）是正确答案。同时可以判断选项 (A)"How expensive some video games are（一些电子游戏有多贵）"、选项 (B)"Where most video games are made（大多数电子游戏是在哪里创作的）"以及选项 (D)"How long ago the first video games were created（最早的电子游戏诞生于多久以前）"均为错误选项。

Questions 19–26

该语篇主要介绍了自由潜水运动（未佩戴呼吸装置的潜水）。

19. (B)。本题为主旨题。本题问"哪个标题能最好地概括该语篇？"。选项 (A)"Deep Divers Study Strange Fish（深海潜水员研究奇怪的鱼）"是错误的，因为语篇中主要讲的是"free diving（自由潜水）"，且语篇中提及"For centuries, fishermen have been free diving to catch fish …（几个世纪以来，渔民一直在以自由潜水的方式捕鱼……）"，说的是捕鱼而不是研究鱼。选项 (C)"Learning to Breathe Deeply（学习深呼吸）"是错误的，因为语篇中只在第三段提到了自由潜水的呼吸技巧"apnea"，并没有对此进行长篇论述。选项 (D)"Looking for Fun on the Ocean Floor（在海底寻找乐趣）"是错误的，因为语篇介绍的是"free diving（自由潜水）"，包括对装备、潜水深度、潜水技巧的介绍。选项 (B)"Extreme Competitors Dive Deep（极限选手深潜入水）"是正确答案，因为语篇介绍了什么是自由潜水、潜水深度和呼吸技巧。

20. (C)。本题为否定事实题。本题问"以下哪项是自由潜水比赛的参赛者不允许使用的？"。根据关键句"The only equipment used by free divers is vests to keep them warm, very long lines to help lower themselves, and weights to help them sink faster.（自由潜水员使用的装备只有让他们保暖的背心、帮助他们下潜的长绳以及帮助他们更快下沉的重物）"可以判断出选项 (A)"Long lines（长绳）"、选项 (B)"Warm vests（保暖的背心）"和选项 (D)"Heavy weights（重物）"都是自由潜水员所需的，要排除，最后得出正确答案是选项 (C)"Oxygen tanks（氧气瓶）"。另外，也可以通过句子"In one free-diving event, athletes compete to see who can dive deepest without using an oxygen tank …（在自由潜水活动中，运动员们比赛看谁能在没有氧气瓶的情况下潜得最深……）"可以判断选项 (C) 不是自由潜水员使用的装备。

21. (A)。本题为细节题。本题问"根据语篇，科学家们的哪种观点曾经是错误的？"。根据语篇中的句子"Scientists had long believed that it was impossible for humans to descend more than 50 meters below the water's surface. … That belief has been clearly proven wrong by the many divers who have long since broken the 50-meter mark.（科学家们以前一直认为人类不可能下潜到水面 50 米以下的深度。……这一观点已经明显被许多早已打破 50 米纪录的潜水者证明是错的了）"可以判断选项(A)"How deep humans are able to dive（人类能潜多深）"是正确答案。选项 (B) "Which animals can dive deepest（哪些动物能够下潜最深）、选项 (C) "Which types of fish need the least amount of oxygen（哪些种类的鱼需要最少的氧气）"以及选项 (D) "How much oxygen is contained in seawater（海水中的含氧量是多少）"在语篇中均未提及，为错误选项。

22. (C)。本题为词汇题。本题问"语篇中第 12 行的'descend'一词与_____意思最为接近"。该词所在的句子是"Scientists had long believed that it was impossible for humans to descend more than 50 meters below the water's surface.（科学家们以前一直不可能_____到水面 50 米以下的深度）"。根据首段可知，"free diving（自由潜水）"是一种"lower themselves（使他们自身下降）"并且"remain underwater（保持待在水下）"的运动，因此这个词可以合理推测为"下潜"或"向下游"等意思。在选项 (A) "sit by（坐在旁边）"、选项 (B) "use up（用完，耗尽）"、选项 (C) "go down（下降）"以及选项 (D) "move from（从……移动）"中，最合适的是选项 (C)，因此为正确答案。

23. (B)。问题为推断题。本题问"关于古代的自由潜水，作者暗示了什么？"。根据语篇中句子"… free diving itself has been practiced since ancient times. For centuries, fishermen have been free diving to catch fish or collect edible plants growing at the bottom of the sea.（……自由潜水本身自古就有。几个世纪以来，渔民一直通过自由潜水来捕鱼或采集生长在海底的可食用植物）"可以判断选项 (B) "It was a practical skill used in finding food.（这是一种用于寻找食物的实用技能）"为正确答案。选项 (A) "It was a well-paid profession.（这是一个高薪职业）"、选项 (C) "It was more competitive then than it is today.（旧时的自由潜水比如今竞争更激烈）"以及选项 (D) "It was a skill passed on from parents to children.（这是一种由父母传给孩子的技能）"在语篇中均未提及，为错误选项。

24. (D)。本题为词汇题。本题问"语篇中第 17 行的'staggering'一词与_____意思最接近"。

该词所在句子是"Nowadays, many free divers can dive to depths of more than 200 meters. To appreciate this staggering distance, imagine a 60-story-high building.（如今，许多自由潜水员可以潜到 200 多米的深度。要体会这种_____的距离，请想象一座 60 层高的建筑）"。根据第 21 题的解析可知，科学家曾一度认为人类不能潜水至 50 米深度以下的地方，而该句却直接说出 200 米的距离，并用 60 层高的建筑做比喻。由此可见，200 米的潜水距离是非常深的、令人惊奇的。在选项 (A)"heavy（重的）"、选项 (B)"available（可获得的）"、选项 (C)"important（重要的）"以及选项 (D)"incredible（不可思议的）"中，最合适的是选项 (D)。

25. **(D)**。本题为作者意图题。本题问"为什么作者会提到 60 层的楼？"。该短语所在句子是"To appreciate this staggering distance, imagine a 60-story-high building.（要体会这种惊人的距离，请想象一座 60 层高的建筑）"。作者想用这种方法让读者体会下潜 200 米是怎样一个深度，所以选项 (D)"To describe how deep some free divers can go（描述一些自由潜水员能潜到多深）"为正确答案。同时可以判断选项 (A)"To explain how free divers practice（来解释自由潜水员是如何训练的）"、选项 (B)"To argue that free diving can be dangerous（来论证自由潜水可能很危险）"以及选项 (C)"To illustrate how some divers jump into water（来说明一些潜水员是如何跳入水中的）"均为错误选项。

26. **(A)**。本题为细节题。本题问"'apnea'是什么？"。出现该词的句子是"Reaching such great depths and remaining there for periods of time is possible because the divers have mastered apnea, the technique of forgoing breathing.（到达如此深的深度并在那里停留一段时间是可以做到的，因为潜水员已经掌握了'apnea'，即屏住呼吸的技能）"。该句中已经给"apnea"做出了解释，是一种屏住呼吸的技能。选项 (A)"The ability to hold one's breath（屏住呼吸的能力）"符合描述，为正确答案。选项 (B)"A sea animal found at great depths（在很深的地方发现的一种海洋动物）"、选项 (C)"The greatest depth reached by divers（潜水员所到达的最大深度）"以及选项 (D)"A piece of equipment used by divers（潜水员使用的一个设备）"均为错误选项。

Questions 27–34

该语篇主要讲述高级绘画班的学生在市中心咖啡馆展出艺术作品的事情。

27. **(B)**。本题为主旨题。本题问"哪个标题能最好地概括这篇文章？"。该语篇主要讲美术生将城镇中心的主要建筑都画了下来，并得到了市中心咖啡馆老板的支持，在那家咖啡馆做展览。另外，根据语篇首段中的"Downtown Café hosted an exhibit for the students in Mr. Romano's advanced drawing class.（市中心咖啡馆为 Romano 先生的高级美术班的学生举办了一场展览）"可以判断选项 (B) "Students Present Art at Downtown Café（学生在市中心咖啡馆展示艺术作品）"为正确答案，同时可以判断选项 (A) "Students Find Jobs at Downtown Café（学生在市中心咖啡馆找到工作）"是错误的。选项 (C) "Teacher Encourages Student Art（老师鼓励学生艺术）"和选项 (D) "Students Donate Drawings to Library（学生向图书馆捐赠画作）"在语篇中均未提及，因此为错误选项。

28. **(B)**。本题为细节题。本题问"为什么 Greenwald 女士要在咖啡馆举办艺术展？"。根据语篇中的句子"'We've been trying to create events that everyone in town can come to and enjoy,' said Ms. Greenwald.（'我们一直在努力打造让镇上每个人都可以参加并喜欢的活动，'Greenwald 女士说）"可以判断选项 (B) "She wanted to hold more events for the community.（她想为社区举办更多活动）"为正确答案。选项 (A) "She wanted to do a favor for Mr. Romano.（她想帮 Romano 先生一个忙）"、选项 (C) "Her daughter was in Mr. Romano's advanced art class.（她的女儿在 Romano 先生的高级美术班中）"以及选项 (D) "She heard the students had no other place to exhibit their art.（她听说学生们没有其他地方可以展出他们的作品）"在语篇中均未提及，为错误选项。

29. **(C)**。本题为代词指代题。本题问"第 9 行中的'it'指的是_____"。该词的上下文是"Mr. Romano's class had been working on a project that involved drawing buildings in town. When the owner of Downtown Café, Lisa Greenwald, heard about it, she knew it was something the café should be involved in.（Romano 先生的班级一直在做一项为城镇建筑作画的项目。当城镇中心咖啡馆的老板 Lisa Greenwald 听说_____时，她知道这是咖啡馆应该参与的事情）"。"it"作为代词，指代的是前文提过的内容且指代内容为单数，由此可以合理判断选项 (C) "project（项目）"为正确答案，即 Lisa Greenwald 听说了这个项目，然后觉得应该要参与。选项 (A) "café（咖啡馆）"、选项 (B) "class（班级）"以及选项 (D) "drawing（绘画）"均为错误选项。

30. **(A)**。本题为细节题。本题问"学生们整个月都在做什么项目？"。根据语篇中句子"The eighth-graders in Mr. Romano's advanced art class have spent the last month walking to different

buildings around the downtown area and drawing them.（在 Romano 先生高级美术班的八年级学生们花费一整月的时间步行到城镇中心周围的不同建筑物，并画下它们）"可以判断选项 (A)"Drawing buildings around town（画城镇周围的建筑物）"为正确答案。同时可以判断选项 (B)"Painting the walls of the new café（粉刷新咖啡馆的墙壁）"、选项 (C)"Making new coffee cups for the café（为咖啡馆制作新的咖啡杯）"以及选项 (D)"Helping Mr. Romano set up his art studio（帮助 Romano 先生建立他的艺术工作室）"均为错误选项。

31. **(B)**。本题为词汇题。本题问"第 19 行中的'fortunate'一词与_____意思最接近"。该词所在的句子是"'We're <u>fortunate</u> that the middle school is within walking distance of so many impressive buildings,' Mr. Romano said.（'让我们感到_____的是，学校距这么多壮观的建筑都很近，'Romano先生说）"。如果这些建筑不在步行距离范围内，学生们就得花更长时间，也会更累，所以相距很近是一件很好的事情。在选项 (A)"bored（厌倦的）"、选项 (B)"lucky（幸运的）"、选项 (C)"worried（担忧的）"以及选项 (D)"surprised（惊讶的）"中，最符合的是选项 (B)，为正确答案。

32. **(D)**。本题为推断题。本题问"关于该中学，哪个选项可能正确？"。四个选项分别是：选项 (A)"It is an older building.（这是一座比较旧的建筑）"，选项 (B)"It has a large art program.（它有一个大型的艺术项目）"，选项 (C)"The students have drawn it in class.（学生们在课堂上画过它）"，选项 (D)"It is located near the downtown area.（它位于市中心附近）"。根据第 30 题的解析可知，学生们一直徒步去给城镇中的各个建筑画画儿，由此可以判断选项 (D) 为正确答案。其他的选项在语篇中均没有足够的信息进行判断。

33. **(D)**。本题为细节题。本题问"为什么 Pauline Kirchner 决定去画展？"。根据语篇中的关键句"… Pauline Kirchner, who was walking by the café when she noticed a poster advertising the art show.（……走路路过咖啡馆的 Pauline Kirchner 注意到了一张宣传艺术展的海报）"可以判断选项(D)"She was interested by a sign she saw.（她对她看到的一个标牌很感兴趣）"为正确答案，这里的"sign"就指语篇中的"poster"。选项 (A)"She was already inside the café.（她已经在咖啡馆里了）"是错误的，因为语篇中说的是"was walking by（路过）"。选项 (B)"She had a drawing at the exhibit.（展览上有她的一幅画儿）"是错的，因为通过第 27 题的解析可知，这次画展是为 Romano 先生的高级美术班的学生举办的。选项 (C)"She thought there would be free coffee.（她以为会有免费的咖啡）"是错误的，语篇中没有提及相关信息。

34. (B)。本题为细节题。本题问"为什么高级艺术班只有十名学生？"。根据语篇中的句子"In order to take the advanced art class, students must submit a portfolio of their previous work and have taken two years of art class.（要参加高级艺术班，学生必须提交一份他们先前的作品集，并且已上过两年的艺术课）"以及 Romano 先生说的"They are each very gifted.（他们每个人都很有才华）"可以合理推断出，这个班对学生有很严格且较高的参加标准，因此选项 (B) "Only the most talented students are invited to take it.（只有最有才华的学生才会受邀上课）"最合适，为正确答案。选项 (A) "Only ten students were interested in taking it.（只有十名学生有兴趣参加）"、选项 (C) "The classroom only has enough space for ten students.（教室只够容纳十名学生）"以及选项 (D) "The class used to be larger, but many students dropped out.（以前这个班比较大，但是有好多学生退出了）"在语篇中均未提及，为错误选项。

Questions 35–42

该语篇是读者写给科学教科书主编的一封信，阐述她对新教科书认可的原因。

35. (A)。本题为作者意图题。本题问"为什么 Ellen 会写这封信？"。根据语篇第一段中的"I disagree that there are too many pictures and graphics in the new books, and I want to explain why.（我不同意一些人认为新书中图片和图形太多的看法，并且我想解释一下原因）"可以判断选项 (A) "To disagree with an opinion she read in the newspaper（不同意她在报纸上读到的观点）"是正确答案。同时可以判断选项 (B) "To explain why some books do not need to include charts and graphs（解释为什么有些书不需要包含图表和图形）"是错误的，因为 Ellen 支持书中有图。选项 (C) "To express her disappointment about the school's selection of new textbooks（表达她对学校所选新教科书的失望）"是错误的，Ellen 不同意一些人认为新书中图片和图形太多的看法，说明 Ellen 对新教科书是支持的。选项 (D) "To encourage other students to write to the newspaper（鼓励其他学生给报社写信）"在语篇中并未提及，为错误选项。

36. (B)。本题为词汇题。本题问"第 3 行中的'bizarre'一词与_____意思最接近"。该词所在的句子是"It seemed <u>bizarre</u> to me that some people apparently do not like the new books because they think the books have too many pictures and graphics.（有些人显然不喜欢新的教科书，因为他们认为这些书中有太多图片和图形，这对我来说似乎很_____）"。根据第 35

题的解析可知，Ellen 支持书中有图表，所以对于不支持的人，她应该是"不理解的"或是"感到奇怪的"，因此选项 (B) "strange（奇怪的）"最合适，为正确答案。同时可以判断选项 (A) "encouraging（鼓舞人心的）"、选项 (C) "exciting（令人兴奋的）"以及选项 (D) "correct（正确的）"为错误选项。

37. **(C)**。本题为细节题。本题问"一些人不喜欢新书的哪个方面？"。语篇中提到，"These people would prefer that books include just words and a lot fewer charts and tables.（这些人更喜欢只包含文字以及较少图表和表格的书）"。有人喜欢字多，有人喜欢图多，这代表人们对书籍呈现信息的方式有偏好，因此选项 (C) "The way they present some information（它们呈现一些信息的方式）"为正确答案。选项 (A) "The poor quality of the printing（不好的印刷质量）"、选项 (B) "The amount of money they cost（它们花费的金额）"以及选项 (D) "The range of topics they include（它们所包含的主题范围）"在语篇中均未提及，为错误选项。

38. **(A)**。本题为代词指代题。本题问"第 9 行中的'they'指的是_____"。该词所在的句子是"But when some ideas are just described in sentences and paragraphs, they are not always easy to understand.（但是当一些想法只用句子和段落来描述时，_____并不总是容易理解的）"。"they"是一个代词，指代前面出现的内容且为复数形式。在选项 (A) "ideas（想法）"、选项 (B) "students（学生）"、选项 (C) "sentences（句子）"和选项 (D) "paragraphs（段落）"中，选项 (A) 最合适。

39. **(C)**。本题为词汇题。本题问"第 16 行中的短语'in visual form'与_____意思最接近"。该短语所在的句子是"Many students agree that it is important to get information in visual form rather than simply read it.（许多学生同意，_____获取信息而不是简单地阅读信息很重要）"。通过句中短语"rather than"可知，其前后内容应是相反的。又因为 Ellen 认为书中的图和图表很有用，可以判断"in visual form"的意思是"以看图和图表的形式"。有同样表达效果的是选项 (C) "as a picture or another graphic（作为图片或其他图像）"，因此为正确答案。另外，选项 (C) 中的介词"as"与画线短语中的"in"意思一致，表示"以……方式"。选项 (A) "during class（在课堂中）"、选项 (B) "outside in nature（在大自然中）"以及选项 (D) "through an experiment or research（通过实验或研究）"均为错误选项。

40. **(C)**。本题为否定事实题。本题问"Ellen 没有说哪件与图表和图形相关的事情来支持她的论点？"。首先要确定 Ellen 的观点是支持书中有图表和图形。为了支持自己的论点，她在语篇第 19—20 行中提及 "Scientists use charts and graphs all the time. Business people do, too …（科学家们一直使用图表和图形。商业人士也这样做……）"，说明图表和图形的使用范围广，同选项 (A)"They are used by people in many jobs.（它们被人们在许多工作中使用）"的表达一致，因此选项 (A) 可排除。其次，她在语篇第 12 行提及 "… they make what the words are saying a lot clearer sometimes.（……有时候它们使文字所表达的内容更清晰）"，同选项 (B) "They make some ideas easier to understand.（它们使一些想法更容易被理解）"的表达一致，因此选项 (B) 可排除。再次，她在语篇第 27 行提及 "… they also have many new diagrams and charts that I think chemistry students will benefit from.（……新书上有很多新的示意图和图表，我认为它们可以让学化学的学生受益）"，同选项(D)"They are helpful to chemistry students.（它们对学化学的学生很有帮助）"的表达一致，因此选项 (D) 可排除。最后，只有选项 (C)"They make textbooks less expensive to buy.（它们使教科书的购买成本更低）"并不是作者支持书中有图表和图形的理由之一，所以选项 (C) 是正确答案。

41. **(D)**。本题为作者意图题。本题问 "为什么 Ellen 在她的信中提到了河流？"。包含该内容的句子是 "For example, I learned that water can exist as a solid, liquid, or gas. A chart in the textbook we were using explained this with pictures of water in different forms, like liquid water in a river, solid water in an ice cube, and water that becomes part of the air, like the steam that rises from hot water.（例如，我学习了水可以以固态、液态和气态的形式存在。我们所使用的教科书里的图表用不同状态的水的图片解释了这一点，如在河里的液态水，在冰块里的固态水，以及成为空气的一部分的水，如从热水中升起的蒸气）"。Ellen 想表达用图表或图形进行展示更有利于理解，因此可以判断选项 (D) "To give an example of a chart she found useful in a book（举一个她在书中发现的有用的图表的例子）"为正确答案。选项 (A) "To share what she learned on a recent field trip（为了分享她在最近一次实地考察中学到的东西）"、选项 (B) "To describe a photograph on the cover of a science book（为了描述一本科学书封面上的照片）"以及选项 (C) "To suggest that charts and graphs are not always appropriate（为了表明图表和图形并不总是合适）"在语篇中均未提及，为错误选项。

42. **(D)**。本题为细节题。本题问 "根据 Ellen 的说法，新旧科学书有什么共同点？"。根据语篇最后一段中的 "The new textbooks have a similar chart about water …（新教科书也有一个关于水的类似的图表……）"可以判断选项 (D) "They include a chart about water.（它们都有一个关于水的图表）"为正确答案。选项 (A)"They include a similar number of diagrams.（它们包含数量差不多的图表）"是错误的，因为根据语篇中提到的"… some people apparently do not like the new books because they think the books have too many pictures and graphics.（……有些人显然不喜欢新的教科书，因为他们认为书中的图片和图形太多了）"，可知新教科书中的图比旧的多。选项 (B)"They were chosen by the same teachers.（它们是由同一批老师选出来的）"和选项 (C) 为"They were written by the same author.（它们是同一个作者写的）"在语篇中均未提及，为错误选项。

全真考题二

Part 1 – Listening

Answer Key			
Question Number	Answer	Question Number	Answer
1.（例题）	A	21.	B
2.（例题）	B	22.	C
1.	C	23.	B
2.	D	24.	B
3.	D	25.	D
4.	D	26.	A
5.	B	27.	C
6.	B	28.	A
7.	A	29.	B
8.	C	30.	A
9.	A	31.	B
10.	D	32.	B
11.	D	33.	A
12.	C	34.	A
13.	A	35.	D
14.	D	36.	D
15.	A	37.	A
16.	D	38.	B
17.	C	39.	C
18.	B	40.	A
19.	C	41.	C
20.	A	42.	B

Answer Explanation

1. （例题）**(A)**。本题为说话者意图题。听力材料大意为老师让同学们友好对待新同学 Sarita。本题问"老师想让学生们做什么？"。根据听力材料中老师说的"Today we have a new student joining our class.（今天我们班来了一名新同学）"，"showing her around the school（带她参观学校）"和"so please be friendly（请表现得友善些）"，可知选项 (A) "Help a new classmate（帮助一名新同学）"为正确答案。选项 (B) "Prepare for gym class（为体育课做准备）"是错误的，因为听力材料提到的是"explaining how to find gym（说明如何找到体育馆）"。选项 (C) "Welcome a guest speaker（欢迎一位演讲嘉宾）"和选项 (D) "Return books to the library（把书还给图书馆）"在听力材料中均未提及，为错误选项。

2. （例题）**(B)**。本题为预测题。听力材料大意为音乐老师让学生们听歌曲中有哪些乐器。本题问"学生们接下来可能会做什么？"。根据关键短语"enjoy the music（欣赏音乐）"可以推测学生们接下来会听老师播放的音乐，因此选项 (B) "Listen to some music（听音乐）"为正确答案。选项 (A) "Sing a song（唱一首歌）"是错误的，因为听力材料中提及"The next song I will play …（接下来我要播放的歌曲……）"，可见老师接下来会播放歌曲而不是让学生们唱歌。选项 (C) "Choose instruments to play（挑选乐器来演奏）"和选项 (D) "Discuss the life of a musician（讨论一位音乐家的一生）"在听力材料中均未提及，因此为错误选项。

1. **(C)**。本题为说话者意图题。听力材料大意为校图书馆更改了还书政策。本题问"这段话的目的是什么？"。根据听力材料中的关键句"… we have changed our policy regarding late and missing books.（……我们更改了有关迟还和遗失图书的政策）"可以判断选项 (C) "To explain a new library policy（对图书馆新政策做出解释）"为正确答案。选项 (A) "To promote a new book（推广一本新书）"、选项 (B) "To locate a missing item（查找一个遗失的物品）"以及选项 (D) "To announce a schedule change（宣布一项日程变更）"在听力材料中均未提及，为错误选项。

2. **(D)**。本题为主旨题。听力材料大意为老师希望学生们把教室打扫干净。本题问"老师要求学生们做什么？"。根据听力材料中的关键句"I'd like each of you to tidy the area around your desks.（我希望你们每个人都把自己课桌周围的区域清扫干净）"可以判断选项 (D) "Clean the

classroom（打扫教室）"为正确答案。选项 (A)"Prepare paper material for an art class（为艺术课准备纸质材料）"是错误的，因为在听力材料中未提及。选项 (B)"Organize an after-school meeting（组织课后会议）"是错误的，因为听力材料中说的是"The teachers are going to have a meeting in here after class ...（老师们课后要在这里开会……）"，并不是让学生们组织课后会议。选项 (C)"Submit completed projects（上交已经完成的作业）"是错误的，因为在听力材料中未提及。

3. (D)。本题为推断题。听力材料大意为篮球教练让学生们从基本动作开始训练。本题问"学生们接下来可能会做什么？"。从听力材料中提及的"So let's all start loosening up.（所以让我们开始放松肌肉吧）"可以判断选项 (D)"Begin stretching exercises（开始做伸展运动）"为正确答案。如果不知道"loosen up"这一短语的意思，也可以通过这一句"But before we do those things, we have to make sure everyone is warmed up and stretched out properly.（在练习投篮和传球之前，我们必须确保每个人都进行了适当的热身和伸展）"同样判断出选项 (D) 为正确答案。选项 (A)"Learn to pass the ball（学习传球）"和选项 (C)"Practice shooting the ball（练习投篮）"是做完热身后才做的事情，因此选项 (A) 和选项 (C) 错误。选项 (B)"Separate into two teams（分成两队）"在听力材料中并未提及，为错误选项。

4. (D)。本题为说话者意图题。听力材料大意为校秘书提醒学生们上交通信信息表。本题问"通知的目的是什么？"。根据材料中句子"I'm sorry to interrupt your lesson, but I want to remind you to return your contact information forms to the main office.（很抱歉打断你们上课，但我想提醒你们，记得把你们的通信信息表交回校务办公室）"可以判断选项 (D)"To remind students to return the contact information form（提醒学生们交回通信信息表）"为正确答案。选项 (C)"To create a list of students in a class（做一个班的学生名单）"是错误的，因为听力材料中提到"I have a list here of the students in this class who have not yet given me their forms.（我这里有一张这个班中没有给我表格的学生名单）"，也就是说校秘书手里已经有了名单。选项 (A)"To apologize for interrupting a class（因打扰到课堂而致歉）"是错误的，因为校秘书所说的"I'm sorry to interrupt your lesson ...（很抱歉打断你们上课……）"是礼貌用语，后面要说的才是打断上课的真正原因。选项 (B)"To ask all students to go to the main office as soon as possible（要求所有学生尽快去校务办公室）"是错误的，因为听力材料中并未提及。

5. (B)。本题为推断题。听力材料大意为老师要在课上为学生们放一段关于古埃及文化的视频。

本题问"关于视频，哪一项可能是正确的？"。根据听力材料中的关键句"Unfortunately, we won't be able to watch the whole thing. If we did, we would be here all night!（可惜我们无法观看整个视频。如果我们观看整个视频，那我们整晚都得在这里！）"可以合理推断出视频很长，因此选项 (B)"It is very long.（视频很长）"是正确答案。选项 (A)"It is very old.（视频很旧）"是错误的，因为听力材料中并未提及相关信息。选项 (C)"It talks about cats in ancient Egypt.（它讲的是古埃及的猫）"和选项 (D)"It shows how animals survive in the desert.（它讲的是动物如何在沙漠中生存）"均是错误的，可根据听力材料中的 "… we'll watch the short part about the culture of ancient Egypt.（……我们将观看一小部分有关古埃及文化的视频）"以及"Tonight, you will read the article about cats in ancient Egypt, and tomorrow you will look at pictures of how people live in the desert.（今晚，你们要阅读有关古埃及猫的文章，明天你们将看一些表现人们如何在沙漠中生活的照片）"来判断。

6. **(B)**。本题为推断题。听力材料大意为校图书馆员带领学生参观图书馆。本题问"讲话者对多数学生的情况做了什么暗示？"。根据听力材料中的句子"After we're finished today, you'll realize that there's much more available to you here than most students think.（今天的参观结束后，你们会认识到这里所提供的比大多数学生想象的要多）"可以推断出大多数学生不认为图书馆有很多资源，因此选项 (B)"They do not know that the library provides a lot of resources.（他们不知道图书馆提供了很多资源）"为正确答案。选项 (A)"They usually visit the library after school hours.（他们通常在放学后参观图书馆）"是错误的，因为听力材料中并未提及。选项 (C)"They do not receive a tour of the library their first year.（他们在入学第一年没有获得参观图书馆的机会）"是错误的，因为根据听力材料中说 "… but the tour you receive at the start of the year really isn't long enough.（……但你们在本学年初的参观时间真的太短了）"可知他们在入学第一年有参观图书馆的机会。选项 (D)"They come to the school library for most of their research.（他们去学校图书馆多数是为了他们的研究）"并未在听力材料中提及，因此为错误选项。

7. **(A)**。本题为说话人意图题。听力材料大意为数学老师邀请学生们参加每天放学后的考前复习。本题问"这段话的目的是什么？"。根据材料中的关键句"I wanted to remind you that I will have study sessions for the exam after school every day this week and everyone is invited.（我想要提醒你们的是，这周每天放学后我都会有备考学习课，所有人都可以参加）"可以判断选项 (A)"To remind students about the review sessions before an exam（提醒学生有考前复习课）"

为正确答案。选项 (B)"To tell students the location of the final exam（告诉学生期末考试的地点）"、选项 (C)"To outline for students what will be discussed in class（给学生概述将在课堂上讨论的内容）"和选项 (D)"To inform students of the results of an exam（通知学生一场考试的结果）"在听力材料中均未提及，为错误选项。

8. **(C)**。本题为主旨题。听力材料大意为通知所有师生科学展的举办地点变更了。本题问"为什么校长要道歉？"。根据听力材料中的关键句"We had to move the science fair because the boys' basketball practice has been scheduled for the gymnasium tonight.（因为体育馆今晚已经安排了男生的篮球训练，所以我们不得不将科学展转移到其他地点）"以及"We apologize for this last-minute change.（我们对这一紧急变更表示歉意）"，可以判断选项 (C)"The location of the science fair has been changed.（科学展的地点改了）"为正确答案。选项 (A)"A basketball game has been rescheduled.（篮球赛被改期）"、选项 (B)"The cafeteria has been closed.（餐厅关门了）"以及选项 (D)"A science lecture has been cancelled.（一场科学讲座被取消了）"在听力材料中均未提及，为错误选项。

9. **(A)**。本题为推断题。听力材料大意为博物馆的导游在介绍一个陶瓷碗。本题问"关于陶瓷碗，哪一项可能是正确的？"。根据听力材料中的关键句"We're very lucky to be able to display this piece, since most museums don't have any Chinese ceramics from this time period.（我们很幸运能够展出这件艺术品，因为大多数博物馆都没有中国这个时期的陶瓷器）"可以合理推断这件陶瓷艺术品非常稀有，因此选项 (A)"It is very rare.（它非常稀有）"为正确答案。选项 (B)"It is very small.（它非常小）"、选项 (C)"It is similar to modern bowls.（它类似于现代的碗）"和选项 (D)"It is borrowed from another museum.（它是从另一个博物馆借来的）"在听力材料中均未提及，为错误选项。

10. **(D)**。本题为主旨题。听力材料大意为老师让学生们做考前复习。本题问"老师在解释什么？"。根据听力材料中的关键句"Let's review for tomorrow's test. Open your books to chapter 10.（让我们为明天的考试复习一下。打开你们的书，翻到第 10 章）"可以判断老师将要帮助学生为明天的考试做复习，所以选项 (D)"Information about tomorrow's test（关于明天考试的信息）"为正确答案。选项 (A)"New facts about birds（关于鸟的新的事实）"、选项 (B)"The previous test the class took（班级上次参加的考试）"以及选项 (C)"Why they are studying about birds（他们为什么要研究鸟）"在听力材料中均未提及，为错误选项。

Questions 11–14

该听力材料大意为女孩想喝瓶装柠檬水但找不到哪里有卖。

11. **(D)。** 本题为推断题。本题问"这一对话最有可能发生在哪里？"。根据听力材料中的关键句"I think the cafeteria staff rearranged where all the drinks go yesterday.（我想是食堂的工作人员昨天将所有饮品重新摆放了）"可以判断谈话的地点应该是食堂，所以选项 (D)"In the school cafeteria（在学校食堂）"是正确答案。选项 (A)"In a hallway（在走廊里）"和选项 (B)"In the schoolyard（在操场）"都是错误的，因为听力材料中未提及。选项 (C)"In the gymnasium（在体育馆里）"是错误的，因为听力材料中女孩说"I just got out of gym class …（我刚上完体育课……）"，所以女孩应该从体育馆出来了，对话不会发生在那里。

12. **(C)。** 本题为主旨题。本题问"女生遇到了什么问题？"。根据听力材料中的关键句"… but do you know where the bottles of lemonade are?（……你知道瓶装柠檬水在哪儿吗？）"以及"… but I can't find them anywhere today.（……但我今天到处都找不到它们）"可以判断选项 (C)"She cannot find a drink she wants.（她找不到她想要的饮料）"为正确答案。选项 (A)"She cannot find her teacher.（她找不到她的老师了）"是错误的，因为听力材料中提到"Why don't you ask Mrs. Higgins? She's the teacher supervising lunch today.（你为什么不去问问 Higgins 老师？她今天看管午饭）"以及"I did, and she told me she doesn't know.（我问了，但是她告诉我说她不知道）"，由此可知女生找到老师了。选项 (B)"She is late for her gym class.（她上体育课迟到了）"以及选项 (D)"She does not like lemonade at school.（她不喜欢学校里的柠檬水）"均是错误的，因为听力材料中并未提及。

13. **(A)。** 本题为推断题。本题问"当女生说'我问了，但是她告诉我说她不知道'时，她可能会是什么感受？"。四个选项分别是：选项 (A)"Frustrated（沮丧的）"，选项 (B)"Surprised（惊讶的）"，选项 (C)"Relieved（感到放心的）"，选项 (D)"Proud（自豪的）"。根据听力材料中的句子"I'm so thirsty!（我太渴了！）"和"… but I can't find them anywhere today.（……但我今天到处都找不到它们）"可以合理推测女生非常想喝柠檬水，因此当 Higgins 老师也不知道哪里能找到柠檬水时，她很可能会感到非常沮丧，因此选项 (A) 最合理，是正确答案。

14. **(D)。** 本题为预测题。本题问"女生接下来可能要做什么？"。根据听力材料中的关键句"Look at that group of students over there. Two of them have bottles of lemonade. Why don't you

go ask where they got them?（你看那边那群学生。有两个学生手里拿着柠檬水。你为什么不去问问他们是从哪里买的？）"以及女生的回答"That's a good idea.（是个好主意）"可知女孩接下来会去询问那两个人，因此选项 (D) "Speak with another student（和另一位学生讲话）"为正确答案。同时可以判断选项 (A) "Go to gym class（去上体育课）"和选项 (B) "Look for a teacher（找老师）"是错误的。选项 (C) "Buy a bottle of lemonade（买瓶柠檬水）"应该发生在女生询问以后，因此也是错误的。

Questions 15–18

该听力材料是两个学生正在谈论历史研究作业，男生无法借到他想要的书，女生帮他出主意，而且两人在知道各自拿到了对方需要的书后计划进行交换。

15. **(A)**。本题为主旨题。本题问"学生们必须要为他们的历史作业做什么？"。听力材料中女生说"Ms. Wilson did talk a lot about that book when she mentioned the different methods of studying history.（当Wilson老师谈到研究历史的不同方法时确实说了很多关于那本书的内容）"以及"There's one chapter that should be helpful for everyone in our class …（书里有一章对我们班的每个人应该都有用……）"。由此可知，所有学生都需要去了解研究历史的方法，所以可以判断选项 (A) "Research one method of studying history（研究一种学习历史的方法）"为正确答案。选项 (B) "Report on a historical event in their town（对他们镇上的一个历史事件进行报道）"、选项 (C) "Write to newspapers and magazines（给报社和杂志社写信）"和选项 (D) "Compare historical information in personal letters and newspapers（比较私人信件和报纸中的历史信息）"在听力材料中均未提及，为错误选项。

16. **(D)**。本题为修辞结构题。本题问"男孩为什么要提到 Wilson 老师？"。根据听力材料中男生说的"Someone had already taken out the book Ms. Wilson mentioned in class.（已经有人借走了 Wilson 老师在课上提到的那本书）"以及女生的回答"You mean that book called *The Making of History*?（你是说那本叫《历史的产生》的书吗？）"可以推测男生可能不记得书名，所以才用"Wilson 老师提到的那本书"来进行描述，因此选项 (D) "To describe the book he was looking for（来描述他要找的书）"为正确答案。选项 (A) "To explain the topic he has been working on（解释他正在研究的主题）"、选项 (B) "To suggest that Ms. Wilson is one of his favorite teachers（暗示 Wilson 老师是他最喜欢的老师之一）"和选项 (C) "To inform the girl that he saw Ms. Wilson at the library（告知女生他在图书馆看到了 Wilson 老师）"在听力材

料中均未提及，为错误选项。

17. **(C)**。本题为细节题。本题问"对于这本书，女生建议男生做什么？"。根据听力材料中女生说的"I think Jason has it.（我觉得书在 Jason 那儿）"以及"Just ask him if you can borrow the book for a few hours.（问问他能不能把这本书借给你几个小时）"可以判断选项 (C) "Borrow it from Jason for a few hours（从 Jason 那里把书借来几个小时）"为正确答案。选项 (A) "Ask Jason where he found it（问 Jason 他在哪里找到的书）"是错误的，Jason 是从图书馆里把书借走的，这是已知事实。选项 (B) "See if the teacher has another copy（看看老师有没有另一本）"以及选项 (D) "Look for it at the library in a few weeks（几周后再去图书馆找找）"在听力材料中均未提及，为错误选项。

18. **(B)**。本题为预测题。本题问"男生和女生随后可能会做什么？"。听力材料中男生说"OK, then we'll swap—because I found one at the library that has lots of information about personal letters and stuff like that.（好的，到时候咱们交换——因为我在图书馆找到了一本书，其中有很多关于私人信件之类的信息）"，即，男生和女生手里分别有对方需要的信息，所以他们打算交换。由此可以判断选项 (B) "Trade library books with each other（相互交换图书馆的书）"为正确答案。同时可以判断选项 (A) "Read each other's history projects（阅读彼此的历史作业）"、选项 (C) "Return their books to the library together（一起到图书馆还书）"以及选项 (D) "Look together for historical letters and newspapers（一起查找历史信件和报纸）"是错误的。

Questions 19–22

该听力材料主要讲述了一对师生正在为重返课堂的学生准备派对。

19. **(C)**。本题为主旨题。本题问"要庆祝什么？"。根据听力材料中的关键句"I think it's really nice that we're welcoming Tania back to class by having a surprise party for her …（我觉得我们为 Tania 举办一个惊喜派对来欢迎她重返课堂特别好……）"可以判断选项 (C) "A student's return to class（一名学生重返课堂）"为正确答案。同时可以判断选项 (A) "A student's birthday（一名学生的生日）"、选项 (B) "A student's award（一名学生的获奖）"和选项 (D) "The end of the school year（学年的结束）"均是错误的。

20. **(A)**。本题为细节题。本题问"派对在哪里举行？"。根据听力材料中的关键句"… having a

surprise party for her right here in the classroom.（……就在这间教室里为她举办一个惊喜派对）"可以判断选项 (A)"In a classroom（在教室里）"为正确答案。同时可以判断选项 (B)"In the cafeteria（在餐厅）"、选项 (C)"At a student's home（在一名学生的家里）"和选项 (D)"At the teacher's home（在老师家）"是错误的。另外，根据听力材料中这句话"So, then I just need to go to the cafeteria to get the ice cream out of the freezer.（所以，我接下来只需去餐厅把冰淇淋从冰箱里拿出来）"可知去餐厅是去拿冰淇淋的，也可以判断选项 (B) 错误。

21. (B)。本题为语用意义题。本题问"当老师说'好了，让我们一起看看。装饰品摆好了——它们看起来很棒——我们也在桌上铺了桌布。现在我们有杯子、餐巾纸和纸盘子'时，她正在做什么？"。可以看出老师是在确认并清点他们已经准备好的东西。在选项 (A)"Telling the student what to go ask for（告诉学生去要什么）"、选项 (B)"Noting things that she and the student have accomplished（记下她和学生已经完成的事情）"、选项 (C)"Suggesting a way to make the room look nicer（建议一种让房间看起来更漂亮的方法）"和选项 (D)"Making a list of things she needs to buy（列出她需要购买东西的清单）"中，最合适的是选项 (B)。

22. (C)。本题为预测题。本题问"老师接下来打算做什么？"。根据听力材料中的关键句"So, then I just need to go to the cafeteria to get the ice cream out of the freezer.（所以，我接下来只需去餐厅把冰淇淋从冰箱里拿出来）"可以判断选项 (C)"Get some ice cream（拿冰淇淋）"为正确答案。选项 (A)"Look for cups（找杯子）"是错误的，因为听力材料中提到"We have cups, napkins, paper plates ...（现在我们有杯子、餐巾纸和纸盘子……）"，杯子已经准备好了。选项 (B)"Pick up the cake（拿蛋糕）"是错误的，因为听力材料中提及"... and one of the parents is bringing in the cake.（……其中一位家长会带蛋糕来）"。选项 (D)"Call a student's parent（给一位学生的家长打电话）"在听力材料中未提及，为错误答案。

Questions 23–26

该听力材料讲述了一个女孩在去上钢琴课还是参加一场音乐会之间犹豫不决，因为两者时间冲突了，幸好有男孩一直在帮她想办法。

23. (B)。本题为细节题。本题问"为什么女孩不想错过合唱音乐会？"。听力材料中女孩说"No, you don't understand. My little brother is in the choir and I promised him I would watch his performance!（不，你不明白。我弟弟在合唱团，我答应过他会看他表演！）"，由此可以判

断选项 (B) "Her brother is in the concert. （她弟弟在音乐会上表演）" 为正确答案。同时可以判断选项 (A) "She loves to sing. （她喜欢唱歌）"、选项 (C) "She is playing the piano with the choir. （她为合唱团演奏钢琴）" 和选项 (D) "Her mother told her to be there. （她的母亲让她去）" 在听力材料中均未提及，为错误选项。

24. **(B)**。本题为细节题。本题问 "为什么女孩担心取消钢琴课？"。根据听力材料中女孩所说 "But I can't miss my lesson. I cancelled two weeks ago … If I miss another one, I'll really be behind schedule. （但我不能错过我的课。我两周前取消过……如果我再错过一节课，我就真的落下了）" 可以判断选项 (B) "She will be behind schedule. （她会落后于日程）" 为正确答案。选项 (A) "She is afraid her teacher will be angry with her. （她怕她的老师生她的气）"、选项 (C) "Her mother does not allow canceling lessons. （她妈妈不允许她取消课程）" 和选项 (D) "She does not want to waste money. （她不想浪费钱）" 在听力材料中均未提及，为错误选项。

25. **(D)**。本题为细节题。本题问 "男孩建议女孩应该怎么做？"。根据听力材料中男孩所说 "How about if you reschedule it for another day? （把上课时间重新安排一下怎么样？）" 可以判断选项 (D) "Move the piano lesson to another day （把钢琴课改在另一天）" 为正确答案。选项 (A) "Find out if her mother is coming （看看她妈妈是否会来）" 是错误的，因为听力材料中提及 "She should be here any minute. （她随时都会到）"，她妈妈会来学校观看音乐会，对于这一点女孩非常确定。选项 (B) "Perform in the concert （在音乐会上表演）" 是错误的，因为听力材料中并未提及。选项 (C) "Miss the choir practice once （错过一次合唱团训练）" 是错误的，因为由第 23 题解析可知，弟弟是合唱团成员，而姐姐不是，所以不存在错过合唱团的训练一说，而且在听力材料中男孩也没有提出这样的建议。

26. **(A)**。本题为语用意义题。本题问 "当女孩说 '如果你不在这儿提醒我这一切，我可怎么办呀' 时，她是什么意思？"。在说这句话前，女孩说 "I am really forgetful today! （我今天真的很健忘！）"，由此可知她今天忘记了很多重要的事情，并感到很懊恼，而男孩的提醒让她有机会重新安排自己的事情，帮她解决了一些问题，所以她应该很庆幸并很感谢有男孩帮她。所以选项 (A) "She is grateful the boy helped her. （她很感激男孩帮了她）" 最合适，为正确答案。选项 (B) "She is worried that she has forgotten something. （她担心自己忘记了什么）"、选项 (C) "She wants to know how she could help the boy. （她想知道她怎样才能帮助男孩）" 和选项 (D) "She does not know what she should do next. （她不知道接下来应做什么）" 均不符合语境，为错误答案。

Questions 27–30

该听力材料讲的是课堂上老师和学生讨论蜜蜂之间是如何传递信息的。

27. (C)。本题为主旨题。本题问"老师和学生们主要在讨论什么？"。根据听力材料中的关键句 "… let's review what we've learned this week about honeybee communication.（……让我们回顾一下本周我们所学的有关蜜蜂之间交流的知识）"可以判断选项 (C) "How bees share information with one another（蜜蜂彼此之间是如何分享信息的）"为正确答案，其中 "communication"相当于 "share information"的另外一种表达形式。选项 (A) "How bees teach one another to dance（蜜蜂如何教另一只蜜蜂跳舞）"在听力材料中并未提及，为错误选项。选项 (B) "How bees warn one another of danger（蜜蜂如何警告另一只蜜蜂有危险）"是错误的，虽然听力材料中提及 "… if a honeybee is attacked while exploring a new food source, it can warn others not to visit that food source.（……如果一只蜜蜂在寻找新的食物源时遭到攻击，它能警告其他蜜蜂不要去那个食物源）"，但只这一处提及了危险，文章并没有展开讲。选项 (D) "How bees tell one another about other beehives（蜜蜂是如何互相谈论其他蜂巢的）"是错误的，因为听力材料中提到的是 "how do they communicate about potential sites for a new hive（蜜蜂找到可能筑新巢的地方时它们会怎样交流）"，而并没有谈论其他蜂巢。

28. (A)。本题为细节题。本题问"为了表达'停止'，蜜蜂会做什么？"。根据听力材料中老师所言 "And we also talked about how bees communicate 'stop' to other bees.（而且我们也讨论了蜜蜂是如何告知其他蜜蜂'停下'的）"以及 "How does the bee do that?（蜜蜂是如何做到这一点的？）"可以锁定答案出自这之后。接着根据学生说的 "… the explorer honeybee will send out a vibrating signal …（……去探索的蜜蜂会发出振动信号……）"可以判断选项 (A) "Give a vibrating signal（发出振动信号）"为正确答案。选项 (B) "Steal food from the dancing bee（从跳舞的蜜蜂那里偷食物）"和选项 (C) "Dance around the other dancing bee（围着另一只跳舞的蜜蜂跳舞）"在听力材料中均未提及，为错误选项。选项 (D) "Bump its tail into that of the dancing bee（用它的尾巴去撞正在跳舞的蜜蜂的尾巴）"是错误的，因为听力材料中说的是 "After it gives the vibrating signal, that honeybee will also either butt its head into the head of the bee that's dancing or it will climb on top of the bee that's dancing.（在发出振动信号后，那只蜜

蜂也会用头去撞正在跳舞的蜜蜂的头，或者它会爬到正在跳舞的蜜蜂的顶上）"。

29. **(B)**。本题为细节题。本题问"蜜蜂用什么来交流新蜂巢的位置？"。根据听力材料中的关键句"Some bees go out to search for a new site for a hive, and when they return, they describe the location through a tail-wagging dance.（有些蜜蜂出去寻找蜂巢的新位置，当它们回来时，它们通过跳摇尾舞来描述位置）"可以判断选项 (B)"A tail-wagging dance（摇尾舞）"为正确答案。选项 (A)"A movement of the head（头部的运动）"和选项 (C)"A vibrating signal（振动信号）"是错误的，因为通过第 28 题的解析可知，蜜蜂"send out a vibrating signal（发出振动信号）"和"butt its head into the head of the bee that's dancing（用头去撞正在跳舞的蜜蜂的头）"是蜜蜂在表达"stop"的方法，而不是交流蜂巢位置的方法。选项 (D)"A round dance（圆圈舞）"是错误的，因为听力材料中提及"As for the location of the food source, bees have two kinds of dances to tell how far away it is—they either do a round dance or a tail-wagging dance.（至于食物源的位置，蜜蜂用两种舞蹈来交流距离有多远——它们要么跳圆圈舞，要么跳摇尾舞）"，所以圆圈舞是描述食物源位置时才跳的。

30. **(A)**。本题为预测题。本题问"学生们接下来很可能会做什么？"。根据听力材料中老师说的第一句话"Before we take our quiz …（在我们进行测试之前……）"和最后一句话"I think you're well prepared for your quiz …（我觉得你们已经准备好测试了……）"可以判断选项 (A)"Take a quiz（进行测试）"为正确答案。同时可以判断选项 (B)"Turn in their homework（交他们的作业）"、选项 (C)"Look for beehives outside（去外面寻找蜂巢）"以及选项 (D)"Watch a movie about bees（看一部关于蜜蜂的电影）"是错误的。

Questions 31–34

该听力材料主要讲了有关电报系统和电报机的知识。

31. **(B)**。本题为主旨题。本题问"这段话的主题是什么？"。整段听力材料讲的都是电报系统和电报机。选项 (A)"Why telegraph systems are no longer used（为什么电报系统不再被使用了）"是错误的，根据听力材料中句子"Telegraph wires were put in place all over the world …（世界各地都有电报线……）"可知电报在过去的使用非常普及，但现在情况如何在听力材料中并未提及，为错误选项。选项 (C)"Why the first telegraph systems were difficult to use（为什么最初的电报系统很难用）"是错误的，听力材料提及"In the very first electric telegraphs

... but these machines didn't always work very well.（在最早的电流式电报机中……但这些机器并不总是运作良好。）"，但仅此一处，不能概括全文。选项 (D)"Why Samuel Morse became interested in telegraphs（为什么 Samuel Morse 对电报感兴趣）"是错误的，因为听力材料中并没有详细解释，不能概括全文。选项 (B)"How telegraph systems have changed over time（电报系统是如何随时间变化的）"为正确答案，因为听力材料中提及了"Early telegraph messages were signals …（早期的电报信息是信号……）"、"Over a thousand years ago in Greece, they used a system …（在一千年前的希腊，他们使用了一个系统……）"以及"In the very first electric telegraphs …（在最早的电流式电报机中……）"，明显讲的是电报系统随时间的改变。

32. **(B)**。本题为修辞结构题。本题问"老师为什么要谈到电视？"。包含这一信息的前后句是"The first part, 'tele-,' comes from the Greek for 'distance,' and 'graph' is from the Greek word for 'write.' So it's writing from a distance. Kind of like 'television,' right? But television is something you watch—that's the 'vision' part—and it's sent from a distance.（这个词的前半部分 'tele-' 来自希腊语，表示 '距离'，'graph' 在希腊语中表示 '写'。所以意思是在远处写。有点儿像 'television'，对吧？但电视是你观看的东西——是 'vision' 的部分——也是从远处来的）"。由此可知，老师在讲 "telegraph" 这一单词由来的过程中，借用 "television" 来辅助学生更好地理解，所以可以判断选项 (B)"To explain the meaning of the word 'telegraph'（解释 'telegraph' 一词的含义）"为正确答案。同时可以判断出选项 (A)"To explain why telegraphs are no longer used（解释为什么不再使用电报机了）"、选项 (C)"To show another way electricity can be used for communication（来展示电可用于通信的另一种方式）"以及选项 (D)"To point out that early televisions were similar to telegraph machines（指出早期电视机类似于电报机）"均是错误的。

33. **(A)**。本题为推断题。本题问"老师觉得 Samuel Morse 有什么令人惊讶的地方？"。根据听力材料中的关键句"The electric telegraph that really succeeded was actually invented by a professor of painting and sculpture, believe it or not! Samuel Morse was an artist who was also interested in electricity.（真正成功的电报机其实是一位绘画和雕塑教授发明的，信不信由你！Samuel Morse 是一位对电也很感兴趣的艺术家）"可知，Samuel Morse 并不是科学家却成功发明电报机，因此选项 (A)"He was not a professional scientist.（他不是专业的科学家）"为正确答案。选项 (B)"He did not like using telegraph machines.（他不喜欢使用电报机）"、选项

(C) "He did not earn much money from inventing the telegraph.（他从发明电报机中没有赚到多少钱）"和选项 (D) "He thought of the telegraph many years before he invented it.（他在他发明电报机前的很多年就想到了）"在听力材料中均未提及，为错误选项。

34. (A)。本题为细节题。本题问"老师对电报员有什么看法？"。根据听力材料中的关键句"Telegraphers sent out messages in code, and then decoded or translated messages coming in. This was a very important job ...（电报员以密码形式发送消息，然后解码或翻译收到的消息。这是一项非常重要的工作……）"可以判断选项 (A) "Their work was very important.（他们的工作非常重要）"为正确答案。选项 (B) "Most of them were also inventors.（他们中的大多数人也是发明家）"、选项 (C) "It was very difficult to become one.（成为其中一员非常难）"和选项 (D) "There were only a few of them.（他们的人数很少）"在听力材料中均未提及，为错误选项。

Questions 35–38

该听力材料主要讲的是太阳大气的最外层——日冕及相关的有趣事实。

35. (D)。本题为主旨题。本题问"老师主要讲了什么？"。根据听力材料首段的句子"And the part of the Sun's atmosphere that's farthest from the Sun's surface is called the corona.（离太阳表面最远的那部分太阳大气称为日冕）"以及听力材料中多次出现的单词"corona"，可知日冕是讲述的主要对象，所以选项 (D) "A part of the Sun's atmosphere（太阳大气的一部分）"为正确答案。选项 (A) "A new discovery about the Sun（关于太阳的新发现）"是错误的，因为听力材料中提及"The corona has some qualities that have interested and puzzled astronomers for a long time.（日冕的一些特性已经让天文学家感兴趣的同时也困惑很长时间了）"，可见日冕并不是天文学家关于太阳的新发现。选项 (B) "Changes in the brightness of the Sun（太阳亮度的变化）"是错误的，因为听力材料中未提及。选项 (C) "Equipment used to study the Sun（研究太阳的设备）"是错误的，虽然听力材料中提及"This can make it hard to observe the corona without special equipment.（这使得在没有特殊设备的情况下很难观察日冕）"，但并不是本篇听力材料的核心，只是一个事实。

36. (D)。本题为修辞结构题。本题问"老师第一次提及壁炉里的火是为什么？"。老师在讲火之前说了这样一句话"Well, remember, the corona is the part of the atmosphere that's the farthest from the Sun's surface.（嗯，要记住，日冕是大气中距离太阳表面最远的那部分）"，然后举了一个常识性的例子：离火源越远越冷。由此让学生更好地理解为什么日冕让人困惑——因为它虽然距离太阳最远，温度却很高，这是违背大众常识的现象。由此可以判断选项 (D)"To discuss the corona's temperature（为了讨论日冕的温度）"为正确答案。选项 (A)"To illustrate how the Sun produces energy（为了说明太阳是如何产生能量的）"、选项 (B)"To compare the Sun to other stars（为了将太阳与其他恒星做对比）"和选项 (C)"To describe the color of the corona（为了描述日冕的颜色）"在听力材料中均未提及，为错误选项。

37. (A)。本题为细节题。本题问"为什么太阳的日冕很暗？"。根据听力材料中的关键句"The corona is hard to see because it's so dim compared to the Sun's surface. Scientists think this is probably because the corona isn't very dense—that means its gas particles are spread out.（日冕很难被看到，因为与太阳表面相比它太暗了。科学家们认为这可能是因为日冕的密度不高——这意味着它的气体粒子是分散的）"可以判断选项 (A)"Its particles are spread out.（它的粒子是分散的）"为正确答案。选项 (C)"It is not very hot.（它的温度不是很高）"错误，因为听力材料中明确提到日冕的温度"is incredibly hot（异常高）"。选项 (B)"It is partly liquid.（它部分是液体）"和选项 (D)"It does not have much energy.（它没有太多能量）"在听力材料中均未提及，为错误选项。

38. (B)。本题为细节题。本题问"为什么在日食期间很容易看到日冕？"。根据听力材料中的关键句"During a total eclipse, the Moon blocks the Sun from our view—only the corona is visible, around the Sun's edges.（在日全食期间，月亮把太阳挡在了我们的视线之外——只能看到太阳边缘的日冕）"可以判断选项 (B)"The Moon blocks the Sun's light.（月亮挡住了太阳的光）"为正确答案。同时可以判断选项(A)"The Sun appears bigger.（太阳看起来更大）"、选项(C)"The corona changes color.（日冕的颜色变化了）"和选项 (D)"Earth gets closer to the sun.（地球离太阳更近了）"在听力材料中均未提及，为错误选项。

Questions 39–42

该听力材料是课上老师在和学生讨论去城市植物园的经历。

39. (C)。本题为细节题。本题问"学生所描述的植物是她在哪里看到的？"。根据听力材料中的句子"I hope everyone enjoyed our field trip yesterday to the city botanical gardens.（我希望大家喜欢我们昨天的城市植物园实地考察之旅）"，可知全班去参观城市植物园了，所以可以判

断选项 (C)"On a class trip（在班级旅行中）"为正确答案。选项 (A)"In a textbook（在教科书上）"、选项 (B)"On a Web site（在一个网站上）"和选项 (D)"On a family vacation（在一次家庭度假中）"均为错误选项。

40. **(A)**。本题为细节题。本题问"据老师介绍，肉质植物为了生存下来是如何适应环境的？"。根据听力材料中的关键句"Remember the thick green body of the cactus you liked so much? It's because of these unique tissues that soak up water that succulents can survive in deserts and other dry and hot environments.（还记得你非常喜欢的那颗仙人掌的厚厚的绿色茎干吗？正是由于这些能够吸收水分的独特组织，肉质植物才能在沙漠等干燥而炎热的环境中生存）"可以判断选项 (A)"They can store water.（它们可以储存水）"为正确答案。选项 (B)"They need little light.（它们不怎么需要光照）"、选项 (C)"They taste bad to animals.（它们对动物来说味道不好）"和选项 (D)"They blend in with their environment.（它们与所处环境融为一体）"在听力材料中均未提及，为错误选项。

41. **(C)**。本题为细节题。本题问"根据老师所言，'succulent'一词指的是什么？"。根据句子"The word 'succulent' actually means 'fat' because of this thick, fleshy appearance.（'succulent'这个词实际上意味着'fat'，因为其厚实、多肉的外表）"，由此可知"succulent"是在描述植物的外表，同"fat"的意思一样，所以选项 (C)"What the plant looks like（植物看上去的样子）"为正确答案。同时可以判断选项 (A)"How the plant tastes（植物的味道如何）"、选项 (B)"Where the plant grows（植物生长的地方）"和选项 (D)"The person who first named the plant（最早为植物命名的人）"均为错误选项。

42. **(B)**。本题为语用意义题。本题问"当女孩说'现在我知道我下一篇科学报告要写什么了'的时候，她在暗示什么？"。在女孩说这句话前，老师解释了"succulent"一词的意思。对此，女孩回答道"Who knew a plant could be so interesting?（谁能想到一种植物竟会如此有趣？）"。由此可以判断选项 (B)"She is interested in learning more about succulent plants.（她对更多地了解肉质植物很感兴趣）"为正确答案。选项 (A)"She has gotten a late start on a science report.（她的科学报告开始得晚了）"和选项 (C)"She did not know that she had so much science homework.（她不知道自己有这么多科学作业）"在听力材料中并未提及，为错误选项。选项(D)"She will decide on the topic of her report later.（她随后会决定她的报告的主题）"是错误的，既然女孩说"Now I know ……（现在我知道……）"，就代表她已经决定好了。

Part 2 – Language Form and Meaning

Answer Key			
Question Number	Answer	Question Number	Answer
1.（例题）	D	21.	D
2.（例题）	D	22.	B
1.	D	23.	C
2.	B	24.	B
3.	C	25.	A
4.	B	26.	B
5.	C	27.	D
6.	D	28.	A
7.	D	29.	D
8.	B	30.	A
9.	C	31.	B
10.	D	32.	C
11.	A	33.	C
12.	B	34.	C
13.	B	35.	B
14.	B	36.	C
15.	C	37.	A
16.	B	38.	D
17.	A	39.	C
18.	C	40.	A
19.	C	41.	B
20.	D	42.	A

Answer Explanation

1. （例题）(D)。本题考查的是副词的含义。此句意为"认为岩石永存并且岩石_____改变的观点不完全正确"。选项处需要选择合适的副词修饰"change（改变）"。选项 (A)"still"表示"仍然"，选项 (B)"very"表示"非常"，选项 (C)"quite"表示"相当"，选项 (D)"never"表示"永不"。第一个同位语从句说"岩石永存"，然后用 and 连接另一个同位语从句，两个同位语从句意思应该一致，推测为"岩石永不改变"最合适。因此选项 (D) 为正确答案。

2. （例题）(D)。本题考查的是表达推测含义的谓语动词。此句意为"如果你曾经站在一条湍急的河边，那么你_____流水击打岩石"。很明显选项处缺少谓语。首先可以判断选项 (B)"seen"错误，因为 seen 是 see 的过去分词，不可以充当句子的谓语。通过分析句意可知，"看到流水击打岩石"的场面不一定人人都会经历，因此句子中要有表达推测含义的情态动词。符合这一要求的是选项 (D)"may have seen"，因此为正确答案。另外，该句中主句的时态要与从句的时态保持一致，都使用现在完成时，而选项 (A)"saw"是一般过去时，选项 (C)"are seeing"是现在进行时，均不符合，为错误选项。

Questions 1–4

该语篇主要讲了 Denville 镇公共图书馆要为初中生举办一场关于提高学习技能的讲座，并提供了时间、地点、主讲人等信息。

1. (D)。本题考查的是谓语动词的时态。此句意为"下周六晚八点，Denville 镇公共图书馆为初中生_____一场关于……的专题讲座"。通过分析句子结构可知，选项处应该是句子的谓语，因此排除选项 (B)"to host"和选项 (C)"hosting"，因为这两个选项均不能做谓语。又因"Next Saturday（下周六）"是表示将来的时间状语，因此句子的时态应用一般将来时，所以选项 (D)"will host"为正确答案，意为"将为初中生举办一场关于……的专题讲座"。选项 (A)"hosted"表示的是一般过去时，故排除。

2. (B)。本题考查的是动名词的用法。根据第 1 题可知图书馆要举办一场讲座，该选项处是对讲座的修饰，说明讲座主题是什么。选项前有"about"，是介词，后面可以跟名词或动名词，因此排除选项 (A)"improve"和选项 (C)"it improves"。选项 (D)"the improvement"是名词，

并可以与 "about" 进行搭配，但是不能与选项后的名词短语 "study skills" 连用，故排除。选项 (B) "improving" 是动名词，代入原文后，意为 "关于提升学习技巧的讲座"，符合句意，为正确答案。

3. **(C)**。本题考查副词的含义。语篇中提到 "Emily Walters 是 Denville 高中的咨询顾问，她将会探讨让学生能更_____利用自己的学习时间的方法……"。四个选项均为副词，选项 (A) "safely" 意为 "安全地"，选项 (B) "instantly" 意为 "立即，马上"，选项 (C) "efficiently" 意为 "效率高地"，选项 (D) "wonderfully" 意为 "非常；令人惊奇地"。由第 1 题的解析可知，Denville 镇公共图书馆举办的讲座是关于提高学习技能的。因此选项 (C) 更符合题意，意为 "更高效地利用自己的学习时间的方法"，因此选项 (C) 为正确答案。

4. **(B)**。本题考查的是定语从句。此句意为 "Walters 老师随后会在现场回答_____关于从初中到高中的转变的问题"。选项处是修饰 "questions" 的成分。观察四个选项，发现选项中都有主语和谓语，因此是个从句，即选项处是修饰 "questions" 的定语从句。其中，只有选项 (B) "that student may have" 符合 "关系代词（that）+ 主语 + 谓语动词" 的语法结构，意为 "回答学生们可能会有的关于从初中到高中的转变的问题"，因此选项 (B) 为正确答案。

Questions 5–8

该语篇主要讲的是老师号召学生们为即将到来的 20 名外国交换生提供住宿。

5. **(C)**。本题考查的是 "there be" 句型。此句意为 "下个月，_____一组来自我们的姐妹城市，法国阿维尼翁（Avignon）的外籍交换生来参观学校"。通过分析句子结构可知，选项处缺少句子的主语和谓语动词，且需要表达 "有" 的含义。选项 (A) "Will be" 缺少主语，故排除。选项 (B) "That there is" 中的 "That" 多余，故排除。选项 (D) "Because there will be" 中有连词 "Because"，但语篇中的句子是个简单句，不需要连词，故排除。选项 (C) "There will be" 是 "there be" 句型的一般将来时，与句中的时间状语 "next month（下个月）" 相符，句意为 "下个月，将有一组来自我们姐妹城市的外籍交换生来参观学校"。因此选项 (C) 为正确答案。

6. **(D)**。本题考查的是句子中主谓宾的顺序。此句意为 "大约有 20 名学生会来，并且_____来暂住"。句中 "and" 是连词，后面可以接一个完整的句子，且顺序应该是 "主语—谓语—宾语"。四个选项中，"they" 为主语，"need" 为谓语，"places" 为宾语，正确顺序应为 "they

need places"，与选项 (D) "they all need places" 一致，句意为 "并且他们都需要地方暂住"。选项 (D) 中的 "all" 是强调代词，意为 "全部，全体"，不影响整体结构。因此选项 (D) 为正确答案。

7. **(D)**。本题考查的是动词的含义及用法。这句话意为 "如果你家可以招待一名交换生，请跟 Duchamp 老师_____"。首先，四个选项都有 "说" 的含义，但用法不同。选项 (A) "ask" 意为 "问"，通常的用法是 "ask sb (about sth)"。选项 (B) "tell" 意为 "告诉"，常用的搭配是 "tell sb sth" 或 "tell sth to sb"。选项 (C) "say" 意为 "说"，常用的搭配是 "say sth to sb"。选项 (D) "speak" 意为 "交谈"，常用 "speak to sb" 表达 "与某人说话"。根据以上四个动词的用法可以判断出选项 (D) 符合题意，为正确答案。

8. **(B)**。本题考查不定式的用法。此句意为 "尤其鼓励学习法语的学生来招待，因为这对学生们来说是一个_____他们语言技能的好机会！"。通过分析句子结构可知，"as" 是连词，后面可以接一个完整的句子，构成原因状语从句。在该从句中，"this" 是主语，"is" 是谓语动词，"a great opportunity" 是表语。通过观察四个选项可知，选项处需要选择 "practice（练习）" 的正确形式。选项 (A) "practiced" 是表示过去时的谓语动词，选项 (C) "are practicing" 是表示现在进行时的谓语动词，选项 (D) "they practiced" 是 "主语 + 谓语动词" 的结构，但是由于该从句中已有了完整的主谓结构，因此这三个选项均错误。选项 (B) "to practice" 是不定式，可以用来说明这是一个 "练习语言技能" 的好机会，因此选项 (B) 为正确答案。

Questions 9–12

该语篇是一则失物招领的通知。

9. **(C)**。本题考查的是定语从句。此句意为 "昨天我在图书馆发现了一块_____手表"。通过分析句子结构可知，主语是 "I"，谓语是 "found"，宾语是 "a wristwatch"，因此选项处应该是修饰 "wristwatch" 的成分，表示 "某人遗失的"。观察四个选项，发现其中有施动者 "someone" 和动作 "leave" 的相关形式，因此该成分应为定语从句，需要有关系代词来引导，因此选项 (C) "that someone left" 为正确答案。选项 (A) "someone left it" 中没有 "that" 是可以的，因为 "that" 在定语从句中做宾语时可以省略，但是这里包含了多余的宾语 "it"，故排除。选项 (B) 也省略了定语从句引导词 "that"，但 "someone leaving" 不构成主谓结构，应该是 "someone left"，故排除。另外，选项处也可以是动词的分词形式，对 "wristwatch"

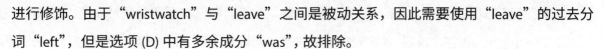

进行修饰。由于 "wristwatch" 与 "leave" 之间是被动关系，因此需要使用 "leave" 的过去分词 "left"，但是选项 (D) 中有多余成分 "was"，故排除。

10. (D)。本题考查的是宾语从句。语篇中说 "如果你认为这块手表可能是你的，那么你需要到学校管理员的办公室"。接着，包含第 10 题的句子意为 "告诉 Bryson 老师，你弄丢了你的手表，并描述_____，这样他可以确定我找到的手表是你的"。句中有连词 "and"，其后可以接一个完整的句子。"describe（描述）" 为谓语，它后面缺少宾语或宾语从句。根据上下文可知，这部分应该想表达 "描述手表是什么样子的"，因此需要用 "what" 表示 "什么"，从而构成 "what + 主语 + 谓语动词" 的从句结构。四个选项中，选项 (D) "what it looks like" 符合语法规则和句意，为正确答案。

11. (A)。本题考查的是动词的含义和用法。此句意为 "此外，即使你没有弄丢手表，也请_____其他学生我找到一块表的事儿"。根据文意合理推测选项处需要的是可以表达 "告知""转告" 或 "传达" 等的动词。四个选项中，选项 (A) "tell" 意为 "告诉"，选项 (B) "hear" 意为 "听说"，选项 (C) "share" 意为 "分享"，选项 (D) "control" 意为 "控制"。将四个选项分别代入，发现选项 (A) "tell" 最合适，且符合它的常用搭配 "tell sb about sth"，即 "告诉其他学生我找到一块表的事儿"，因此选项 (A) 为正确答案。

12. (B)。本题考查的是 "would like to do sth" 的用法。此句意为 "这是一块好表，而且我确定失主应该想要_____"。选项处前面是 "would like"，常用 "would like to do sth" 的搭配，表达 "想要做某事"，所以此处应选择选项 (B) "to get it back"，意为 "想要把它（手表）找回来"。选项 (C) "back to get it" 中 "back" 的位置不正确，因此排除选项 (C)。选项 (A) "it getting back" 和选项 (D) "it got back" 不符合 "would like to do sth" 的结构，故排除。

Questions 13–18

该语篇主要讲的是书签的使用历史悠久，在过去，书签用很昂贵的材料制成。

13. (B)。本题考查的是不定式的用法。此句意为 "如今我们使用的书签通常只是窄窄的厚纸片，我们将其插入书页中_____我们回到我们上次阅读结束的地方"。通过分析句意可知，选项处需要解释插入书签的目的是什么，因此需要用不定式表目的。四个选项中，将选项 (B) "to help" 代入选项处，意为 "将其插入书页中来帮助我们回到我们上次阅读结束的地方"，选项

(B) 为正确答案。选项 (A)"helps"是谓语动词，然而句中已有谓语动词"are"，故排除。选项 (C)"but help"中"but"表达的是转折关系，与题意不符，故排除。选项 (D)"they help"是一个"主语＋谓语"的结构，与题意不符，故排除。

14. **(B)**。 本题考查的是同级比较"as + 形容词 + as"的用法。此句意为"或许会令人感到惊奇的是，书签存在的时间与人们拥有书_____"。通过分析句意可知，此句在比较书签和书存在的时间长短。选项处前有一个"as"，选项 (B)"long as"中有一个"as"，能够构成"as long as"的结构，表示"书签和书存在的时间一样长"，是同级比较，因此选项 (B) 为正确答案。选项 (A)"long"后缺少"as"，结构不完整，故排除。选项 (C)"longingly"是副词，意为"渴望地"，不符合题意，故排除。选项 (D)"longer than"不能与选项前的"as"连用，故排除。

15. **(C)**。 本题考查的是谓语动词的使用。此句意为"随着时间的推移，书签极大地_____"。通过分析句子结构可知，句子缺少谓语。又因"over time"意为"随着时间的推移"，表示从过去的某个时间一直持续到现在，所以谓语应该用现在完成时，即"have/has + 动词的过去分词"。选项 (C)"have changed"符合语法规则，意为"书签已经发生了极大变化"，因此为正确答案。选项 (A)"changes"是一般现在时，故排除。选项 (B)"to change"和选项 (D)"to have changed"是不定式，不能充当句子的谓语，故排除。

16. **(B)**。 本题考查的是主语和谓语动词的使用。此句意为"现在，_____常用廉价的纸制成"。通过分析句子结构可知，该句描述的对象跟上一句一样都是"bookmarks"，因此主语应该使用指代名词复数的代词"they"，而非指代名词单数的"it"，故排除选项 (C)"it does"和选项 (D)"it is"。由于"bookmarks"和"make"之间是被动关系，因此谓语应该使用被动语态，即"be 动词 + 动词的过去分词"，因此选项 (B)"they are"为正确答案，意为"书签常用廉价的纸制成"。选项 (A)"they have"不能构成被动语态，故排除。

17. **(A)**。 本题考查的是动词的过去分词的用法。此句意为"在过去，书签一般是由精细的布料或装饰精美的皮革_____的昂贵物品"。通过分析句子结构可知，该句子是主系表结构，主语是"Bookmarks"，系动词是"were"，表语是"expensive items"，因此选项处应该是修饰"expensive items"的成分。此成分可以是定语从句，也可以是动词的分词。由于"expensive items"和"make"之间是被动关系，所以需要用动词的过去分词形式，即 made，因此选项 (A)"made"正确，表示"由精细的布料或装饰精美的皮革制成"。选项 (B)"making"表主动关系，故排除。选项 (C)"that made"缺少 be 动词，不能构成被动语态，故排除。选项 (D)"were made"虽然为被动语态，但是缺少定语从句引导词"that"（"that"在定语从句中做主语时不能省略），故排除。

18. (C)。本题考查的是表语从句的结构。此句意为"书签相对比较珍贵的一个原因或许是_____必须与其所标记的书相匹配"。通过分析句子结构可知，此句的主语是"one reason"，谓语动词是"is"，"bookmarks were relatively precious objects"是定语从句，修饰"reason"。很明显，选项处是一个表语从句，需要引导词"that"且"that"不可以省略。从句中"quanlity"是主语，"had to suit"是谓语，"the books"是宾语。所以选项 (C)"that their quality"为正确答案，其他选项均不符合表语从句的语法结构，故排除。

Questions 19–26

该语篇主要讲的是动植物的灭绝很普遍，但也存在复活效应（Lazarus effect）。

19. (C)。本题考查的是谓语动词的使用。此句意为"科学家们_____每个月有十多种植物和动物灭绝"。通过分析句子结构可知，此句主语为"Scientists"，"that"引导的是宾语从句，所以选项处应是谓语。四个选项中，选项 (B)"estimating"是现在分词，选项 (D)"to estimate"是不定式，都无法充当句子的谓语，故排除。另外，由于主语"Scientists"是名词的复数形式，因此选项 (C)"estimate"为正确答案，意为"科学家们估计每个月有十多种植物和动物灭绝"。选项 (A)"estimates"是动词的第三人称单数形式，主谓不一致，故排除。

20. (D)。本题考查的是动词的含义。此句意为"在某些情况下，人类活动因一个物种的消失而被_____"。四个选项中，选项 (A)"failed"是"fail"的过去分词，意为"失败"，选项 (B)"scored"是"score"的过去分词，意为"得分；获得胜利"，选项 (C)"caused"是"cause"的过去分词，意为"导致"，选项 (D)"blamed"是"blame"的过去分词，意为"指责"。分别将这四个选项代入，发现选项 (D)"blamed"的含义最合适，"be blamed for sth"表示"因某事而被指责"，意为"人类活动因一个物种的消失而被指责"，因此选项 (D) 为正确答案。

21. (D)。本题考查的是谓语动词的使用。语篇中说"然而，灭绝也是自然发生的"，接着又说"它（物种灭绝）是一个过程，一个_____整个地球历史的过程"。通过分析句子结构可知，"a process"后面是"that"引导的定语从句。在定语从句中，"that"是从句的主语，所以选项处应该是从句的谓语。选项 (A) "it took" 是 "主语 + 谓语" 的结构，故排除。选项 (B) "to have taken" 是不定式，不能充当谓语，故排除。另外，此句的时间状语是 "throughout Earth's history"，意为 "贯穿整个地球历史"，所以从句的时态应为现在完成进行时，强调动作是一直持续的，其谓语动词的结构应为 "have/has been + 动词的现在分词"，因此选项 (D) "has been taking" 为正确答案。选项 (C) "has to be taken" 并非现在完成进行时的结构，且 "take place（发生）" 无须使用被动形式，故排除。

22. **(B)**。本题考查的是 "occasion" 的副词形式。语篇中提到，"在人类存在的很长一段时间之前，一些植物和动物物种就消失了"。接着说，"然而，科学家们_____发现……"。通过分析句子结构可知，选项处缺少修饰 "discover" 的副词，四个选项中只有选项 (B) "Occasionally" 是副词，意为 "然而，科学家们有时候发现……"，因此选项 (B) 为正确答案。

23. **(C)**。本题考查的是动词的过去分词的用法。此句的意思为 "然而，科学家们有时候发现，一些_____消失的物种并没有真的灭绝"。通过分析句子结构可知，"that" 引导的从句做 "discover" 的宾语，这个宾语从句中，主语是 "some species"，谓语动词是 "are"，表语是 "extinct"，因此选项处应该是用于修饰从句主语 "some species" 的成分。通过分析句意可知，这里想表达的是 "一些被认为消失了的物种"，"some species" 与 "think" 之间是被动关系，这里应该用 "think" 的过去分词 "thought"，所以选项 (C) "thought to have" 为正确答案。选项 (B) "thinking it had" 和选项 (D) "having thought it" 都是动词的现在分词形式，表达主动的含义，故排除。选项 (A) "they thought it" 是 "主语 + 谓语动词 + 宾语" 的结构，是完整的句子，故排除。

24. **(B)**。本题考查的是名词短语做主语的用法。此句意为 "_____以前被认为灭绝了的被称为复活效应"。通过分析句子结构可知，"is known" 是句子的谓语，所以选项处应该是句子的主语。四个选项中，选项 (A) "It was a live animal discovered"、选项 (C) "They discovered a live animal" 和选项 (D) "A live animal was discovered" 均包含 "主语 + 谓语" 结构，故排除。选项 (B) "The discovery of a live animal" 是一个名词短语，可以充当句子的主语，意为 "发现以前被认为灭绝的动物还活着，这被称为复活效应"，因此选项 (B) 为正确答案。

25. **(A)**。本题考查的是名词短语做宾语的用法。此句意为 "复活效应的一个最近的例子发生在老挝，在那里，探索者发现_____，被叫作 *Laonastes aenigmamus*"。通过分析句子结构可知，

"where" 引导定语从句，修饰 "Laos（老挝）"。在定语从句中，"explorers" 是主语，"found" 是谓语，所以选项处应是宾语。四个选项中，选项 (A) "a mouse-sized animal" 是语序正确的名词短语，可以做句子的宾语，意为 "一只像老鼠那么大的动物"，因此为正确答案。选项 (B) "that was a mouse-sized animal" 的意思是 "那是一个像老鼠那么大的动物"，此选项有完整的 "主语 + 系动词 + 表语" 的结构，无法充当句子宾语，故排除。选项 (C) "an animal that the size a mouse" 和选项 (D) "out an animal the size of a mouse" 的表达不通顺，结构也不符合语法规则，因此排除。

26. **(B)**。本题考查的是与时间连用的介词的用法。此句意为 "在发现它之前，这种动物被认为已经灭绝了一千一百万年了"。通过分析句子结构可知，选项处缺少与时间连用的介词。四个选中，选项 (A) "in" 一般后跟 "一段时间"，表示 "在一段时间之内"；选项 (B) "for" 一般后跟 "一段时间"，表示 "某事已经存在或发生了一段时间"；选项 (C) "since" 一般后跟 "某个时间点"，表示 "从某个时间点开始一直持续到现在"；选项 (D) "near to" 一般后跟 "某个时间点"，表示 "接近某个时间点"。题目中 "eleven million years" 是一个时间段，因此排除选项 (C) "since" 和选项 (D) "near to"。通过分析句意可知，这种动物被认为灭绝的现象已经存在了一千一百万年，而不是在一千一百万年之内，因此正确答案为选项 (B) "for"。

Questions 27–34

该语篇主要讲的是小语种也可以对历史产生重要影响，并介绍了其中的一种——劳伦系语（Laurentian）。

27. **(D)**。本题考查的是名词做主语。此句意为 "极少数人说的_____通常被称为小语种"。通过分析句子结构可知，"are referred to" 是句子的谓语，选项处应该是句子的主语。选项 (D) "Languages" 是名词的复数形式，与 "are" 搭配，主谓一致，可以做句子的主语，意为 "极少数人说的语言"，因此选项 (D) 为正确答案。选项 (C) "It is a language" 是 "主语 + 系动词 + 表语" 的结构，无法充当句子的主语，故排除。选项 (A) "Because languages" 的 "Because" 是多余成分，语法不正确，故排除。选项 (B) "There languages" 包含多余的成分 "There"，语法不正确，故排除。

28. **(A)**。本题考查的是动词的过去分词做伴随状语的用法。此句意为 "即使只被少数人_____，这些语言也能够产生重大的历史影响"。通过分析句意可知，选项处是用来修饰句子主语"these languages（这些语言）"的，"languages"与"speak（说）"之间是被动关系，意为"被少数人说的语言"，应该使用"speak"的过去分词形式"spoken"。另外，选项后的"by"也可以证明二者之间是被动关系。四个选项中，选项 (A)"spoken"为正确答案。选项 (B)"that spoke"、选项 (C)"it had spoken"和选项 (D)"they are speaking"均表达主动关系，故排除。另外，通过观察发现，由"though"引导的让步状语从句中没有主语和谓语动词，这是因为当从句和主句中的主语一致，且谓语动词为 be 动词的相应形式时，从句中可以省略主语和谓语动词。

29. (D)。本题考查的是"so … that …"结构。此句意为"在北美洲，有一些语言使用范围_____小，以至于除了研究这些语言的专家几乎没人知道这些语言的名字"。通过分析句意可知，选项处缺少副词来修饰"small（小）"。四个选项中，选项 (A)"quite（相当）"、选项 (B)"very（非常）"、选项 (C)"too（太）"、选项 (D)"so（如此）"都可以用来修饰"small"，以加深程度，但因选项处后有"that"，只有"so"能够与之组成"so + 形容词 + that"的结构，表示"如此……以至于……"，所以选项 (D) 为正确答案。

30. (A)。本题考查的是限定词的含义。此句意为"_____像这样的语言，劳伦系语，在北美洲东部的几十个村庄中使用"。四个选项中，选项 (A)"One"表示"一个"，用于强调某人或某事；选项 (B)"Any"表示"任何的，任一的"；选项 (C)"Some"表示"某个"，用于表示不知道确切是哪个人或事物；选项 (D)"Another"表示"另一"。前文提到，一些小语种几乎不为人知，此句以劳伦系语为例子加以说明，这个例子非常具体，不是"任何的，任一的"，故选项 (B)"Any"排除；不是"某个"，故选项 (C)"Some"排除；从文中可知，这个例子是作者所举的唯一的例子，不存在"另一"的说法，故选项 (D)"Another"排除。最后，将选项 (A)"One"代入原文，意为"一种像这样的语言"，符合题意，因此为正确答案。

31. (B)。本题考查的是"there be"句型。此句意为"到 16 世纪末，这种语言消失了；现在_____劳伦系语"。根据选项可知，此句想要表达的是"没有说劳伦系语的人了"，需要使用"there be"句型的否定形式。基本结构应为"there be + no + 名词"。四个选项中只有选项 (B)"there are no speakers"符合该结构，因此为正确答案。其他三个选项均不符合上述结构，故排除。

32. (C)。本题考查的是名词短语做宾语的用法。此句意为"然而，虽然不再被使用了，但劳伦系语在当今所有的语言中都留下了_____"。通过分析句子结构可知，该句是复合句，前面

是由 "even though" 引导的让步状语从句，后面为主句。在主句中，主语是 "Laurentian"，
谓语是 "has left"，因此选项处应该是宾语。四个选项中，只有选项 (C) "a lasting mark" 是
名词短语，可以做句子的宾语，意为 "持久的痕迹"，因此为正确答案。选项 (A) "a mark
lasted"、选项 (B) "to last a mark" 和选项 (D) "was a lasting mark" 都不能做 "has left" 的宾语，
故排除。

33. (C)。本题考查的是代词的用法。此句意为 "16 世纪中期，法国探险家 Jacques Cartier 与说劳
伦系语的人接触的时候，他们教给_____ 'kanata' 这个单词，意思是'村庄'"。通过分析
句意可知，这位法国探险家 Jacques Cartier 是被教授的对象，那么此处应使用表达单数的人
称代词 "him"，因此选项 (C) 为正确答案。选项 (A) "it" 通常指代动物或事物，且指代内容
需为单数，故排除。选项 (B) "that" 意为 "那个"，在句中指代不明，故排除。选项 (D) "them"
意为 "他们 / 她们 / 它们"，指代内容应为复数，故排除。

34. (C)。本题考查的是定语从句的结构。此句意为 "'kanata' 这个单词成了一个国家名字的由
来，这个国家_____加拿大"。通过分析句子结构可知，选项处是修饰 "the country" 的定
语从句，其结构为 "关系代词（that）+ 主语 + 谓语"，因此选项 (C) "that today we call" 符合
结构，意为 "我们如今称之为加拿大的国家"，其中的 "today" 用于表达时间，不影响整体
结构。其他选项均不符合定语从句的语法结构，故排除。

Questions 35–42

该语篇主要讲的是最硬的岩石也能被温柔的力量（比如水）在长久的作用下改变形状。

35. (B)。本题考查的是谓语动词的使用。此句意为 "当我们捡起一块石头并_____在我们手中
时，会感觉它很坚硬、很结实"。通过分析句子结构可知，该句包含由 "and" 连接的两个并
列的谓宾结构，它们拥有相同的主语 "we"。第一个谓宾结构是 "pick up a rock"，第二个谓
宾结构即为需要填入的选项。四个选项中，选项 (B) "hold it" 最合适，其中 "it" 指代的是 "a
rock"，意为 "把岩石拿在手里"。其他选项均不能满足谓宾结构的要求，故排除。

36. (C)。本题考查的是 "have difficulty (in) doing"（介词 in 可以省略）的用法。此句意为 "一些岩
石非常坚硬以至于我们可能_____如何能将其破坏"。通过分析句意可知，此处想要表达的
含义是 "很难想象……"，需要使用 "have difficulty (in) doing" 的结构。选项 (C) "difficulty

imagining" 可以与选项前的 "have" 组成这一结构，因此选项 (C) 为正确答案。其他选项都不能表达确切的含义，故排除。

37. **(A)。** 本题考查的是名词短语做主语。此句意为 "然而，_____，无论它们多么巨大，也会被侵蚀"。注意句子中有多个逗号，可以将 "however" 和 "no matter how large they are" 视为插入语，从而提炼出句子的主干为 "_____ can be worn away"。由此可知选项处应该是句子的主语。四个选项中，选项 (B) "Even rocks are the hardest" 和选项 (D) "There are even the hardest rocks" 都是完整的句子，不能做句子的主语，故排除。选项 (C) "The hardest rocks even though" 中的 "even though" 是连词，后面需要跟句子，此选项无法与后面的内容构成句子，也无法充当句子主语，故排除。选项 (A) "Even the hardest rocks" 是名词短语，其中的 "even" 是副词，表示 "即使"，起到修饰作用，意为 "即使最坚硬的岩石也能被侵蚀"，因此选项 (A) 为正确答案。

38. **(D)。** 本题考查的是 "as little as" 的用法。此句意为 "_____滴在岩石上的一滴水就足以……"。通过分析句子结构可知，此句为主系表结构，选项处应为定语修饰主语 a drop of water。"as little as" 是一个习语，表示 "一个数字或数量小得令人惊讶"。因此正确答案为选项 (D)。

39. **(C)。** 本题考查的是 "be enough to do sth" 的用法。此句意思是 "就像滴在岩石上的一滴水那么微小（的力量）就足以_____"。从上题的句意分析可知，此句表达的是 "滴水足以穿石"。选项前接 "is enough"，那么根据 "be enough to do sth（足以做某事）" 这一用法，应选择选项 (C) "to remove tiny bits"，意为 "足以移除掉岩石上的小碎块儿"。其他选项都不能与 "is enough" 连用，故排除。

40. **(A)。** 本题考查的是 "too + 形容词 + for sb to do sth" 的用法。此句意为 "当然，一滴水滴到坚硬的岩石上的效果_____小以至于我们无法看到"。通过分析句意可知，选项处修饰 "small"，选项后还有不定式结构 "to see"，因此这里是用 "too + 形容词 + for sb to do sth（太……以至于某人不能……）" 的结构来表达 "效果太小以至于我们无法看到"，因此选项 (A) "too" 为正确答案。选项 (B) "that"、选项 (C) "ever" 和选项 (D) "how" 都无法进行合理搭配，故排除。

41. **(B)。** 本题考查与时间连用的介词的用法。此句意为 "然而，当即使看似轻柔的力量作用于坚硬的岩石上_____数百万年时，所产生的变化也是惊人的"。选项处应该填一个与"millions of years"一起使用的介词。四个选项中，选项 (A)"at"、选项 (C)"to"和选项 (D)"from"通常与具体的时间点连用，只有选项 (B)"over"通常与一段时间连用。题目中"millions of years"是一个时间段，因此选项 (B)"over"为正确答案，表示"在数百万年中"。

42. **(A)**。本题考查的是动词的过去分词。此句意为"事实上，现在在世界上一些最坚硬的岩石中_____深洞和地道就是数百万年来的降雨和流水造成的"。通过分析句子结构可知，选项处是用来修饰"the deep caves and tunnels"的成分。由于"find"与"the deep caves and tunnels"之间是被动关系，此处需要使用 find 的过去分词，因此选项 (A)"now found"为正确答案，意为"当下所发现的深洞和地道"。选项 (B)"to find now"、选项 (C)"finding now"和选项 (D)"that now find"均表示主动，故排除。

Part 3 – Reading

Answer Key

Question Number	Answer	Question Number	Answer
1.（例题）	C	21.	B
2.（例题）	A	22.	B
1.	C	23.	C
2.	C	24.	B
3.	D	25.	A
4.	B	26.	C
5.	D	27.	D
6.	C	28.	A
7.	A	29.	A
8.	B	30.	D
9.	D	31.	D
10.	C	32.	C
11.	C	33.	B
12.	C	34.	B
13.	B	35.	A
14.	B	36.	A
15.	D	37.	D
16.	C	38.	C
17.	B	39.	D
18.	A	40.	C
19.	D	41.	A
20.	A	42.	C

Answer Explanation

（例题）**Questions 1-2**

该语篇主要描述了金门大桥以及其周围的风景。

1. （例题）(C)。本题为主旨题。本题问"文本主要讲的是什么？"。语篇中第一句是"The Golden Gate Bridge is a famous bridge in San Francisco.（金门大桥是一座位于旧金山的著名大桥）"，接着具体介绍了金门大桥周围的风景以及人们在此的活动。由此可以判断选项 (C)"A famous bridge（一座著名的桥）"为正确答案。选项 (A)"Gray clouds（灰色的云）"、选项 (B)"San Francisco（旧金山）"以及选项 (D)"Taking photographs（拍照）"均是错误的，因为它们只是在描述金门大桥过程中所提及的片面信息。

2. （例题）(A)。本题为细节题。本题问"金门大桥是什么颜色的？"。根据文中句子"The bridge has a red color …（桥身是红色的……）"可以判断选项 (A)"Red（红色）"为正确答案。选项 (B)"Green（绿色）"、选项 (C)"Blue（蓝色）"以及选项 (D)"Gray（灰色）"均为错误选项。

Questions 1-4

该语篇是 Berkfield 社区中心夏季艺术课程的安排表。

1. (C)。本题为细节题。本题问"有几位老师教摄影课？"。首先可以确定关于摄影的课程有两门，分别是"Photography Basics（摄影基础）"和"Photographing Nature（拍摄自然）"。这两门课的授课老师是"Mr. Stefan Hendershot""Ms. Beth Beranski"和"Ms. Sheila Jackson"。所以一共是三位教摄影课的老师，所以选项 (C)"Three（三位）"是正确答案。同时可以判断选项 (A)"One"（一位）、选项 (B)"Two（两位）"和选项 (D)"Four（四位）"均错误。

2. (C)。本题为细节题。本题问"哪门课与 Beth Beranski 老师的课在同一时间？"。首先要知道 Beth Beranski 老师只教一门课，即"Photography Basics – Section 2（摄影基础——第二部分）"，时间在"Monday, Thursday: 6:30 P.M.–8:30 P.M.（周一、周四下午 6：30 至晚上 8：30）"，所以要找到在这个时间段进行的另一门课。其中选项 (C)"Beginning Drawing（素描入门）"为正确答案。选项 (A)"Oil Painting（油画）"的上课时间为"Saturday, July 12, and

Sunday, July 13（7 月 12 日星期六和 7 月 13 日星期日）"。选项 (B) "Advanced Drawing（高级绘画）"的上课时间为 "Wednesday, Friday: 2 P.M.–5 P.M.（周三、周五下午 2 点至下午 5 点）"。选项 (D) "Photographing Nature（拍摄自然）"的时间为 "Tuesday, Thursday: 7 P.M.–9 P.M. and Saturday: 10 A.M.–12 P.M.（周二、周四晚上 7 点至晚上 9 点和周六上午 10 点至中午 12 点）"。这三门课与 Beth Beranski 老师的课程时间都不同，因此选项 (A)、(B)、(D) 错误。

3. **(D)**。本题为否定事实题。本题问"哪位老师最有可能不会长期在该中心授课？"。根据安排表发现 Stefan Hendershot 老师是 "visiting artist（客座艺术家）"，即只会任教一段时间，所以选项 (D) "Mr. Stefan Hendershot" 是正确答案。同时可以判断选项 (A) "Ms. Beili Zheng"、选项 (B) "Mr. Arthur Bellini" 和选项 (C) "Ms. Sheila Jackson" 均为错误选项。

4. **(B)**。本题为细节题。本题问"哪门课对学生有年龄要求？"。在安排表中 "Sculpting with Clay（黏土雕刻）"对应着一条星号信息 "**students must be 14 or older（** 学生必须在 14 岁或 14 岁以上）"。由此可以判断选项 (B) "Sculpting with Clay（黏土雕刻）"为正确答案。同时可以判断选项 (A) "Oil Painting（油画）"、选项 (C) "Advanced Drawing（高级绘画）"和选项 (D) "Photographing Nature（拍摄自然）"均为错误选项。

Questions 5–7

该语篇主要是 School World 商店为各年级返校学生整理出的购物说明，列出了各年级所需的用品和购买区域等。

5. **(D)**。本题为细节题。本题问"学生会在商店的哪个区找到美术工具？"。在表格中 "Supplies（供应用品）"一栏可以找到 "Crayons, paints, brushes, sketchbooks（蜡笔、颜料、画笔、速写本）"。这些美术用品是在 "Store Section 4（商店 4 区）"售卖，因此选项 (D) "Four（4 区）"为正确答案。同时可以判断选项 (A) "One（1 区）"、选项 (B) "Two（2 区）"以及选项 (C) "Three（3 区）"均为错误选项。

6. **(C)**。本题为推断题。本题问"3 区中的用品最有可能被用于以下哪门课？"。首先 3 区中售卖的是 "Calculators, rulers, protractors（计算器、尺子、量角器）"，这些工具都是数学课所需，因此可以判断选项 (C) "Seventh-grade math（七年级的数学课）"为正确答案。同时可以判断选项 (A) "Fourth-grade English（四年级的英语课）"、选项 (B) "Fifth-grade social studies（五

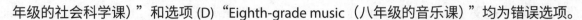

年级的社会科学课）"和选项 (D) "Eighth-grade music（八年级的音乐课）"均为错误选项。

7. **(A)**。本题为推断题。本题问"学生应该怎么做才能享受折扣？"。根据信息 "Students with current school ID cards are eligible for a 10 percent discount on their purchases.（持有现行学生证的学生有资格在购买时享受 10% 的折扣）"可以判断选项 (A) "Present a student identification card（出示学生证）"为正确答案。同时可以判断选项 (B) "Ask a store employee for help（向商店员工寻求帮助）"、选项 (C) "Visit all sections of the store（参观商店的所有区域）"和选项 (D) "Bring a school-supplies list（带上一张学校用品清单）"均为错误选项。

Questions 8–11

该语篇为社区图书馆发布的一则通告，要举办售旧书筹钱的活动，并希望大家积极捐书。

8. **(B)**。本题为细节题。本题问"图书馆过去举办了多少次图书售卖？"。根据语篇中关键句 "Last year we held a similar sale …（去年我们举办了一个类似的销售活动……）"可以判断选项 (B) "One（一次）"为正确答案，同时可以判断选项 (A) "None（零次）"、选项 (C) "Two（两次）"和选项 (D) "Three（三次）"均为错误选项。

9. **(D)**。本题为细节题。本题问"作者希望人们做什么？"。根据语篇中关键句 "We're asking members of the community to give us books they no longer need.（我们请求社区成员把他们不再需要的书送给我们）"可以判断选项 (D) "Provide used books（提供旧书）"为正确答案。选项 (A) "Donate money（捐钱）"是错误的，虽然语篇中提及 "The Community Library is holding a used book sale to raise money for our new weekly program …（社区图书馆正在举办旧书销售活动，以便为我们新的每周项目筹集资金……）"，但是并没有让人们直接捐钱。选项 (B) "Work at the sale（在售卖会上工作）"和选项 (C) "Read to children（为孩子们阅读）"在听力材料中均未提及，为错误选项。

10. **(C)**。本题为否定事实题。本题问"根据通知中的信息，什么书很可能不会出售？"。根据语篇中的关键句 "It doesn't matter how old your books are, as long as they are in good condition.（只要你的书状况良好，无论有多旧都没有关系）"可知图书馆不要破损的书，由此可以判断选项 (C) "Damaged books（损坏的书）"是正确答案。同时可以判断选项 (B) "Very old books（非常旧的书）"是错误的，因为图书馆要旧书。选项 (A) "Cookbooks（食谱）"是错误的，因为语篇中提及"Practically anything you have we will take, including novels, nonfiction books, picture books, and even cookbooks.（事实上，你拥有的任何书籍我们都会要，包括小说、非小说类书籍、图画书，甚至食谱）"，也就是说图书馆也要食谱。选项 (D)"Children's books（儿童书）"并未在语篇中直接提及，但也可以包含在"anything you have"的概念内。

11. **(C)**。本题为细节题。本题问"售卖从哪天开始？"。根据语篇中的关键句"The following Thursday, Friday, and Saturday are the sale dates.（接下来的星期四、星期五和星期六是售卖时间）"可知售卖会从星期四开始，所以选项 (C)"Thursday（星期四）"为正确答案。选项 (D)"Saturday（星期六）"是错误的，因为星期六是售卖的最后一天。选项 (A)"Monday（星期一）"和选项 (B)"Wednesday（星期三）"是错误的，因为语篇中提及"Drop-off dates are this Monday through Wednesday.（从周一到周三是送书日）"，人们可以在这几天把旧书拿给图书馆。

Questions 12–18

该语篇主要讲了四名学生一起合作煮汤的故事。

12. **(C)**。本题为主旨题。本题问"这个故事的最佳标题是什么？"。根据整个语篇可知，四个同学看到一幅汤羹的图后决定尝试做出来。接下来，有的学生回家拿菜，有的学生量取调料，还有的煮水，最终成功做出了汤。由此可以判断选项 (C)"Friends Cook a Dish Together（朋友们一起做一道菜）"为正确答案。选项 (A)"David's Shopping List（David 的购物清单）"、选项 (B)"Choosing the Best Vegetables（选择最好的蔬菜）"和选项 (D)"Students Write Their Own Recipe（学生们编写自己的食谱）"均不能概括该语篇的内容，为错误选项。

13. **(B)**。本题为代词指代题。本题问"文中第 5 行中的'it'指的是_____"。"it"所在句是对前面问题的回答："Doesn't that soup look delicious?（那汤看起来很美味，不是吗？）""It does!（它确实美味！）"。由此可以判断选项 (B)"soup（汤）"为正确答案。同时可以判断选项 (A)"page（页）"、选项 (C)"book（书）"和选项 (D)"recipe（食谱）"为错误选项。

14. **(B)**。本题为细节题。本题问"学生们为什么做饭？"。根据语篇中关键句"The students had been asked to make a special dish for the upcoming school picnic.（学生们被要求为即将到来的学校野餐做一道特别的菜）"可以判断选项 (B)"They were asked to make a dish for a picnic.（他

们被要求为野餐做一道菜。）"为正确答案。同时可以判断选项 (A) "They were hungry.（他们饿了）"、选项 (C) "They wanted to test their cooking skills.（他们想测试一下他们的厨艺）"和选项 (D) "They wanted to cook a special dinner for their parents.（他们想为他们的父母做一顿特别的晚餐）"均为错误选项。

15. **(D)**。本题为推断题。本题问"谁家有一个菜园？"。语篇中 Maria 问"Do you have carrots, David?（David，你有胡萝卜吗？）"，David 回答"Yes. I just picked some from our garden in the back of the house.（有，我刚从我们家后面的菜园里摘了一些）"。由此可知家里有菜园的是 David，因此选项 (D) "David" 为正确答案，选项 (A) "John"、选项 (B) "Anna" 和选项 (C) "Maria" 为错误选项。

16. **(C)**。本题为细节题。本题问"故事中 Anna 和 John 去哪儿了？"。语篇中 Anna 说"Hey, I think we have some corn at my house!（嘿，我觉得我们家有一些玉米）"以及"I'll go get it right now.（我马上回去拿）"，由此可知 Anna 回家拿菜去了。同样，John 说"And my mother just bought a big bag of potatoes.（我妈妈刚买了一大袋子土豆）"以及"Could you boil some water while Anna and I go get the vegetables?（你能在我和 Anna 去拿菜的时候烧一些水吗？）"。综上可以判断选项 (C) "To their own homes（回他们自己的家）"为正确答案。同时可以判断选项 (A) "To a farm（去一个农场）"、选项 (B) "To a grocery store（去一个杂货店）"和选项 (D) "To a teacher's house（去老师家）"均为错误选项。

17. **(B)**。本题为词汇题。本题问"第 22 行中的短语'in no time'与_____意思最接近"。语篇中提到，"Anna and John came back in less than ten minutes with the corn and potatoes.（Anna 和 John 不到十分钟就拿着玉米和土豆回来了）"，然后 David 说"It's nice that your houses are so close to mine. Now the soup will be done in no time.（你们的家离我的家这么近真好。现在汤_____就做好了）"。由此可知 Anna 和 John 回家拿菜很快，有了这些菜，汤也能做得很快，所以 David 说的应该是"汤马上就做好了"，选项 (B) "very quickly（很快）"为正确答案。选项 (A) "while away（消磨）"、选项 (C) "without help（不需要帮忙）"和选项 (D) "with no effort（毫不费力）"均不合适，为错误选项。

18. **(A)**。本题为词汇题。本题问"第 23 行中的'aroma'一词与_____意思最接近"。包含这个单词的句子是"The soup was finished cooking in just half an hour and had such a nice aroma

that David's mother came into the kitchen, saying, 'Mmm. Something smells delicious! ...'（汤半个小时就煮好了，有如此好的 'aroma' 以至于 David 的妈妈走进厨房就说道：'嗯，闻着很美味啊！……'）"。David 的妈妈是因为闻到汤的味道才发出的感叹，因此可以推测这里讲的是"汤闻上去很美味"，所以选项 (A) "smell（气味）" 为正确答案。选项 (B) "color（颜色）"、选项 (C) "taste（滋味）" 和选项 (D) "smoothness（顺滑）" 均不合适，为错误选项。

Questions 19–27

该语篇主要讲述了太空垃圾（常被称为轨道碎片）给宇航员带来了危险，同时表达了对其继续增加的担忧。

19. **(D)**。本题为主旨题。本题问"哪个标题能最好地概括文章？"。作者在首段明确了主旨是"space junk（太空垃圾）"，并在下面的段落中阐述了它们 "are dangerous to astronauts（对宇航员很危险）"，以及目前科学家的应对方式是 "record the size, the speed, and the direction of movement of these objects（记录这些物体的大小、速度和运动方向）"，然后在最后一段阐明了 "steps must be taken soon not only to clean up the existing orbital debris but also to keep more from entering space（必须尽快采取措施，不仅要清理现有的轨道碎片，还要防止更多的轨道碎片进入太空）"。综上，最合适的应该是选项 (D) "Mess in Space Creates Problems for Scientists（太空的凌乱给科学家们带来了问题）"。选项 (A) "Bright Stars Light the Night Sky（明亮的星星照亮夜空）"、选项 (B) "Space Flights Available to Tourists（供游客体验的太空航行）" 和选项 (C) "Faster Rockets Make Space Research Easier（更快的火箭使太空研究更容易）" 均与语篇主题不符，为错误选项。

20. **(A)**。本题为细节题。本题问"什么是轨道碎片？"。语篇首段说太空中有我们看不见的太空垃圾，接着第二段开始说这些太空垃圾是什么。第二段第一句话提到，"These unwanted objects made by humans, often referred to as orbital debris, do not fall to Earth.（这些由人类制造的、不需要的东西常被称为轨道碎片，它们不会落到地球上）"，紧接着说 "... they circle the planet ...（……它们环绕着地球……）"。所以 "orbital debris（轨道碎片）" 是环绕着地球的垃圾，选项 (A) "Garbage that circles Earth（环绕着地球的垃圾）" 为正确答案。选项 (B) "Planes that are used to carry astronauts（用于运载宇航员的飞机）"、选项 (C) "Distant stars that can be seen from Earth（从地球上可以看到的遥远的恒星）" 和选项 (D) "Meteors that can be seen from Earth（从地球上可以看到的流星）" 均为错误选项。

21. **(B)**。本题为代词指代题。本题问"第 9 行中的'they'指的是_____"。包含该词的句子在主要讲述轨道碎片的第二段中："Moving faster than airplanes, these objects must be avoided because <u>they</u> can injure astronauts or damage the equipment they use.（这些物体移动得比飞机快，必须要避开，因为它们会弄伤宇航员或损坏他们使用的装备）"。"they"是代词，指代前文中的复数名词，由句意可知这里指代的是"objects"。所以选项 (B)"objects（物体）"为正确答案。选项 (A)"tools（工具）"、选项 (C)"scientists（科学家）"和选项 (D)"astronauts（宇航员）"均不合适，为错误选项。

22. **(B)**。本题为词汇题。本题问"第 11 行中'accumulates'一词与_____意思最接近"。包含该词的句子是"Because more and more orbital debris <u>accumulates</u> every year, astronauts must be increasingly careful when they work in space.（由于每年会_____越来越多的轨道碎片，宇航员在太空工作时必须越来越小心）"。可以根据句意合理猜测出，宇航员要越来越小心，有可能是因为轨道碎片越来越大或越来越多。在选项 (A)"opens（打开）"、选项 (B)"collects（积聚）"、选项 (C)"prepares（准备）"和选项 (D)"repairs（修复）"中，最合适的是选项 (B)，为正确答案。

23. **(C)**。本题为推断题。本题问"文中提到了观察太空中物体的航天局科学家们，他们的目的是什么？"。根据语篇中的关键句"They then use this information to calculate where the debris will be when astronauts are scheduled to work in space.（然后他们利用这些信息来计算出当宇航员被安排在太空工作时碎片的位置）"，可知科学家们需要确保宇航员的工作轨迹和碎片轨迹不重合，由此可以判断选项 (C)"To predict the locations of the objects（预测物体的位置）"为正确答案。选项 (A)"To reduce the weight of the objects（减轻物体的重量）"、选项 (B)"To increase the speed of the objects（提高物体的速度）"以及选项 (D)"To determine where the objects came from（确定物体来自哪里）"在语篇中均未提及，因此为错误选项。

24. **(B)**。本题为因果题。本题问"根据文章，对于太空中的宇航员而言，日益严重的问题是什么？"。根据第 22 题的解析可知，由于太空垃圾每年越来越多，宇航员们在太空工作时也要越来越小心。而且"With time, though, there will be too many objects to keep track of.（然而，随着时间的推移，太空里的垃圾会多到无法跟踪）"，也就是说当太空垃圾日益增多，宇航员会因此而更加危险。由此可以判断选项 (B)"The unsafe working conditions as they do their jobs（宇航员工作时不安全的工作条件）"为正确答案。同时可以判断选项 (A)"The length

of time they are away from home（他们离家的时间长度）"、选项 (C)"The many international regulations they must follow（他们必须遵守的许多国际法规）"和选项 (D)"The amount of technical knowledge they need to have（他们需要具备的技术知识储量）"是错误的，且这些选项内容在语篇中也均未提及。

25. (A)。本题为细节题。本题问"关于轨道碎片移动的速度，作者是怎么说的？"。因为第二段都在讲轨道碎片，所以要从该段入手。根据关键句"Moving faster than airplanes, these objects must be avoided because they can injure astronauts or damage the equipment they use.（这些物体移动得比飞机快，必须要避开，因为它们会弄伤宇航员或损坏他们使用的装备）"可以判断选项 (A)"It is extremely fast.（它速度极快）"为正确答案，同时可以判断选项 (D)"It is slower than that of airplanes.（它比飞机慢）"是错误的。选项 (B)"It is difficult to measure.（速度很难测量）"和选项 (C)"It is affected by Earth's weather.（它受地球气候的影响）"在语篇中均未提及，为错误选项。

26. (C)。本题为词汇题。本题问"第 18 行中的'dodge'一词与_____意思最接近"。包含该词的句子是"For now, this strategy is sufficient to help astronauts dodge trouble.（就目前而言，这种策略足以帮助宇航员_____麻烦）"。其中"strategy"是指科学家们跟踪轨道碎片这件事情。也就说，用科学家们跟踪轨道碎片并定位的方法是可以保证宇航员的安全的。由此可以判断选项 (C)"avoid（避开，避免）"最合适，表示"足以帮助宇航员避开麻烦"，为正确答案。选项 (A)"hide（躲藏）"、选项 (B)"repair（修理）"和选项 (D)"doubt（怀疑）"均不符合语境，为错误答案。

27. (D)。本题为细节题。本题问"根据文章，一些官员希望在未来做些什么？"。根据语篇中的关键句"Officials in many countries are now considering other solutions to this problem.（许多国家的官员现在正在考虑解决这个问题的其他方法）"以及"They also believe that steps must be taken soon not only to clean up the existing orbital debris, but also to keep more from entering space.（他们还认为必须尽快采取措施，不仅要清理现有的轨道碎片，还要防止更多的轨道碎片进入太空）"可以判断选项 (D)"Remove unwanted objects from space（从太空中移除废弃物）"为正确答案。选项 (A)"Build stronger rockets（建造更厉害的火箭）"、选项 (B)"Send more astronauts into space（将更多宇航员送入太空）"和选项 (C)"Increase funding for space research（增加研究太空的经费）"在语篇中均未提及，为错误选项。

Questions 28–34

该语篇主要讲述了伊巴丹（Ibadan）这座城市的发展进程。

28. **(A)**。本题为主旨题。本题问"文章主要讲了什么？"。该语篇讲的是尼日利亚的重要城市之一伊巴丹。语篇提及了它"began in the nineteenth century（始于 19 世纪）"，如今变成了"an enormous city（一座大城市）"。因此选项 (A)"The development of a city（一座城市的发展）"是最贴合语篇的描述，为正确答案。同时可以判断选项 (D)"The history of a small country（一个小国的历史）"是错误的，因为伊巴丹是一个城市，不是国家。选项 (B)"Trade in an African region（一个非洲地区的贸易）"和选项 (C)"The life of a farming family（一个农民家庭的生活）"在语篇中均未提及，为错误选项。

29. **(A)**。本题为细节题。本题问"根据文章，什么是'compound'？"。根据语篇中的关键句"At first the people there lived in compounds, neighborhoods of houses surrounded by walls.（起初，那里的人们住在'compounds'中，即用墙围起来的住宅区）"可以判断"compound"是由许多房子组成的，外面有一圈围墙，因此选项 (A)"A group of houses（一片房子）"符合语篇中的描述，为正确答案。同时可以判断选项 (B)"The founder of a city（一座城市的缔造者）"、选项 (C)"A meeting of farmers（一次农民会议）"以及选项 (D)"A line of railway tracks（一条铁路线）为错误选项。

30. **(D)**。本题为细节题。本题问"住在伊巴丹的人从这座城市中移除了什么？"。根据文章中关键句"As the city grew, however, people decided to tear down the walls around the compounds …（然而，随着城市的发展，人们决定拆除住宅区的围墙……）"可以判断选项 (D)"The walls around neighborhoods（街区周围的围墙）"为正确答案。同时可以判断选项 (A)"Food markets（菜市场）"、选项 (B)"Old railroad lines（旧的铁路线）"和选项 (C)"The farms within its borders（城内的农场）"为错误选项。

31. **(D)**。本题为词汇题。本题问"第 8 行中的'enormous'一词与_____意思最接近"。包含该词的句子是"Today Ibadan is an <u>enormous</u> city with its own university and national airport.（如今，伊巴丹是一座拥有自己的大学和国家机场的_____城市）"。语篇中提到旧时的伊巴丹是"a small settlement consisting only of a small number of families living in a few mud houses（一个非常小的居民点，只有寥寥几户人家，他们生活在几座用泥土做的房子里）"，而现在伊巴

丹既有大学还有机场，可见城市发展了也扩大了，变成了一座大城市，所以选项 (D)"large（大的）"为正确答案。选项(A)"famous（著名的）"、选项(B)"serious（严肃的）"和选项(C)"empty（空的）"为错误选项。

32. (C)。本题为词汇题。本题问"第 13 行中的 'erected' 一词与_____意思最为接近"。包含该词的句子是"In today's Ibadan many more houses have been <u>erected</u>.（如今的伊巴丹已经_____了更多房屋）"。句中使用了被动语态，"erected"作为动词与"house"搭配，猜测表达的意思可能是建房子、修房子或拆房子。从接下来一句"the city's newer houses are made of brick instead of mud（城市中较新的房子都是用砖头建造的而不是泥巴）"可知这些房子是较新的，也就是新建的，所以选项 (C)"built（建造）"符合描述，为正确答案。选项 (A)"entered（进入）"、选项 (B)"filled（充满）"和选项 (D)"met（遇见）"为错误选项。

33. (B)。本题为推断题。本题问"文章暗示伊巴丹的天气一般是怎样的？"。根据文章最后一段的句子"Given Ibadan's weather throughout most of the year, tin is an ideal material. It is durable, so residents can go many years without worrying about leaks during the region's heavy rains.（鉴于伊巴丹一年中大部分时间的天气，锡是一种理想的材料。它经久耐用，因此居民可以使用多年而不必担心在该区的大雨期间漏雨）"。从屋顶使用的材料可知伊巴丹多雨，所以选项(B)"It is rainy.（多雨）"为正确答案。选项 (A)"It is cold.（寒冷）"、选项 (C)"It is foggy.（多雾）"和选项 (D)"It is windy.（多风）"均为错误选项。

34. (B)。本题为细节题。本题问"文中提到了锡的什么优势？"。根据对第 33 题的解析可知，锡是一种很耐用的材料，因此选项 (B)"It lasts a long time.（它可以用很久）"为正确答案。选项 (A)"It is lightweight.（它很轻）"、选项 (C)"It keeps a house cool.（它使房间保持凉爽）"和选项 (D)"It does not cost much.（它成本不高）"在听力材料中均未提及，为错误选项。

Questions 35–42

该语篇主要讲述了一种食肉植物捕蝇草。

35. (A)。本题为主旨题。本题问"文章主要讲了什么？"。语篇首段提到，"The Venus flytrap has long fascinated plant enthusiasts.（捕蝇草长期以来一直让植物爱好者着迷）"，紧接着讲了捕蝇草的特点是"not very sticky（不很黏）"，用"incredible speed（不可思议的速度）"捕食，以及捕蝇草并不会在每次被触碰的时候都合上叶子。综上，可以判断文章介绍了捕蝇草及其一些特点，因此选项 (A) "An unusual kind of plant（一种不寻常的植物）"为正确答案。选项 (B) "A newly discovered insect（一种新发现的昆虫）"、选项 (C) "A harmful species of insect（一种有害昆虫）"和选项 (D) "A plant created by scientists（由科学家创造的植物）"均不能概括语篇，为错误选项。

36. **(A)**。本题为代词指代题。本题问"第 2 行中'them'一词指的是_____"。包含该词的句子是 "The Venus flytrap has amazing leaves that are able to suddenly snap shut when an insect crawls on them.（捕蝇草有令人惊奇的叶子，当昆虫在它们上面爬时可以突然合上）"。这里描述的是捕蝇草捕食昆虫的过程，"them"是代词，指代的是前面出现的复数名词。根据句意可以推测出昆虫爬到捕蝇草的叶子上时，叶子会快速合上，所以选项 (A) "leaves（叶子）"为正确答案。选项 (B) "insects（昆虫）"、选项 (C) "carnivores（食肉植物）"和选项 (D) "enthusiasts（狂热者）"均不符合描述，为错误选项。

37. **(D)**。本题为细节题。本题问"什么是'carnivore'？"。该词第一次出现在句子 "The Venus flytrap is a carnivorous plant, and like all carnivores, it eats meat.（捕蝇草是一种食肉植物，和所有'carnivores'一样，它吃肉）"中。即使"carnivorous"和"carnivores"都不认识，也可以通过"it eats meat"判断出两个单词一定跟食肉有关。因此选项 (D) "A species that eats meat（一个食肉的物种）"为正确答案，同时可以判断选项 (A) "An insect that feeds on plants（一种以植物为食的昆虫）"、选项 (B) "The sticky surface of a leaf（叶子有黏性的表面）"和选项 (C) "A plant that can trap water（一种能吸收水分的植物）"为错误选项。

38. **(C)**。本题为词汇题。本题问"第 7 行中的'consumed'一词与_____意思最接近"。包含该词的句子是 "The insect, once caught, is then slowly consumed by the plant.（昆虫一旦被抓，就会被植物慢慢_____）"。根据第 37 题的分析可知，捕蝇草是一种食肉动物，一旦抓住食物应该会吃掉对方。由此可以判断选项 (C) "eaten（吃掉）"为正确答案。选项 (A) "smelled（嗅到）"、选项 (B) "saved（挽救）"和选项 (D) "felt（感觉到）"均不符合描述，为错误选项。

39. **(D)**。本题为细节题。本题问"捕蝇草在植物中保持着什么样的纪录？"。根据文章中的关键句 "The leaves of a Venus flytrap can shut in less than a second, which makes them the fastest moving part of any known plant.（捕蝇草的叶子可以在不到一秒的时间内合上，这使它们成为

221

所有已知植物组织器官中速度最快的）"可以判断选项 (D)"Its leaves move the fastest.（它的叶子移动得最快）"为正确答案。同时可以判断选项 (A)"It is the world's largest.（它是世界上最大的）"、选项 (B)"It drinks the most water.（它饮水最多）"和选项 (C)"Its smell is the strongest.（它的气味是最重的）"为错误选项。

40. **(C)。** 本题为细节题。本题问"研究人员对捕蝇草的叶子有什么了解？"。根据文章中的关键句 "Researchers who study the plant have found that its leaves are actually covered with tiny hairs.（研究这种植物的研究人员发现，它的叶子实际上被许多细小的茸毛覆盖）"可以判断选项 (C)"They contain tiny hairs.（叶子上有细小的茸毛）"为正确答案。选项 (A)"They reflect light.（叶子反光）"和选项 (B)"They absorb water.（叶子吸收水）"是错误的，因为在听力材料中均未提及。选项 (D)"They are coated with a sticky substance.（叶子上覆有一层黏性物质）是错误的，因为文中提到"The Venus flytrap, though, is not very sticky.（然而捕蝇草并不是很黏）"，根据该信息判断捕蝇草叶子上应该没有一层黏性物质。

41. **(A)。** 本题为词汇题。本题问"第 14 行中的 'trigger' 一词与_____意思最接近"。包含该词的关键句是"It is these hairs that <u>trigger</u> the shutting of the trap.（正是这些茸毛_____陷阱关闭）"。这一段首句就提到，"... the Venus flytrap does not simply close up every time it is touched.（……捕蝇草并不是每次被触碰时都会合上）"，而是当叶子上的至少两根小茸毛被弄乱后，捕蝇草才会合上叶子。由此可以判断选项 (A)"cause（导致）"意思最合适，为正确答案。选项 (B)"avoid（避免）"、选项 (C)"guard（保卫）"和选项 (D)"locate（定位）"均不符合描述，为错误选项。

42. **(C)。** 本题为因果题。本题问"根据文章，是什么决定了昆虫是否会被捕蝇草抓住？"。根据最后一段中的关键句 "... the plant is likely to shut only when it feels an insect moving and not for other reasons, like when it is hit with a raindrop or blown by the wind.（……该植物很可能只有在感觉到昆虫在移动时才会合上叶子，而不是出于其他原因，比如被雨滴击中或被风吹动）"，可以判断选项 (C)"The manner in which the insect moves on a leaf（昆虫在叶子上移动的方式）"为正确答案。同时可以判断选项 (A)"How large the insect is（昆虫有多大）"、选项 (B)"Whether the wind is blowing（有没有风）"和选项 (D)"What time of day it is when the insect lands on the plant（昆虫落在植物上时是一天中的什么时间）"均为错误选项。

第 10 章

听力文本

全真考题一

This is the listening section of the *TOEFL Junior*® Standard Form **4RTJPT1**.

Raise your hand if you cannot hear my voice clearly.

The listening section has 42 questions. Follow along as you listen to the directions to the listening section.

Directions. In this section of the test, you will hear a teacher or other school staff member talking to students. Each talk is followed by one question. Choose the best answer to each question and mark the letter of the correct answer on your answer sheet. You will hear each talk only one time.

Here is an example:

(Narrator): Listen to a teacher speaking to a class.

(Woman): Today we have a new student joining our class. Her name is Sarita and she just moved here with her family. I'd like you to all make Sarita feel welcome by showing her around the school and explaining how to find the gym and library. Remember that she doesn't know anyone here, so please be friendly.

(Narrator): What does the teacher want the students to do?

Now read the answer choices.

The correct answer is A, "Help a new classmate."

Here is another example:

(Narrator): Listen to a music teacher talking to a class.

(Man): The next song I will play will feature some very interesting instruments. I'll turn up the volume a little bit so you can hear these instruments in the background. So sit back and enjoy the music. When this piece is over, we'll have a discussion about it.

(Narrator): What will the students probably do next?

Now read the answer choices.

The correct answer is B, "Listen to some music."

Go on to the next page and the test will begin with question number one.

(Narrator): Number 1. Listen to a speaker talking to a group of students.

(Man): Welcome to the Ocean Aquarium. Instead of visiting our regular exhibits or attending one of our shows on underwater life, we've planned a special activity for you. Today you'll be working with our staff members. First, you'll take water samples from each of our fish tanks. Then we'll show you how we analyze the water to make sure the chemical balance is safe for the fish and other sea creatures here.

(Narrator): What will the students be doing at the aquarium?

(Narrator): Number 2. Listen to a teacher talking to students on a class trip.

(Man): While we're here at the zoo today, I'd like each of you to pick out one animal and write down some notes about what makes it special. Once we get back to the classroom, you're going to tell the rest of the class why you think the animal is interesting. When deciding which creature to look at, try to choose one that you didn't already know about. We will meet at the zoo's entrance in one hour.

(Narrator): What will the students probably do next?

(Narrator): Number 3. Listen to a message from a school nurse.

(Woman): I'd like to remind all of you that your health information forms are due in my office tomorrow before the end of the school day. We sent them to your home address and asked your parents to answer questions about your medical histories and to provide us with an emergency phone number in case we have to contact your parents. Please talk to your parents tonight and come in tomorrow with the form all filled out. You can drop it off in my office.

(Narrator): What does the nurse remind the students to do?

(Narrator): Number 4. Listen to the principal making an announcement.

(Man): Attention, students. Please be reminded that there will be a staff meeting after school today. Because all teachers are required to attend, there will be no after-school activities and all students must leave the school building immediately after their last lesson. The only students who may stay in the building are the students in the Mathematics Club. They will be attending a competition later this afternoon. Thank you all for your cooperation.

(Narrator): What is the purpose of the announcement?

(Narrator): Number 5. Listen to a teacher talking to a class.

(Man): As you have already heard, we will have twenty exchange students visiting our school for one month starting tomorrow. They'll want to learn about our daily life and school culture. When you meet the students for the first time, you should remember that they may ask some surprising questions, or [that] they may do things differently than you expect. You should always be polite and helpful to our guests. Of course you can talk to them about life in their countries, too. The idea is to learn from one another!

(Narrator): Why is the teacher talking about the visiting students?

(Narrator): Number 6. Listen to a teacher talking in a science class.

(Woman): Today, I'll show you how to grow salt crystals—like the ones I'm holding in front of you. As you can see, they're big and they're quite pretty. Now, you may think it's difficult to get such nice-looking salt crystals. But in fact, all you need to do is hang a piece of thread over a glass of salt water and wait a few days!

(Narrator): What does the teacher imply about the experiment?

(Narrator): Go on to the next page.

(Narrator): Number 7. Listen to a librarian talking to a class.

(Woman): Since some of you have been asking me about books to bring home and read during winter vacation, I've decided to hold a book fair at the library today. I'd like to invite each of you to come to the fair after lunch. If you want, you can borrow some of the year's best books for all of winter vacation. It would be wonderful if you would stop in, since I hope you'll be reading during your time away from school.

(Narrator): What is the purpose of the librarian's talk?

(Narrator): Number 8. Listen to a teacher talking in an art class.

(Man): I've heard that some of you are having a hard time working with the paint because it's been so messy. I'm sorry that I didn't realize it would take so long for this paint to dry. Since we don't want your paintings to drip on the floor, I've put newspaper on the ground to avoid making a mess. I know these paints have been sloppy, so next time we'll use different ones.

(Narrator): Why is the teacher apologizing?

(Narrator): Number 9. Listen to a teacher talking to the school science club.

(Woman): Well class, it looks like I have bad news. For the first time in a few years, we didn't win the science competition. The judges didn't like our presentation poster this year. They said it had too many pictures and not enough explanation of the experiments. So we only earned half the points possible for the competition. We need to concentrate more on these posters if we want to start winning competitions again. To start, we can look at last year's poster as an example.

(Narrator): What is probably true about last year's poster?

(Narrator): Go on to the next page.

(Narrator): Now you will hear some conversations. Each conversation is followed by three or more questions. Choose the best answer to each question and mark the letter of the correct answer on your answer sheet. You will hear each conversation only one time.

(Narrator): Questions 10 through 13. Listen to a conversation between a teacher and a student at school.

(Woman): Hey Jim. I just wanted to thank you for the cake that you brought to the spring picnic for the music club. It was delicious. Did you bake it yourself?

(Boy): Oh no! My mother did. I'm glad you enjoyed it.

(Woman): Oh, I did. But I wasn't the only one!

(Boy): Really? Well, I'll have to tell my mother. She's a great cook, but she wasn't sure about baking. She did want to try baking that cake, but she was afraid people might not like it.

(Woman): Well, that certainly wasn't the case. It was the first dessert to go! I went up for a second helping, but it was completely gone! In fact, I'd love to try baking it myself. Could you ask your mother to write down the recipe and bring it to me tomorrow?

(Boy): Sure. It looked pretty complicated to me, but I'm sure you'll be able to handle it.

(Woman): Well, I'll certainly try! And you know what? If you bring the recipe, I'll bake it this weekend and bring a piece for you and your mother on Monday.

(Boy): That sounds great. I'd better make sure I get the recipe for you!

(Narrator): Now answer the questions.

(Narrator): Number 10. What does the teacher imply when she says, "But I wasn't the only one"?

(Narrator): Number 11. What was the boy's mother afraid of?

(Narrator): Number 12. What does the teacher ask the boy to do?

(Narrator): Number 13. What will the teacher do on Monday?

(Narrator): Go on to the next page.

(Narrator): Questions 14 through 17. Listen to a conversation between two students as they leave school.

(Boy): Hey Judy, do you want to come over to my house to play my new video game?

(Girl): Oh, I would love to, but can we do it tomorrow? Today I have my first karate class.

(Boy): No kidding! I didn't know they had a karate class here at school.

(Girl): Actually, it's not school-sponsored; it's offered by the city at the community center.

(Boy): I'd love to learn karate, especially after just seeing that movie about the kid who learns to defend himself.

(Girl): I know—I think seeing that movie is why so many other kids have signed up for the class this year. So, I'm glad I signed up on the first day the class was announced.

(Boy): Oh, no! That means there's probably no room for me!

(Girl): Well, don't give up yet. Why don't you go on the city's Web site and click on the link to the karate class. That's how I registered. If the class is full, the Web site will tell you.

(Boy): OK, I'll give it a try, but I don't have much hope.

(Girl): I have a feeling there might be some cancellations after today's first class.

(Boy): Really? Why do you say that?

(Girl): Because the instructor is very demanding—he makes you work and wants you to be 100 percent committed to the class.

(Boy): That's fine with me. Remember how I had Coach Peters for volleyball?

(Girl): Oh, yeah. He was tough—he wouldn't let my friend stay on the team after he missed just one practice!

(Boy): Exactly. But it was worth it for those willing to work hard—we won the league championship!

(Narrator): Now answer the questions.

(Narrator): Number 14. What is the main topic of the conversation?

(Narrator): Number 15. What caused the boy to be interested in karate?

(Narrator): Number 16. What does the girl imply when she says there might be cancellations after the first class?

(Narrator): Number 17. Why does the boy mention Coach Peters?

(Narrator): Questions 18 through 21. Listen to a conversation between a teacher and a student.

(Girl): Excuse me, Mr. Sonder. May I ask you a question about the final project?

(Man): Sure. What's your question?

(Girl): Well, during class today you announced that our final project will be on ancient civilizations such as the Egyptians, the Mesopotamians, and the Chinese.

(Man): That's right. Since we could only survey each briefly in class, I wanted to give you all a chance to study at least one of the civilizations in depth. Are you worried about it?

(Girl): No, not at all. I'm actually very interested in pyramids and everything, but the ones I'm most excited about are ones that you hadn't mentioned, the ones from the ancient Mayan culture. You see, my parents are from Yucatán, Mexico, and my grandparents still live there. In fact, I'll be going there to visit them over spring break. So I was wondering …

(Man): OK, I get it. You'd like to know if you could do your project on Mayan history since you can actually visit their ruins, right? Absolutely! That would be fantastic!

(Girl): Really? Oh, that's great! I'll visit the ruins and bring back all kinds of souvenirs to show everyone in class!

(Man): I'd like that a lot, Amy. Just remember though, you still have to follow the guidelines about completing the project. You should start with a research question, gather facts based on evidence, and document all your sources.

(Girl): Don't worry, Mr. Sonder. I'll make sure I do all that—and more!

(Narrator): Now answer the questions.

(Narrator): Number 18. What are the speakers mainly discussing?

(Narrator): Number 19. What subject does the teacher most likely teach?

(Narrator): Number 20. Where is the girl's family originally from?

(Narrator): Number 21. What does the girl mean when she says, "So I was wondering"?

(Narrator): Go on to the next page.

(Narrator): Questions 22 through 26. Listen to a conversation between two students.

(Girl): Is something wrong, Greg? You look a little upset.

(Boy): I can't find my permission slip for the field trip to the science museum tomorrow! I was sure I put it in this folder last night, but now it's not here!

(Girl): Maybe it fell out. Why don't you look in your backpack? I'm sure it's in there somewhere.

(Boy): I already did that. I can't find it anywhere!

(Girl): Hmm … well I'm sure Ms. Gomez will give you another copy of the permission slip if you ask her for one. You can have your parents sign it tonight and turn it in tomorrow.

(Boy): But she said the permission slip is due today. Oh, I really want to go on that trip— the science museum is so cool! I kept forgetting to give the permission slip to my mom to sign, but I finally remembered to have her sign it last night. I can't believe I lost it!

(Girl): Well, Ms. Gomez is really nice. If you ask her, maybe you can turn it in tomorrow and still come on the trip.

(Boy): Yeah, I guess that's my only option.

(Girl): If you want, I'll go with you. I'm going to her classroom now to hand in my permission slip anyway.

(Boy): Yeah, that'd be great, thanks!

(Narrator): Now answer the questions.

(Narrator): Number 22. What did the boy lose?

(Narrator): Number 23. Why didn't the boy turn in his permission slip sooner?

(Narrator): Number 24. How does the boy probably feel when he says, "I already did that. I can't find it anywhere"?

(Narrator): Number 25. What does the boy imply when he says, "Yeah, I guess that's my only option"?

(Narrator): Number 26. What will the students probably do next?

(Narrator): Go on to the next page.

(Narrator): Now you will hear some talks and discussions about academic topics. Each talk or discussion is followed by three or more questions. Choose the best answer to each question and mark the letter of the correct answer on your answer sheet. You will hear each talk or discussion only one time.

(Narrator): Questions 27 through 30. Now you will hear a tour guide speaking in an art museum.

(Woman): Thank you for coming to our museum's newest exhibition, called *Frames in Art*. Usually when people come to the museum, they spend a lot of time looking at art in frames—that is, paintings in fancy gold frames, simple black frames, maybe, or perhaps clear plastic frames. This exhibition, as you will see momentarily, is a little different. All you will see are the frames themselves. "Why would a museum put on an exhibition of frames?" you might ask. "Aren't they just there to hold the painting?" Well, it's true that frames have a practical function—to hold and protect a work of art. But a frame also has an artistic value in itself, as an object. Each frame is unique. You'll see from our collection that the frames vary widely in style and materials used, in size and in weight, and [that] many are very beautiful.

After you see the collection, our tour will also take you through part of our conservation department. There you'll see some of our experts at work. Part of their job is to maintain and repair frames from paintings in our major art collections. What you probably don't realize is that frames can be helpful when you're trying to learn the history of a work of art. They often provide clues about the artwork they hold. We have a painting by a famous artist here at our museum that shows a group of children around a table. People thought it was painted before 1850 because of the style of the table and the children's clothing. Our conservation experts looked at the frame using some scientific methods, like examining it with special microscopes and analyzing the chemicals in the varnish on the frame. They discovered that the frame was in fact the original frame—it was as old as the painting. And they were able to determine its age: it was made after 1900, not in the 1850s. So the frame, not the painting itself, gave us the answer regarding the age of the painting!

(Narrator): Now answer the questions.

(Narrator): Number 27. What is the speaker mainly talking about?

(Narrator): Number 28. What does the speaker say about the materials used to make frames?

(Narrator): Number 29. What will visitors see at the end of the tour?

(Narrator): Number 30. What did the museum learn about the painting of the children?

(Narrator): Go on to the next page.

(Narrator): Questions 31 through 34. Listen to part of a discussion in a science class.

(Man): We've been learning about land … things like cliffs, beaches, valleys … and how some of these landforms have mostly been created by—what? Who remembers? Kate?

(Girl): Water, right?

(Man): That's right. Can you give us a few quick examples to review?

(Girl): Well, beaches are made of sand, and sand is just bits of rock and shells and things that have been worn away by water. And valleys—well, some valleys are formed by rivers and streams. The water running between the hills or mountains washed away the rock and made the valley bigger. But—I heard of an example that's kind of related. It's not land, though.

(Man): Tell us about it.

(Girl): Well, I was looking at this magazine we get at home, and there was this whole article on how they use water to cut steel—to cut through metal. I mean, it's kind of the same idea as the water forming beaches and carving out the sides of rock into cliffs and caves and stuff.

(Man): So … they spray water at the metal for a long time? Until it wears the metal away?

(Girl): Well, not quite. What they use is this tool called a water jet. It's like a hose, but the water comes out really, really fast and hard—hard enough to cut right through metal. Oh, yeah—and they use it for stone, too … like really hard stone, like marble—you know, for marble floors and stuff.

(Man): It's interesting that you say this water jet is also used on stone. Because, basically that's what's happening when, for example, the ocean pounds away at rock along the shore. It wears that stone away. And like you said, what's left is sand. But not immediately—it takes a while. So that water in the water jet must be coming out with a tremendous force.

(Girl): Yeah, it comes out really hard. The article made the point that it's loud—so loud that workers using it have to wear things over their ears to protect them!

(Man): Well that makes sense. Think about the sound of waves hitting rocks.

(Narrator): Now answer the questions.

(Narrator): Number 31. Why are the teacher and student talking about cliffs, beaches, and valleys at the beginning of the discussion?

(Narrator): Number 32. Why does the student talk about sand?

(Narrator): Number 33. What is the tool called a water jet used for?

(Narrator): Number 34. According to the student, what is one problem with the water jet?

(Narrator): Go on to the next page.

(Narrator): Questions 35 through 38. Listen to part of a discussion in a history class.

(Man): We've been studying ancient history for a few weeks now. Based on what you've learned, where do we get much of the information we have about ancient cultures?

(Girl): From artifacts—from things archaeologists have found. Like pottery and stone tablets with writing on them. And from ruins—like, the remains of ancient houses or towns.

(Man): Good. And how do they find those artifacts and ruins?

(Girl): Well, it seems like a lot of times they get discovered by accident. Like, maybe someone hiking in the mountains sees an old pot sticking out of the ground.

(Boy): Yeah, or a farmer digging in a field hits a part of an old wall. And then the archaeologists do some more digging and discover an ancient palace or something.

(Man): Yes, that's right. But archaeologists also have ways of looking for evidence of ancient cultures without digging in the ground. Strange as it may sound, archaeologists can go in the opposite direction to search for clues. And by opposite direction, I mean up. Archaeologists regularly get information from aerial photography. They examine photographs taken from airplanes and helicopters to look for ancient sites. Aerial photography has been used by archaeologists for over a hundred years, even just by attaching cameras to balloons or a kite.

(Boy): But how is that helpful? What could you see from way up high that you can't see up close on the ground?

(Man): First, you can see a much bigger area. And what archaeologists often look for are certain patterns on the ground. Here's an example. Imagine a farm field with a crop growing on it—say, wheat or corn. That crop needs water and nutrients to grow, right? Imagine now that there's an ancient village buried beneath that field. In places where the ancient people, say, dug a trench or a pit or even something like a fish pond, over time, new and looser soil will settle in those spots. That soil has more nutrients and holds water better than surrounding soil that hasn't been disturbed. So what happens to the plants growing above?

(Boy): They'd get more water? And more nutrients?

(Man): Exactly—so those particular plants might be bigger and greener. And in places where the ancient people might have built a high stone wall, the crop plants might not grow as well, because there's less soil underneath them. So how would that look from above—in an aerial photograph?

(Girl): I guess some plants would look greener than others? Ohh—I get it! And you could see the pattern of greener plants and taller plants. So the plants would kinda be like a map of the ancient village underneath.

(Man): Yes! Those kinds of patterns are called crop marks. You might not notice the pattern when you're standing on the ground. But crop marks are much more noticeable from above. Once they find the crop marks, archaeologists then need to investigate the area for more clues.

(Narrator): Now answer the questions.

(Narrator): Number 35. What is the main topic of the discussion?

(Narrator): Number 36. Why does the teacher talk about balloons and kites?

(Narrator): Number 37. What can archaeologists learn from some aerial photographs?

(Narrator): Number 38. What are crop marks?

(Narrator): Go on to the next page.

(Narrator): Questions 39 through 42. Listen to a teacher talking in a biology class.

(Woman): Thousands of different species of ocean animals can be found in almost any part of the sea at any given time. In coastal waters, however, where the ocean waves meet the land, there are fewer fish and other sea animals. Why is there less animal life here? The problem is that the waves make it hard for plants to grow near the shore. The plants would be easily uprooted and washed away. Without ocean plants on the seafloor to hide in, small animals are more exposed to the predators that hunt them for food. This makes coastal regions particularly unsafe. But some creatures, like crabs, clams, sea snails, and sea worms, have adapted to life near the beach.

Now, a person walking along the beach might not see many small animals moving in the shallow waters along the shore, but this doesn't mean they are not there. Animals that live in these coastal waters often hide underground, buried in the sand. In fact, many of these animals almost never come out of the sand, and when they do, it's only for a very short time.

The masked crab, for example, may occasionally dig itself up and spend a few minutes walking on the seafloor. If you try to touch it, though, it will immediately bury itself again, for protection. To find a masked crab, you'd have to dig down deep in the sand at low tide, when more of the shoreline is exposed. Other sea animals live closer to dry land. Beach hoppers are tiny creatures that dig into the sand in areas only barely reached by the waves. Because birds like to eat them, though, the beach hoppers only come out at night, when they feed on seaweed that has been left on the beach by the tide.

(Narrator): Now answer the questions.

(Narrator): Number 39. What is the teacher mainly talking about?

(Narrator): Number 40. What is mentioned about ocean plants in coastal waters?

(Narrator): Number 41. Where can masked crabs usually be found?

(Narrator): Number 42. Why does the beach hopper only come out at night?

(Narrator): Stop. This is the end of the Listening section.

全真考题二

This is the listening section of the *TOEFL Junior®* Standard Form **4RTJPT2**.

Raise your hand if you cannot hear my voice clearly.

The listening section has 42 questions. Follow along as you listen to the directions to the listening section.

Directions. In this section of the test, you will hear a teacher or other school staff member talking to students. Each talk is followed by one question. Choose the best answer to each question and mark the letter of the correct answer on your answer sheet. You will hear each talk only one time.

Here is an example:

(Narrator): Listen to a teacher speaking to a class.

(Woman): Today we have a new student joining our class. Her name is Sarita and she just moved here with her family. I'd like you to all make Sarita feel welcome by showing her around the school and explaining how to find the gym and library. Remember that she doesn't know anyone here, so please be friendly.

(Narrator): What does the teacher want the students to do?

Now read the answer choices.

The correct answer is A, "Help a new classmate."

Here is another example:

(Narrator): Listen to a music teacher talking to a class.

(Man): The next song I will play will feature some very interesting instruments. I'll turn up the volume a little bit so you can hear these instruments in the background. So sit back and enjoy the music. When this piece is over, we'll have a discussion about it.

(Narrator): What will the students probably do next?

Now read the answer choices.

The correct answer is B, "Listen to some music."

Go on to the next page and the test will begin with question number one.

(Narrator): Number 1. Listen to a message from a school librarian.

(Woman): We've noticed that a large number of books are missing from our library's collection. Because this has been an ongoing issue, we have changed our policy regarding late and missing books. Starting this year, if a book is returned more than six months after its due date, the student borrowing the item will be required to pay for a new copy of that book.

(Narrator): What is the purpose of the talk?

(Narrator): Number 2. Listen to an art teacher talking to a class.

(Woman): Since most of you have completed your projects, I'd like each of you to tidy the area around your desks. The teachers are going to have a meeting in here after class, so I'd like the room to be spotless. It would also be great if some students could help to sweep the floor, since there are some scraps of paper left on the ground.

(Narrator): What does the teacher request that the students do?

(Narrator): Number 3. Listen to a basketball coach talking to students on the first day of basketball practice.

(Man): I know you're all eager to play a real game, but during our first few practices we're going to work on the basic skills you'll need. Today we're going to practice shooting and then we'll learn how to pass the ball. But before we do those things, we have to make sure everyone is warmed up and stretched out properly. So let's all start loosening up.

(Narrator): What will the students probably do next?

(Narrator): Number 4. Listen to the school secretary making an announcement in a class.

(Woman): I'm sorry to interrupt your lesson, but I want to remind you to return your contact information forms to the main office. It's very important that we have the most updated contact information for you and your family. I have a list here of the students in this class who have not yet given me their forms. Please check the list, and if your name is on it, don't forget to give me your form as soon as possible.

(Narrator): What is the purpose of the announcement?

(Narrator): Number 5. Listen to a social studies teacher talking to a class.

(Man): Because you have asked so many questions about ancient Egypt, today we're going to watch part of an interesting video. Unfortunately, we won't be able to watch the whole thing. If we did, we would be here all night! Since we have only about 20 minutes of class left, we'll watch the short part about the culture of ancient Egypt. Tonight, you will read the article about cats in ancient Egypt, and tomorrow you will look at pictures of how people live in the desert.

(Narrator): What is probably true about the video?

(Narrator): Number 6. Listen to a school librarian talking to a group of students.

(Man): I know this is your first year at the school, and I'm so glad that your history teacher, Mr. Wilson, brought you here today during your class time. I like to show our new students everything our library has to offer, but the tour you receive at the start of the year really isn't long enough. After we're finished today, you'll realize that there's much more available to you here than most students think. Let's start with the history section.

(Narrator): What does the speaker imply about most students?

(Narrator): Go on to the next page.

(Narrator): Number 7. Listen to a math teacher speaking to her class.

(Woman): As you all know, your final exam is next week. I wanted to remind you that I will have study sessions for the exam after school every day this week and everyone is invited. We won't have time to go over everything that we learned in class this year, so make sure that you write down some specific things that you want to review.

(Narrator): What is the purpose of the talk?

(Narrator): Number 8. Listen to a principal's announcement over the intercom.

(Man): Attention, all teachers and students. Tonight's science fair will now be held in the cafeteria. We had to move the science fair because the boys' basketball practice has been scheduled for the gymnasium tonight. We apologize for this last-minute change.

(Narrator): Why is the principal apologizing?

(Narrator): Number 9. Listen to a museum tour guide speaking to a group of students.

(Woman): This next piece is a ceramic bowl from ancient China, specifically the Tang Dynasty. We're very lucky to be able to display this piece, since most museums don't have any Chinese ceramics from this time period. If you look closely, you can see the detailed painting used to illustrate the bowl.

(Narrator): What is probably true about the ceramic bowl?

(Narrator): Number 10. Listen to a science teacher speaking to his class.

(Man): Let's review for tomorrow's test. Open your books to chapter 10. Since we've been talking about birds for a few weeks now, you will want to go back and read through the important parts of the chapter. Make sure that you study the new vocabulary words! Good luck studying!

(Narrator): What is the teacher explaining?

(Narrator): Go on to the next page.

(Narrator): Now you will hear some conversations. Each conversation is followed by three or more questions. Choose the best answer to each question and mark the letter of the correct answer on your answer sheet. You will hear each conversation only one time.

(Narrator): Questions 11 through 14. Listen to a conversation between two students at school.

(Girl): Excuse me, Tim, but do you know where the bottles of lemonade are? They're usually right next to the beverage machine, but I can't find them anywhere today. I just got out of gym class and I'm so thirsty!

(Boy): I don't know, Katy. I think the cafeteria staff rearranged where all the drinks go yesterday. Everything's somewhere different now. Why don't you ask Mrs. Higgins? She's the teacher supervising lunch today.

(Girl): I did, and she told me she doesn't know. I'm worried that they've stopped selling bottles of lemonade at school.

(Boy): They've got to still sell them here. Look at that group of students over there. Two of them have bottles of lemonade. Why don't you go ask where they got them?

(Girl): That's a good idea. Thanks, Tim!

(Narrator): Now answer the questions.

(Narrator): Number 11. Where does the conversation probably take place?

(Narrator): Number 12. What is the girl's problem?

(Narrator): Number 13. How does the girl probably feel when she says, "I did, and she told me she doesn't know"?

(Narrator): Number 14. What will the girl probably do next?

(Narrator): Go on to the next page.

(Narrator): Questions 15 through 18. Listen to a conversation between two students after school.

(Boy): Will I see you at the public library this afternoon?

(Girl): No, I got what I needed for the history research project on Monday—I went there after school.

(Boy): I went there Monday, too, but I went there at night. They didn't have what I was looking for. Someone had already taken out the book Ms. Wilson mentioned in class.

(Girl): You mean that book called *The Making of History*?

(Boy): Yes, that one.

(Girl): Ms. Wilson did talk a lot about that book when she mentioned the different methods of studying history. I took a look through it. There's one chapter that should be helpful for everyone in our class, but the rest of it wasn't very helpful for the method I chose for my project.

(Boy): Wait—are you the person who took it out? The librarian told me to come back in a couple of days to see if it had been returned. Was that you?

(Girl): No. I saw it on the library shelf and looked through it. I think Jason has it. He was in the library, too, and the book has a lot of information about the method he picked. I don't think the book will be back at the library for a while.

(Boy): What's Jason writing about? I'm doing my project on researching history through newspapers.

(Girl): Oh, then don't worry about waiting for the book. It's mostly about archaeology and digging up artifacts and dating them—studying history that way. That's what Jason's working on. Just ask him if you can borrow the book for a few hours. That should be enough time to read that one chapter that's helpful.

(Boy): That's a good idea.

(Girl): You know, I did get one library book that you might be able to use. It's about historical information in diaries and letters—that's my topic. But it also covers magazines, newspapers … anything that's printed. I'm almost finished with it.

(Boy): OK, then we'll swap—because I found one at the library that has lots of information about personal letters and stuff like that. You can borrow it as soon as I'm done.

(Narrator): Now answer the questions.

(Narrator): Number 15. What must the students do for their history projects?

(Narrator): Number 16. Why does the boy mention his teacher, Ms. Wilson?

(Narrator): Number 17. What does the girl suggest that the boy do regarding the book?

(Narrator): Number 18. What will the boy and girl probably do later?

(Narrator): Go on to the next page.

(Narrator): Questions 19 through 22. Listen to a conversation between a teacher and a student.

(Woman): Mike, thank you for skipping your free period to come help me set up the room for our special party this afternoon.

(Boy): It's no problem, Ms. Casey. I think it's really nice that we're welcoming Tania back to class by having a surprise party for her right here in the classroom.

(Woman): Yes, I think it will be fun. Her mother told me she really missed being with us in class the last few days. But apparently, the doctor had recommended that she stay home and rest.

(Boy): Will she be able to do everything at school—I mean, since she has a broken arm?

(Woman): Well, she broke her left arm, and since she writes with her right hand, she'll still be able to take notes in class. So that's good. But she'll need to take it easy … so no gym class, of course, and she will probably need some help carrying books and things like that.

(Boy): Well, all of us in class will be happy to help out.

(Woman): I know you will. I'm sure she'll appreciate that. All right, let's see. The decorations are up—they look great—and we've put a tablecloth on the table. We have cups, napkins, paper plates …

(Boy): What about the food and drinks?

(Woman): There are bottles of soda in a bag behind my desk—maybe you could put those out on the table … and one of the parents is bringing in the cake. So, then I just need to go to the cafeteria to get the ice cream out of the freezer.

(Boy): Mmm, ice cream!

(Woman): If you could finish setting out everything on the table, I'll go do that now and be back in a few minutes. OK?

(Boy): OK, Ms. Casey.

(Narrator): Now answer the questions.

(Narrator): Number 19. What is being celebrated?

(Narrator): Number 20. Where is the party being held?

(Narrator): Number 21. What is the teacher doing when she says, "All right, let's see. The decorations are up—they look great—and we've put a tablecloth on the table. We have cups, napkins, paper plates …"?

(Narrator): Number 22. What is the teacher going to do next?

(Narrator): Questions 23 through 26. Listen to two students talking in front of school at the end of the day.

(Boy): Hey Alison, where are you going?

(Girl): What do you mean? School's over so I'm leaving.

(Boy): But today the school choir is performing their end-of-the-year concert. Aren't you going to come and watch?

(Girl): Oh, no! I totally forgot! I have a piano lesson this afternoon.

(Boy): Oh, that's a shame. I guess you can't be in two places at once though.

(Girl): No, you don't understand. My little brother is in the choir and I promised him I would watch his performance!

(Boy): Well, is it possible to cancel your piano lesson just this once? The end-of-the-year concert only happens, well … once a year!

(Girl): But I can't miss my lesson. I cancelled two weeks ago because I had to meet with a teacher after school. If I miss another one, I'll really be behind schedule.

(Boy): I know what you mean. If I missed two violin lessons in the same month, then I would get really confused about what I should be practicing and forget all the things my teacher told me to improve. How about if you reschedule it for another day? Then you could watch the choir performance today, but still have your piano lesson before the end of the week.

(Girl): Hmm … well my teacher did say that she was available to teach my lesson either today or tomorrow. I'll have to ask if she still has time for our lesson tomorrow. But first I'd better talk to my mother and make sure it's okay with her. I'm going to go call her.

(Boy): Isn't your mother coming to watch your brother sing?

(Girl): Oh yeah! She should be here any minute. Wow, I am really forgetful today! What would I do if you weren't here to remind me of everything? Let's go to the auditorium right now and find my mother.

(Narrator): Now answer the questions.

(Narrator): Number 23. Why does the girl not want to miss the choir concert?

(Narrator): Number 24. Why is the girl worried about canceling her piano lesson?

(Narrator): Number 25. What does the boy suggest that the girl should do?

(Narrator): Number 26. What does the girl mean when she says, "What would I do if you weren't here to remind me of everything"?

(Narrator): Go on to the next page.

(Narrator): Now you will hear some talks and discussions about academic topics. Each talk or discussion is followed by three or more questions. Choose the best answer to each question and mark the letter of the correct answer on your answer sheet. You will hear each talk or discussion only one time.

(Narrator): Questions 27 through 30. Listen to a discussion in a biology class.

(Woman): Before we take our quiz, let's review what we've learned this week about honeybee communication. One thing that we've talked about is how honeybees communicate about food sources. After a honeybee discovers a new source of food and returns to the hive, how do the other bees figure out the kind of food source the bee has just visited?

(Girl): They use their antennas. The food leaves a scent on the body of the bee that discovers the food, and the other bees use their antennas to figure out what kind of food it is.

(Woman): Great. And how does the honeybee communicate about the quality, quantity, and location of the food source?

(Boy): It does a kind of dance. The other bees pay attention to how long and how lively the dance is to figure out how good the source is and how much food there is. As for the location of the food source, bees have two kinds of dances to tell how far away it is—they either do a round dance or a tail-wagging dance.

(Woman): That's right. And we also talked about how bees communicate "stop" to other bees. For example, if a honeybee is attacked while exploring a new food source, it can warn others not to visit that food source. How does the bee do that?

(Girl): Well, the explorer honeybee will send out a vibrating signal and interrupt the dance of bees who are telling the other bees about that food source. After it gives the vibrating signal, that honeybee will also either butt its head into the head of the bee that's dancing or it will climb on top of the bee that's dancing.

(Woman): Very good. And how about when they move to a new hive—how do they communicate about potential sites for a new hive?

(Boy): Some bees go out to search for a new site for a hive, and when they return, they describe the location through a tail-wagging dance. The better the site, the more they wag their tails when they dance.

(Woman): Great. I think you're well prepared for your quiz, so go ahead and put away your books and take out a piece of paper and pencil.

(Narrator): Now answer the questions.

(Narrator): Question 27. What are the teacher and students mainly talking about?

(Narrator): Question 28. To communicate "stop," what will a honeybee do?

(Narrator): Question 29. What do honeybees use to communicate about the location for a new hive?

(Narrator): Question 30. What will the students probably do next?

(Narrator): Go on to the next page.

(Narrator): Questions 31 through 34. Listen to a teacher talking in a history class.

(Woman): During the nineteenth century, new machines were invented at an amazing rate. Some of the most important new technology was in communication. You'll probably think right away of the telephone—but the telegraph actually came much earlier.

Now, when we hear the word telegraph, we usually think of the machine that sends electric signals over a wire. A lot of people don't realize, though, that telegraph systems have been around for hundreds of years. Early telegraph messages were signals that could be seen from far away, like fires that were visible at night, or smoke signals by day. These allowed people to pass basic messages from one location to another. Over a thousand years ago in Greece, they used a system that allowed them to communicate over 800 kilometers!

In fact, the word "telegraph" comes from the Greek language. The first part, "tele-," comes from the Greek for "distance," and "graph" is from the Greek word for "write." So it's writing from a distance. Kind of like "television," right? But television is something you watch—that's the "vision" part—and it's sent from a distance.

Now the problem with early telegraph methods, like the fires and smoke and others that followed, is that you need good weather in order to use them. The solution to this problem came with the discovery of electricity. In the very first electric telegraphs, electrical currents caused arrows on a machine to point to different letters of the alphabet, but these machines didn't always work very well. The electric telegraph that really succeeded was actually invented by a professor of painting and sculpture, believe it or not! Samuel Morse was an artist who was

249

also interested in electricity. He consulted with several scientists, and he invented a telegraph machine. He also invented a system of dots and dashes that stood for letters that could be sent and received over a wire. People at either end translated words into the dot-and-dash code.

Telegraph wires were put in place all over the world, even across the Atlantic Ocean. So of course, many people were employed as telegraphers. Telegraphers sent out messages in code, and then decoded or translated messages coming in. This was a very important job, especially for companies like newspapers, who needed information quickly. Without a telegrapher on either end of the wire, the information would just remain a series of electronic signals—the message couldn't get through!

(Narrator): Now answer the questions.

(Narrator): Number 31. What is the main topic of the talk?

(Narrator): Number 32. Why does the teacher talk about televisions?

(Narrator): Number 33. What does the teacher think is surprising about Samuel Morse?

(Narrator): Number 34. What point does the teacher make about telegraphers?

(Narrator): Go on to the next page.

(Narrator): Questions 35 through 38. Listen to a teacher talking in a science class.

(Woman): You might be used to hearing about the atmosphere of Earth, but the Sun has an atmosphere, too—like Earth, the Sun is covered in gases. And the part of the Sun's atmosphere that's farthest from the Sun's surface is called the corona. The corona has some qualities that have interested and puzzled astronomers for a long time.

For one thing, the corona is incredibly hot—hundreds of times hotter than the surface of the Sun. Why does this puzzle astronomers? Well, remember, the corona is the part of the atmosphere that's the farthest from the Sun's surface.

Think about it … if you were sitting near a fire in a fireplace, you would feel warm—maybe even hot, right? Now, imagine if you moved away from the fire—you'd expect to feel cooler. So why is the corona—the outermost layer of the Sun's atmosphere—actually hotter than the Sun's surface, not cooler? Here's one idea scientists have: a space mission discovered that bundles of extremely hot material—what they call heat bombs—move out from the Sun to the corona. When the heat bombs reach the corona, they explode and release heat. This idea is just one possible reason why the corona's so hot—scientists aren't certain whether there are other possible explanations.

There's something else scientists wonder about the corona. Think about that fireplace again. When a fire gets bigger, it gets hotter—and brighter, too … If there's more fire, there's more light. But despite the corona's high temperature, it's not as bright as scientists would think. It's pretty dim—even dimmer than the Moon. The corona is hard to see because it's so dim compared to the Sun's surface. Scientists think this is probably because the corona isn't very dense—that means its gas particles are spread out. Because the particles aren't close together, the corona doesn't give off a lot of light. This can make it hard to observe the corona without special equipment. We can see it best during an eclipse, when the Moon comes between Earth and the Sun. During a total eclipse, the Moon blocks the Sun from our view—only the corona is visible, around the Sun's edges. At that time astronomers can easily observe the corona. It's clear that sometimes it bulges out in certain spots, then gets smaller. Sometimes it flares way out far into the solar system. Scientists continue to study the Sun's corona and hope to find answers to some of their questions.

(Narrator): Now answer the questions.

(Narrator): Number 35. What is the teacher mainly talking about?

(Narrator): Number 36. Why does the teacher first talk about a fire in a fireplace?

(Narrator): Number 37. Why is the Sun's corona dim?

(Narrator): Number 38. Why is the corona easy to see during an eclipse?

(Narrator): Go on to the next page.

(Narrator): Questions 39 through 42. Listen to a discussion in a science class.

(Man): I hope everyone enjoyed our field trip yesterday to the city botanical gardens. Even though we live in a fairly small city, the botanical gardens here are among the best in the country. The gardens have a huge number of different plant and tree species. And some are extremely rare—in fact, some of the trees we saw yesterday don't exist anywhere else in the country. What did you all think?

(Girl): My favorite part of the trip was going into that big building with all the strange-looking desert plants. I loved that one huge plant with all the sharp needles, er, spines, on it. And it kind of looked like it had arms!

(Man): I know which one you mean—that was quite a remarkable plant. Was it in the succulent plant building?

(Girl): Succulent plants? I thought it was a kind of cactus. Weren't all the plants in that building cactus plants?

(Man): That particular one was a cactus, yes, but not all the other plants in the building were. You see, cacti are just one kind of succulent plant—the succulents are a broader category. Basically, succulents are plants with thick tissue that can store water. Remember the thick green body of the cactus you liked so much? It's because of these unique tissues that soak up water that succulents can survive in deserts and other dry and hot environments.

(Girl): So does that mean then that succulent plants don't have any leaves?

(Man): Well, some do and some don't. But still, if they do have leaves, they're generally pretty thick—not thin and papery, like the leaves of most other kinds of plants. The word "succulent" actually means "fat" because of this thick, fleshy appearance.

(Girl): Huh! Who knew a plant could be so interesting? Now I know what I'll be doing my next science report on!

(Narrator): Now answer the questions.

(Narrator): Number 39. Where did the student see the plant she describes?

(Narrator): Number 40. According to the teacher, how have succulents adapted in order to survive?

(Narrator): Number 41. According to the teacher, what does the word "succulent" refer to?

(Narrator): Number 42. What does the girl imply when she says, "Now I know what I'll be doing my next science report on"?

(Narrator): Stop. This is the end of the Listening section.

附　　录

1. *TOEFL Junior*® 标准考试总分数等级描述

以下表格展示了 *TOEFL Junior*® 标准考试的总分等级、总分数、整体能力描述和 CEFR（欧洲语言共同参考标准）描述。

总分等级	总分数	*TOEFL Junior*® 标准考试整体能力描述 （这些描述代表在使用英语作为教学语言的中学中考生的表现）	对应的 CEFR 分数
5 级 卓越	845—900	始终可以理解复杂的书面和口语材料，运用复杂的语言结构和词汇知识	所有部分为 B2
4 级 娴熟	785—840	通常可以理解复杂的书面和口语材料，运用复杂的语言结构和词汇知识	所有部分为 B1
3 级 突破	730—780	可以理解一些复杂的书面和口语材料，运用基本的语言结构和词汇知识	所有部分大多为 B1，但是偶尔为 A2
2 级 进步	655—725	偶尔可以理解基本的书面和口语材料，运用基本的语言结构和词汇知识	所有部分大多为 A2，但是阅读和听力偶尔为 A1
1 级 新生	600—650	可以理解一些非常基础的书面和口语材料，使用基本的语言结构和词汇知识，但是需要进一步培养这些语言技能和理解能力	阅读和听力大多为 A1；语言形式与含义大多为 A2

TOEFL Junior® 标准考试各部分考试分数与欧洲语言共同参考标准（CEFR）的对应关系

考试的各部分分数可以对应到欧洲语言共同参考标准（CEFR），以帮助考生理解分数的含义。

考试部分	CEFR A2 级别以下	CEFR A2 级别	CEFR B1 级别	CEFR B2 级别
听力理解	210 分以下	210—240	245—285	290—300
语言形式与含义	210 分以下	210—245	250—275	280—300
阅读理解	210 分以下	210—240	245—285	290—300

2. *TOEFL Junior*® 标准考试分数等级描述

听力理解

得分在 290—300 分数段的考生通常能做到以下几点：

- 听较长的学术和非学术口头表达时，不论主旨表达清晰还是委婉，他们都能理解。
- 他们能从较长的学术和非学术口头表达中找出重要细节。
- 他们能根据说话者的语调及重读做出推测。
- 他们能在篇幅较长、较为复杂的演讲中理解习惯用语。
- 他们能在较长的学术和非学术口头表达中理解说话者表达一段信息的意图（如进行对比或为支持某一论点提供依据）。

得分在 245—285 分数段的考生通常能做到以下几点：

- 他们能在较长的、用语简单的、语境清晰的学术和非学术口头表达中理解被明确表达的主旨。
- 他们能在较长的、用语简单的、语境清晰的学术和非学术口头表达中找出重要细节。
- 他们能在听完较短的、用语简单的、语境清晰的口语表达后做出推断。
- 他们能理解中等难度口语语段中的若干常见习语。
- 在熟悉的语境中，他们能理解说话者表达一段信息的意图（如进行对比或为支持某一论点提供依据）。

得分在 210—240 分数段的考生通常能做到以下几点：

- 如果表达清晰，他们能够理解一则简短的课堂通知的主旨。
- 他们能理解在较短的表述和对话中被清楚表达并强调的重要细节。
- 当用语简单、语境清晰时，他们能理解口语信息的直白的改述。
- 当用语简单、语境清晰时，他们能理解一段较短表述中说话者的意图。

得分在 210 分以下的考生通常需要提高以下技能：

- 理解通知、短发言以及简单对话的大意和重要细节。
- 在用语简单、语境清晰时，可以理解说话者在一段短发言中的意图。
- 在用语简单、语境清晰时，可以改述口语信息。

语言形式与含义

得分在 280—300 分数段的考生通常能做到以下几点:

- 他们通常能在学术和非学术文本中准确判断出较复杂的语法结构(如,关系从句)的含义和用法。
- 他们展现出较大的词汇储备,其中包括主要用于学术文本的词汇。
- 他们通常能识别出在非学术和学术文本中的句子是如何形成连贯、具有意义的段落的。

得分在 250—275 分数段的考生通常能做到以下几点:

- 他们通常能够在非学术和学术文本中准确判断出基本语法结构(如,形容词比较级)的意义和用法,但不能一贯准确判断出较复杂结构的意义和用法。
- 他们展现出通常使用于日常、非学术文本中的词汇储备。
- 他们通常能识别出在非学术文本中的句子是如何形成连贯、有意义的段落的,但有时对于学术文本难以实现这一点。

得分在 210—245 分数段的考生通常能做到以下几点:

- 他们有时能够在非学术文本中识别出最基本语法结构(如一般现在时或一般过去时动词时态)的意义和用法。
- 他们展现出对常见的、用于非学术文本的初级词汇的储备。
- 他们有时能识别出在非学术文本中的句子是如何形成连贯、有意义的段落的,但通常对于学术文本难以实现这一点。

得分在 210 分以下的考生通常需要以如下方式来提升语言掌握程度:

- 提升他们的综合词汇量。
- 加强他们对基本语法结构(如,主谓一致或简单介词)的了解和使用。
- 理解句子是如何形成连贯、有意义的段落的。

阅读理解

得分在 290—300 分数段的考生通常能做到以下几点:

- 他们能理解非学术和学术文本的主旨,其中包括主旨未被明确陈述的文本。
- 他们能准确领会非学术和学术文本中的重要细节,其中包括语言难度较高的文本。

- 他们能在阅读非学术和学术文本时做出有效推断，其中包括理解作者为何提及某些信息（如，为做对比或为支撑论点提供依据）。

- 他们通常能推断出虚构类故事中某一角色的态度或观点。即便是语言复杂的学术文本，他们通常也能理解比喻性语言，并能根据上下文确定陌生单词的词义。

得分在 245—285 分数段的考生通常能做到以下几点：

- 他们能理解在非学术和学术文本中明确表达的主旨。

- 他们通常能在非学术和学术文本中找出重要细节，包括在上下文不明了以及包含陌生单词的情况下。

- 他们有时能在阅读非学术和学术文本时准确做出推断，其中包括理解作者为何提及某些信息（如，为做对比或为支撑论点提供依据）。

- 他们通常能在虚构类叙事中确定事件并理清情节。

- 他们通常能在阅读结构简单的文本时通过上下文确定陌生单词的词义。

得分在 210—240 分数段的考生通常能做到以下几点：

- 他们有时能理解在非学术文本中明确表达的主旨。

- 当用语简单、语境清晰时，他们有时能在非学术和学术文本中找出基本细节。

- 在如时间表、菜单这类日常使用的非学术、非线性文本中，他们通常能定位基本信息。

- 他们有时能在直白的非学术文本中做出推断。

- 他们有时能通过上下文确定结构简单的非学术文本中陌生单词的词义。

得分在 210 分以下的考生通常需要提高以下技能：

- 在语言简明的文本中确定主旨及重要细节。

- 基于语言简明的文本做出推断。

- 在非线性阅读材料（如时间表、菜单等）中定位基本信息。

- 通过上下文确定陌生单词词义。

3. *TOEFL Junior*® 口语考试分数等级描述

一名成绩在 14—16 分的考生能做到以下所有描述:

- 几乎总是表达流畅。

- 几乎总能有效运用语调。

- 所讲内容总能让听者明白,稍有发音不当。

- 所用词汇、语法几乎总是准确的、多样的并有效的,仅有少量几处错误。

- 所讲内容完整、连贯,描述细致、有细节。

- 理解一场学术讲座的所有主要观点和起证实作用的细节信息,并能逐一准确复述,几乎没有遗漏。

一名成绩在 11—13 分的考生能做到以下所有描述:

- 通常能流畅地进行口语表达,偶有停顿或迟疑。

- 通常能有效运用语调。

- 所讲内容通常能让听者明白,但有若干发音错误。

- 所用词汇、语法通常准确、有效,但包含若干错误。

- 所讲内容大体完整、连贯,但若干细节不够准确或被略去。

- 理解并能复述一场学术讲座的主要观点,但若干起证实作用的细节可能被遗漏或复述不准确。

一名成绩在 8—10 分的考生能做到以下所有描述:

- 能流畅地表达几小段时间。

- 有时能有效运用语调。

- 所讲内容时而能让听者明白,但有明显发音错误。

- 经常使用基本词汇和简单语法结构。

- 所讲内容有限,偶尔提供细节。

- 理解并复述一场学术讲座的有限信息,但很可能遗漏大量起证实作用的细节。

得分不足 8 分的考生可能需要提高下列技能:

- 至少流畅地表达几小段时间。

- 有效运用语调。

- 所讲内容能让听者明白。
- 运用基本词汇和简单的语法结构。
- 所讲内容中有若干细节。
- 理解并复述一场学术讲座的若干信息。

4. TOEFL Junior® 标准考试答题纸

ETS® TOEFL® Junior™

EXAMPLE

CORRECT	INCORRECT	INCORRECT	INCORRECT	INCORRECT
Ⓐ Ⓑ ● Ⓓ	Ⓐ Ⓑ Ⓧ Ⓓ	Ⓐ Ⓑ Ⓧ Ⓓ	Ⓐ Ⓑ Ⓒ Ⓓ	Ⓐ Ⓑ Ⓒ Ⓓ

Print your name in your first language:

Test Center Name:

Form Code:

Test Date:

SCHOOL USE ONLY
Is Consent Form on file? ◯ Yes ◯ No

1. NAME: Print your name. Using one box for each letter, first print your family name, then your first (given) name. Leave one box blank between names. Then, below each box, use a No. 2 pencil and fill in the circle matching the same letter.

2. STUDENT NUMBER
— Start here

SAMPLE

MUST BE COMPLETED FOR SCORING

6. GENDER
- FEMALE ◯
- MALE ◯

7. WHAT IS YOUR CURRENT GRADE LEVEL?
- ◯ Elementary School
- ◯ Middle School — 1st Year
- ◯ Middle School — 2nd Year
- ◯ Middle School — 3rd Year
- ◯ High School
- ◯ Other

8. HOW MANY TIMES HAVE YOU TAKEN THE TOEFL JUNIOR TEST IN THE PAST?
- ◯ None
- ◯ Once
- ◯ Twice
- ◯ Three or more times

9. INCLUDING THIS YEAR, HOW MANY YEARS HAVE YOU BEEN STUDYING ENGLISH AT A SCHOOL?
- ◯ 1–2
- ◯ 3–5
- ◯ 6–8
- ◯ 9 or more

10. HOW MANY HOURS PER WEEK DO YOU STUDY ENGLISH IN YOUR REGULAR SCHOOL?
- ◯ 1–2
- ◯ 3–5
- ◯ 6–8
- ◯ 9 or more

11. HOW MANY HOURS PER WEEK DO YOU STUDY ENGLISH OUTSIDE OF YOUR REGULAR SCHOOL?
- ◯ 0
- ◯ 1–3
- ◯ 4–6
- ◯ 7 or more

12. HAVE YOU LIVED IN AN ENGLISH-SPEAKING COUNTRY?
- ◯ No
- ◯ Yes, I stayed less than 3 months
- ◯ Yes, I stayed between 3 months and 12 months
- ◯ Yes, I stayed over 1 year

3. DATE OF BIRTH

YYYY	MM	DD

4. COUNTRY CODE

5. LANGUAGE CODE

PAGE 1   94491-94491 • TF912E100 • Printed in U.S.A.   Q3463/1-2

766625

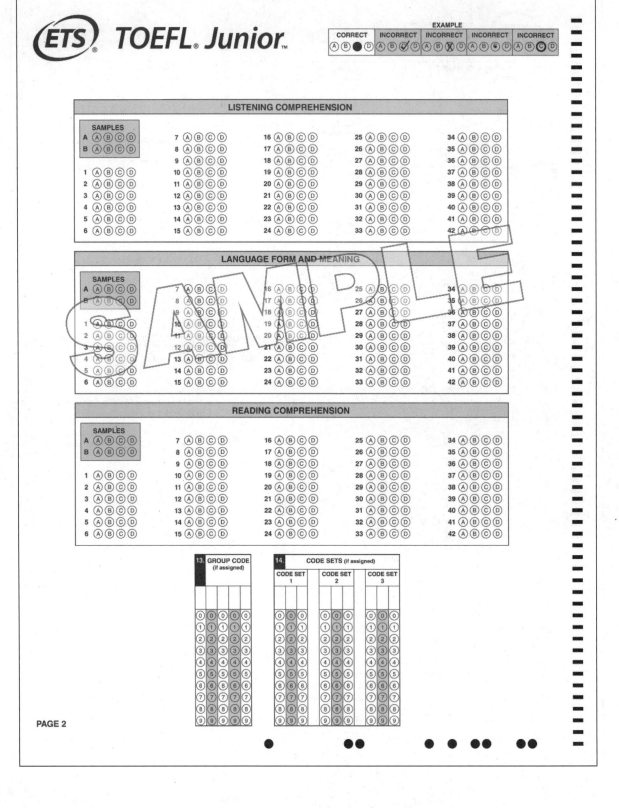

5. TOEFL Junior® 标准考试成绩单

TOEFL Junior.
S T A N D A R D

Official Score Report

Student Name: Your Name

Student Number: 1122334455667788　　**Date of Birth:** 7-Jul-1997

Test Date: 29-May-2014

Gender: F

Test Center: Your Test Center United States of America
Your ETS Preferred Network - TOEFL Junior Representative

Overall Score Level　　　Accomplished　　　Total Score: 835

4

0　　　　　　　　5

A typical student at Level 4 often demonstrates comprehension of complex written and spoken materials, drawing on knowledge of complex language structures and vocabulary.

Listening Comprehension

Test takers who score between 290 and 300 typically have the following strengths:

290

200　　　　300

CEFR Level **B2**

- They can understand main ideas, whether they are clearly stated or implied, in both academic and non-academic extended spoken texts.
- They can identify important details in both academic and non-academic extended spoken texts.
- They can make inferences based on a speaker's intonation or stress.
- They can usually understand idiomatic language used in longer, more complex speech.
- They can understand how information is being used by a speaker (e.g., to make a comparison or to provide evidence to support an argument) in academic and non-academic extended spoken texts.

Language Form and Meaning

Test takers who score between 250 and 275 typically have the following strengths:

275

200　　　　300

CEFR Level **B1**

- They usually recognize the accurate meaning and use of basic grammatical structures (e.g. comparative adjectives) in non-academic and academic texts but do not consistently recognize the accurate meaning and use of more advanced structures.
- They demonstrate knowledge of vocabulary typically used in everyday, non-academic texts.
- They usually recognize how sentences combine to create cohesive, meaningful paragraphs in non-academic texts, but sometimes have difficulty doing so with academic texts.

Reading Comprehension

Test takers who score between 245 and 285 typically have the following strengths:

Lexile Measure **910L**

270

200　　　　300

CEFR Level **B1**

- They can understand main ideas that are explicitly stated in non-academic and academic texts.
- They can usually identify important details in non-academic and academic texts, even when the context is not always clear and the vocabulary may be unfamiliar.
- They can sometimes make inferences accurately, including inferences needed to understand why an author includes certain information (e.g., to make a comparison or to provide evidence to support an argument) in non-academic and academic texts.
- They can usually identify events and plotlines in a fictional narrative.
- They can usually determine the meaning of unfamiliar vocabulary words from context in simply constructed texts.

778483

ETS® Security Guard

Understanding Your Score Report

Overall Score Level, Section Scores and Performance Descriptors

Your score report provides both an overall score level and individual section scores. Overall score levels range from 1 to 5 and are accompanied by overall performance descriptors. The scaled score for each section ranges from 200 to 300 and is reported in 5-point increments. Scores from 3 different sections should not be directly compared because each measure is scaled separately. The total score is a sum of the 3 section scores and ranges from 600 to 900. Section scores are accompanied by section performance descriptors. For more detailed information about scores, visit *www.ets.org/toefl_junior*.

The following table shows all of the TOEFL Junior® Standard overall score levels, overall performance descriptors and CEFR profiles.

TOEFL Junior Standard Overall Score Level	Overall Performance Descriptors These descriptors represent performance in middle schools which use English for instruction. A typical student at this level:	CEFR Profile A typical student at this level achieved these section-level CEFR scores
5 Superior	consistently demonstrates comprehension of complex written and spoken materials, drawing on knowledge of complex language structures and vocabulary.	B2 for all sections
4 Accomplished	often demonstrates comprehension of complex written and spoken materials, drawing on knowledge of complex language structures and vocabulary.	B1 for all sections
3 Expanding	demonstrates comprehension of some complex written and spoken materials and most basic materials, drawing on knowledge of basic language structures and vocabulary.	Mostly B1 for all sections, but occasionally A2.
2 Progressing	occasionally demonstrates comprehension of basic written and spoken materials, drawing on knowledge of basic language structures and vocabulary.	Mostly A2 for all sections, but occasionally A1 for Reading and Listening.
1 Emerging	can comprehend some very basic written and spoken texts, drawing on knowledge of basic language structures and vocabulary, but needs to further develop these language skills and comprehension abilities.	Mostly A1 for Listening and Reading; mostly A2 for Language Form and Meaning.

NOTE: If an NS is received, an overall score could not be produced due to insufficient test taker responses in some sections. The test taker did not respond in an entire section or sections.

CEFR Levels

The Common European Framework of Reference for Languages (CEFR) is a widely-used tool for understanding different stages of language learning. It covers six proficiency levels: A1, A2, B1, B2, C1 and C2, with C2 being the highest level. The performance descriptors for each section of TOEFL Junior are adapted from the CEFR level descriptors to reflect the TOEFL Junior test content and the age of the test takers. For more detailed information on how TOEFL Junior test scores relate to the CEFR, please visit *www.ets.org/toefl_junior*.

Lexile Measure

Lexile measure matches English-Language readers with appropriate texts. Use your Lexile measure to find books at your reading level. To begin, visit *toefl_junior.lexile.com*.

Recommended Score Validity — 2 Years

TOEFL Junior measures a test taker's current level of English language proficiency and is not designed to be a predictor of future *TOEFL iBT*® scores. Because of the rapid development of English proficiency by test takers within the TOEFL Junior recommended age range, it is recommended that scores not be used beyond 2 years. However, scores can be considered valid beyond 2 years if the test taker has provided evidence of having maintained the same level of English language learning.

Copyright © 2022 by ETS. All rights reserved. ETS, the ETS logo and TOEFL Junior are registered trademarks of ETS in the United States and other countries.

6. *TOEFL Junior®* 标准考试证书

CERTIFICATE OF ACHIEVEMENT

This is to certify that

Nine ALTRD

achieved the following score on the

TOEFL Junior® Standard Test

Listening:	280
Language Form and Meaning:	275
Reading:	265
Overall Score:	820

ETS UAT Center (AD New Test Forms)
at: Princeton, United States
date: 10 Feb 2022

Joanna S. Gorin

Joanna S. Gorin
Vice President of Global Language Learning,
Teaching & Assessment
Chief Operating Officer, Global Language Markets

Silver
ETS CMD Staging, United States
08408166

TOEFL Junior® Standard Scale Scores

Test Section	Score Range
Listening Comprehension	200-300
Language Form and Meaning	200-300
Reading Comprehension	200-300

TOEFL Junior® Standard Overall Score Level	Certificate Color	TOEFL Junior Standard Overall Performance Descriptors These descriptors represent performance in middle schools which use English for instruction. A typical student at this level	CEFR Profile * A typical student at this level achieved these section-level CEFR scores
5 Superior	Gold	consistently demonstrates comprehension of complex written and spoken materials, drawing on knowledge of complex language structures and vocabulary.	B2 for all sections.
4 Accomplished	Silver	often demonstrates comprehension of complex written and spoken materials, drawing on knowledge of complex language structures and vocabulary.	B1 for all sections.
3 Expanding	Bronze	demonstrates comprehension of some complex written and spoken materials and most basic materials, drawing on knowledge of basic language structures and vocabulary.	Mostly B1 for all sections, but occasionally A2.
2 Progressing	Green	occasionally demonstrates comprehension of basic written and spoken materials, drawing on knowledge of basic language structures and vocabulary.	Mostly A2 for all sections, but occasionally A1 for Reading and Listening.
1 Emerging	Blue	can comprehend some very basic written and spoken texts, drawing on knowledge of basic language structures and vocabulary, but needs to further develop these language skills and comprehension abilities.	Mostly A1 for Reading and Listening; mostly A2 for Language Form and Meaning.

Recommended Score Validity - *TOEFL Junior* test scores are available for reporting for 2 years after the test date. Because English-language proficiency can change rapidly depending on additional learning or development since the time of testing, decisions involving scores will be most valid when scores are obtained close to the point at which the decisions are made. Institutions can choose to use scores that are more than 2 years old as a record of an individual's English-language proficiency at the time the test was taken.

* The CEFR levels provided are context dependent. They are based on the language abilities of middle-school students and lower-level high-school students. They should not be compared to the CEFR levels on other *TOEFL®* tests.

Disclaimer: This is NOT an official score report and cannot be used for admissions purposes.

Copyright © 2022 by Educational Testing Service. All rights reserved. ETS, the ETS logo, TOEFL and TOEFL JUNIOR are registered trademarks of ETS in the United States and other countries.

124338-124338 • SS18E20 • Printed in U.S.A

804866

7. *TOEFL Junior®* 口语考试成绩单

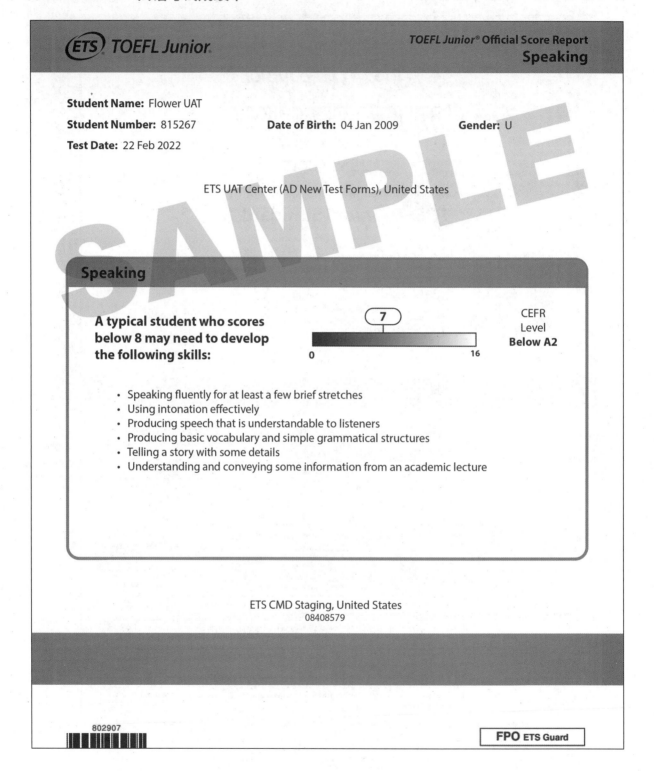

Understanding Your Score Report

Score and Performance Descriptors

Your score report provides your *TOEFL Junior®* Speaking test score, along with performance descriptors. The score ranges from 0 to 16; these scores are linked to the scoring guides used to score the speaking tasks to help you better understand the meaning of your score. For more detailed information about scores, visit ***www.ets.org/toefl_junior***.

CEFR Levels

The Common European Framework of Reference for Languages (CEFR) is a widely used tool for understanding different stages of language learning. The Speaking test covers 4 proficiency levels: Below A2, A2, B1 and B2. The performance descriptors are adapted from the CEFR level descriptors to reflect the test content and the age of the test takers. A CEFR level is not reported for a score of 0. For more information on how TOEFL Junior test scores relate to the CEFR, visit ***www.ets.org/toefl_junior***.

The following table shows the Speaking test score ranges, performance descriptors and CEFR levels.

TOEFL Junior Speaking Test Score Range	Performance Descriptors	CEFR Level
A typical student who scores between 14 and 16 can do all of the following:	• Almost always speak in a fluent and sustained way • Almost always use intonation effectively • Produce speech that is always understandable to listeners, with only minor errors in pronunciation • Almost always produce vocabulary and grammar that is accurate, varied and effective, with only a few errors • Tell a complete and coherent story with elaboration and detail • Understand and accurately convey all main ideas and supporting details from an academic lecture, with almost no omissions	B2
A typical student who scores between 11 and 13 can do all of the following:	• Usually speak in a fluent and sustained way, with some stops or hesitations • Usually use intonation effectively • Produce speech that is usually understandable to listeners, but with some pronunciation errors • Usually produce vocabulary and grammar that is accurate and effective, although with some errors • Tell a story that is mostly complete and coherent, although some details are inaccurate or left out • Understand and convey main ideas from an academic lecture, although some supporting details may be left out or inaccurate	B1
A typical student who scores between 8 and 10 can do all of the following:	• Speak fluently for a few brief stretches • Sometimes use intonation effectively • Produce speech that is at times understandable to listeners, but with obvious pronunciation errors • Often produce basic vocabulary and simple grammatical structures • Tell a limited story, occasionally providing details • Understand and convey limited information from an academic lecture, but probably leave out many supporting details	A2
A typical student who scores below 8 may need to develop the following skills:	• Speaking fluently for at least a few brief stretches • Using intonation effectively • Producing speech that is understandable to listeners • Producing basic vocabulary and simple grammatical structures • Telling a story with some details • Understanding and conveying some information from an academic lecture	Below A2

Note: If the responses for this test could not be properly recorded, a score of NS will be produced.

Recommended Score Validity
- TOEFL Junior test scores are available for reporting for 2 years after the test date. Because English-language proficiency can change rapidly depending on additional learning or development since the time of testing, decisions involving scores will be most valid when scores are obtained close to the point at which the decisions are made. Institutions can choose to use scores that are more than 2 years old as a record of an individual's English-language proficiency at the time the test was taken.

Copyright © 2017 by Educational Testing Service. All rights reserved. ETS, the ETS logo, TOEFL IBT and TOEFL JUNIOR are registered trademarks of Educational Testing Service (ETS) in the United States and other countries.

121810-86427 • I.N. 802907

8. *TOEFL Junior®* 口语考试证书

CERTIFICATE OF ACHIEVEMENT

This is to certify that

Cookie UAT

achieved the following score on the

TOEFL Junior® **Speaking Test**

Speaking: 11

ETS UAT Center (AD New Test Forms)
at: Princeton, United States
date: 15 Feb 2022

Joanna S. Gorin

Joanna S. Gorin
Vice President of Global Language Learning,
Teaching & Assessment
Chief Operating Officer, Global Language Markets

Silver
ETS CMD Staging, United States
08408579

TOEFL Junior® Speaking Test Score Range: (0-16)	TOEFL Junior® Speaking Test Certificate	Performance Descriptors	CEFR Level
A typical student who scores between 14 and 16 can do all of the following:	Gold	• Almost always speak in a fluent and sustained way • Almost always use intonation effectively • Produce speech that is always understandable to listeners, with only minor errors in pronunciation • Almost always produce vocabulary and grammar that is accurate, varied and effective, with only a few errors • Tell a complete and coherent story with elaboration and detail • Understand and accurately convey all main ideas and supporting details from an academic lecture, with almost no omissions.	B2
A typical student who scores between 11 and 13 can do all of the following:	Silver	• Usually speak in a fluent and sustained way, with some stops or hesitations • Usually use intonation effectively • Produce speech that is usually understandable to listeners, but with some pronunciation errors • Usually produce vocabulary and grammar that is accurate and effective, although with some errors • Tell a story that is mostly complete and coherent, although some details are inaccurate or left out • Understand and convey main ideas from an academic lecture, although some supporting details may be left out or inaccurate	B1
A typical student who scores between 8 and 19 can do all of the following:	Bronze	• Speak fluently for a few brief stretches • Sometimes use intonation effectively • Produce speech that is at times understandable to listeners, but with obvious pronunciation errors • Often produce basic vocabulary and simple grammatical structures • Tell a limited story, occasionally providing details • Understand and convey limited information from an academic lecture, but probably leave out many supporting details	A2
A typical student who scores below 8 may need to develop the following skills:	Blue	• Speak fluently for at leat a few brief stretches • Using intonation effectively • Producing speech that is understandable to listeners • Producing basic vocabulary and simple grammatical structures • Telling a story with some details • Understand and convey some information from an academic lecture	Below A2

Recommended Score Validity - TOEFL Junior test scores are available for reporting for 2 years after the test date. Because English-language proficiency can change rapidly depending on additional learning or development since the time of testing. Decisions involving scores will be most valid when scores are obtained close to the point at which the decisions are made. Institutions can choose to use scores that are more than 2 years old as a record of an individual's English-language proficiency at the time the test was taken.

The CEFR levels provided are context dependent. They are based on the language abilities of middle-school students and lower-level high-school students. They should not be compared to the CEFR levels on other *TOEFL®* tests.

Disclaimer: This is <u>NOT</u> an official score report and cannot be used for admissions purposes.

Copyright © 2022 by Educational Testing Service. All rights reserved. ETS, the ETS logo, TOEFL and TOEFL JUNIOR are registered trademarks of ETS in the United States and other countries.